Organizational Behavior Modification

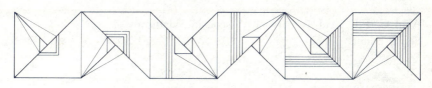

Management Applications Series

Alan C. Filley, University of Wisconsin, Madison
Series Editor

Performance in Organizations: Determinants and Appraisal
L. L. Cummings, University of Wisconsin, Madison
Donald P. Schwab, University of Wisconsin, Madison

Leadership and Effective Management
Fred E. Fiedler, University of Washington
Martin M. Chemers, University of Utah

Managing by Objectives
Anthony P. Raia, University of California, Los Angeles

Organizational Change: Techniques and Applications
Newton Margulies, University of California, Irvine
John C. Wallace, University of California, Irvine

Interpersonal Conflict Resolution
Alan C. Filley, University of Wisconsin, Madison

*Group Techniques for Program Planning: A Guide to Nominal
   Group and Delphi Processes*
Andre L. Delbecq, University of Wisconsin, Madison
Andrew H. Van de Ven, Kent State University
David H. Gustafson, University of Wisconsin, Madison

Organizational Behavior Modification
Fred Luthans, University of Nebraska, Lincoln
Robert Kreitner, Western Illinois University

Organizational Behavior Modification

Fred Luthans
University of Nebraska, Lincoln

Robert Kreitner
Western Illinois University

Scott, Foresman and Company · Glenview, Illinois
Dallas, Tex. · Oakland, N.J. · Palo Alto, Cal. · Tucker, Ga.
Brighton, England

To Kay and Margaret

Library of Congress Catalog Number: 74-21906
ISBN: 0-673-07966-X

Copyright © 1975 Scott, Foresman and Company.
Philippines Copyright 1975 Scott, Foresman and Company
All Rights Reserved.
Printed in the United States of America.

Foreword

The Management Applications Series is concerned with the application of contemporary research, theory, and techniques. There are many excellent books at advanced levels of knowledge, but there are few which address themselves to the application of such knowledge. The authors in this series are uniquely qualified for this purpose, since they are all scholars who have experience in implementing change in real organizations through the methods they write about.

Each book treats a single topic in depth. Where the choice is between presenting many approaches briefly or a single approach thoroughly, we have opted for the latter. Thus, after reading the book, the student or practitioner should know how to apply the methodology described.

Selection of topics for the series was guided by contemporary relevance to management practice, and by the availability of an author qualified as an expert, yet able to write at a basic level of understanding. No attempt is made to cover all management methods, nor is any sequence implied in the series, although the books do complement one another. For example, change methods might fit well with managing by objectives.

The books in this series may be used in several ways. They may be used to supplement textbooks in basic courses on management, organizational behavior, personnel, or industrial psychology/sociology. Students appreciate the fact that the material is immediately applicable. Practicing managers will want to use individual books to increase their skills, either through self study or in connection with management development programs, inside or outside the organization.

Alan C. Filley

Preface

Organizational behavior is a function of its consequences. We feel this is a significant statement in human resource management. The importance of consequences in the study of organizational behavior has been largely overlooked. Management scholars and practitioners have depended primarily upon theories of motivation while searching for the elusive causes of organizational behavior. As a result, they have attempted to look "inside" the individual to identify such causes as attitudes, drives, desires, and motives. However, none of these are directly observable. They are only inferred from organizational behavior which, however, *is* observable. Thus, our focus is on observable organizational behavior and the external environment rather than on the individual's internal motivational state. In particular, we believe that organizational behavior is a function of its *contingent* consequences.

The classic goals of any scientific endeavor are understanding, prediction, and control. Studying the motivation of organizational participants is a step toward understanding organizational behavior. However, can the study of human motivation accomplish the goals of prediction and control? Or, going one step further, should human resource management even be concerned with these goals? The answers to these questions seem clear to us. We do not believe that the study of motivation will lead directly to prediction and control, but we do believe that these are desirable goals for human resource management. Therefore, we have turned to operant learning theory and the principles of behavior modification as a means of achieving better understanding, prediction, and control of organizational behavior.

We do not feel that the extensive work done in psychology and education on an operant-based approach to human behavior can be directly applied to human resource management. We certainly realize that human resource management deals with much more complex settings, subjects, and problems than have been dealt with by either behavioral psychologists or behavior modification advocates in education. On the other hand, we are convinced that much can be learned from their theories, research, and applications. Because of these convictions we have attempted to integrate operant learning theory and the principles of behavior modification with the management field of organizational behavior. The result of this integration is what we call organizational behavior modification or, simply, O. B. Mod.

The book consists of ten chapters. The first chapter emphasizes the external, scientific approach to the study and practice of human resource management. Chapter 2 gives a comprehensive overview of learning theory. The contributions of Watson, Thorndike, and Skinner are given primary emphasis. Chapter 3 is devoted to the principles of behavior modification, which are derived from operant learning theory. The identification of observable behavioral events, the use of frequency of behavioral events as the basic datum, and the importance of viewing behavior within a contingency context are given major attention. Chapter 4 presents and gives examples of the five-step problem-solving model of behavioral contingency management (BCM). This five-step model (identify, measure, analyze, intervene, and evaluate) represents a specific application of O. B. Mod. for more effective human resource management. Chapters 5 and 6 consist of a close examination of the positive (reinforcement) and negative (punishment) control of organizational behavior. Chapter 7 provides a detailed study of shaping and modeling intervention strategies. Chapter 8 reports some actual cases of using O. B. Mod. and related approaches. Production, service, total organizational development, and non-business applications are included. Ethical implications of O. B. Mod. are raised and analyzed in Chapter 9. Finally, Chapter 10 discusses both academic and organization/management preconditions for the future development of O. B. Mod.

This book represents the combined ideas and efforts of many of our colleagues. First of all, we are grateful to Professor Robert Ottemann, University of Nebraska, Omaha. He has been involved from the beginning in our theoretical development, research, and application of O. B. Mod. We would also like to thank David Lyman for his contributions to the early formulation of our ideas. We are indebted to Dr. John Fry, Human Resources Research Organization, for allowing us to adapt some of his work in a case in Chapter 8. The same is true of Sam McPherson and Robert Esposito. These two practitioners of O. B. Mod. have contributed both to our ideas and to the book itself. We thank Professor Art Baars, Western Illinois University, for reading portions of the manuscript. Finally, thanks go to our lovely wives for providing us with the necessary positive reinforcement to write the book.

Fred Luthans
Robert Kreitner

Contents

1   *A New Perspective*   1

A Scientific Perspective   2
Organizational Behavior: Internal to External   3
Motivation: The Traditional Internal Explanation   7
Learning: An Alternative Approach   11
Organizational Behavior Modification   12
A Preliminary Word on Behavior Control   15

2   *Learning Theory Background*   17

Definition of Learning   18
Watsonian Behaviorism   19
Reinforcement Learning Theories   22
Skinnerian Behaviorism   24
Behavior Modification   29
O. B. Mod.: Historical Integration   32

3   *Principles of Behavior Modification*   33

Fundamental Principles   34
Specific Procedures and Techniques   44
Application of Principles and Techniques   56

4   *Behavioral Contingency Management*   60

The Practicing Manager as a Behavioral Scientist   60
Organizational Behavior
     versus Organizational Activities   62
The Emery Air Freight Experience   67
The Behavioral Contingency Management Model   68

5   *Positive Control*   84

Technical Refinements of Reinforcement   84
Positive Reinforcement
       and Human Resource Management   89
Identifying Positive Reinforcers   91
Money as a Reward for Performance   104

6   *Negative Control*   108

Functional Definitions of Terms   108
The Popularity of Negative Control   115
The Case Against Negative Control   117
Alternatives for More Effective Application   123

7   *Shaping, Modeling, and Self-Control*   130

The Shaping Process   130
The Modeling Process   137
Self-Control in O. B. Mod.   143

8   *Organizational Behavior Modification:*
Some Actual Cases   150

The Production Case   150
The Service Case   159
The Total Organizational Development Case   164
The Military Case   170

9   *Analyzing Ethical Issues*   174

The General Issue of Behavioral Control   174
The Role of O. B. Mod.
       in Human Resource Management   181
O. B. Mod.: Management or Manipulation?   183
A Specific Issue:
       Measuring On-The-Job Behavior   184

10 *Preconditions for Future Development*   186

Academic Preconditions   186
Organizational Preconditions   188

References   198

Index   207

A New Perspective 1

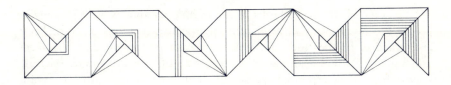

Like everything else in the world today, the behavioral approach to management is undergoing drastic change. Old approaches to managing people in modern organizations are no longer adequate. Traditional human relations approaches that attempt to make employees happy through money, conditions, and security are just not working. First of all, the traditional methods have not resulted in satisfied employees and, secondly, the assumption that happy employees are productive employees has not been borne out by research or common practice.

Today, human problems in organizations abound. A recent comprehensive government report on *Work in America* (1973, p. xvi.) notes that the productivity of the worker is low—as measured by absenteeism, turnover rates, wildcat strikes, sabotage, poor-quality products, and a reluctance by workers to commit themselves to their work tasks. These problems are not restricted to blue-collar workers and, as the report points out, could be a major contributing factor to the decline in physical and mental health, family stability, community participation and cohesiveness, and "balanced" sociopolitical attitudes and an increase in drug and alcohol addiction, aggression, and delinquency.

There is little doubt that human work effectiveness is important from both an organizational and a societal standpoint. While the old theories and techniques of human resource management are certainly not entirely wrong, there seems to be enough justification to explore new alternatives and develop new techniques. The purpose of this book is to provide the student and practitioner of management with a new perspective as well as some specific techniques for more effectively managing people in modern organizations.

A SCIENTIFIC PERSPECTIVE

One of the major faults of the traditional approaches to managing people has been a lack of a scientific perspective in terms of both theory and practice. In the study of human behavior in general there has been a definite shift from a philosophical to a scientific perspective. A scientific approach is characterized by operational definitions, precise problem formulation, and rigorous data collection, analysis, and interpretation. In the relatively short span of the last century, behavioral scientists have carried out what their name implies, i.e., a scientific study of human behavior. As with most academic disciplines, behavioral scientists have fragmented into divisions and subdvisions with each group embracing its own philosophies, tenets, and techniques. Today, the behavioral sciences include psychology, sociology, and anthropology, with respective emphasis given to individual behavior, social behavior, and impact of culture on behavior.

In the past, management theorists have generally ignored a scientifically based explanation of behavior and the role that the behavioral sciences could play. Today, however, the behavioral sciences are receiving much more attention. Starting about fifteen years ago with the popular writings of Douglas McGregor, behavioral science has become increasingly important and now is the recognized theoretical and research base for the behavioral approach to management. Yet, despite the widespread recognition of behavioral science as a whole, there has been a decided imbalance regarding the possible explanations of organizational behavior.

In behavioral science, and more specifically in psychology, there are two general explanations of human behavior. One approach, which could be called the *internal approach,* explains behavior in terms of mental states and cognitive processes. In this explanation, the internal states *cause* behavior. The other approach, which could be called the *external approach,* explains behavior in terms of environmental consequnces. (The internal approach is primarily a "motivational" explanation of human behavior and the external approach is mainly a "learning" explanation.) Thus, the external approach, which does not deal with unobservable inner states, is much more adaptable to scientific explanation than the internal approach. However, management has almost totally ignored the external explanation of organizational behavior, even though one of the hallmarks of a scientific perspective is to deal with observables.

The external explanation of behavior with its scientific orientation is the perspective taken by this book. The book is firmly based on the premise that *behavior is a function of its consequences.* The precise meaning of this significant statement will unfold in later chapters. For now it can be said that the external approach is based on a scientifically derived body of knowledge variously known as behaviorism, behavioral learning theory, operant psychology, behavior modification, and applied behavior analysis.

ORGANIZATIONAL BEHAVIOR: INTERNAL TO EXTERNAL

Armed with a new scientific perspective, the behavioral approach to management, usually labeled organizational behavior, has undergone a flurry of theory, research, and teaching. Too often, however, the search has been one-sided, centering on the theoretical causes of behavior. The practicing manager, on the other hand, has been faced with the pragmatic realities of controlling on-the-job behavior. The introductory remarks suggest that the internal approach has not yielded results. Because of this, a movement has been started to get both management scholars and practitioners to deal directly with overt behavior and its consequences instead of internal states.

Awareness of the external approach

Consider the following depiction of organizational behavior as an illustration of this new (external) approach. An individual comes to an organization (large or small, public or private) with the capacity to behave in many ways. Based upon prior experience, training, formal education, and general life style, the person possesses a unique behavioral repertoire. From the organization's viewpoint, some of the employee's behavior may be consistent with formal stated objectives and some of it may not be. Armed with the knowledge of what behavior is desirable (that required to attain organizational objectives), the practicing manager can attempt to accelerate the new employee's desirable behavior and decelerate the undesirable behavior. This important aspect of a manager's job can be accomplished through the knowledge of some scientifically validated laws of learning.

FIGURE 1–1.   A Word Recognition Test.

INSTRUCTIONS: After carefully considering each of the following terms
as it relates to on-the-job behavior, rate each term with a '2,' '1,' or '0.'

2 = Very familiar term
1 = Vaguely or somewhat familiar term
0 = Unfamiliar term

_____ 1.   Expectancy

_____ 2.   Extinction

_____ 3.   Reinforcer

_____ 4.   Drive

_____ 5.   Attitude

_____ 6.   Motive

_____ 7.   Behavioral event

_____ 8.   Need

_____ 9.   Contingency

_____10.   Hygiene factors

At this point it should prove interesting for the reader to take
the simple test found in Figure 1–1. (Please take the test now.) Regardless of whether the reader has had a lot, some, or no formal management
training there is a high probability that items 1, 4, 5, 6, 8, and 10 will
have a higher average score than items 2, 3, 7, and 9.[1] The former group
of terms comes from the language of the internal approach to explaining
behavior with its emphasis on mental states, cognitive processes, and

1. As a corollary point of interest, the following will give the reader a
basis for comparing his/her score with the scores of others who have
taken the same test. As a general pretest of the instrument in Figure 1-1,
the authors surveyed ninety-two undergraduates with no formal management course work and fifty-eight others with one or more courses in
management. In order of diminishing familiarity, the first group ranked
the terms as follows: (1) Attitude, (2) Motive, (3) Drive, (4) Reinforcer,
(5) Expectancy, (6) Need, (7) Hygiene factors, (8) Extinction, (9) Contingency, and (10) Behavioral event. The second, more experienced group
ranked the terms in the following order of diminishing familiarity: (1)
Attitude, (2) Motive, (3) Drive, (4) Need, (5) Reinforcer, (6) Expectancy,
(7) Hygiene factors, (8) Contingency, (9) Extinction, and (10) Behavioral
event. Both groups of undergraduates expressed greater familiarity with
the psychoanalytic and cognitive terminology than with the behaviorist
terminology. This point is made convincingly by the eighth, ninth, and
tenth place finishes, in both groups, of three of the four behaviorist terms.

hypothetical constructs. The latter group of terms, on the other hand, comes from the language of the external approach with its emphasis upon overt behavior, antecedent conditions, and environmental consequences.

Whether we are aware of it or not, most of us speak the cognitive language of the internal approach in explaining human behavior. Not surprisingly, it is simply the result of steady exposure to the language of the psychoanalytic and cognitive schools of thought—the internal approach. It is a matter of culture and conditioning or, as the behaviorist would say, a matter of the differential reinforcement of the use of mentalistic terminology.

The reader may want to try the following as a personal experiment. For the next few days listen carefully to yourself, your professors or supervisors, peers, and subordinates and record how many times the words "need," "motive," "attitude," "drive," "purpose," and "desire" are used when the behavior of people, especially organizational participants, is being discussed. Then, going one step further, shift your attention to the four behaviorist words in Figure 1-1, "reinforcer," "extinction," "behavioral event," and "contingency," and record the number of times each is heard in regard to behavior. If our little test is a reliable indicator, you will end up with many more of the former than of the latter.

Consequences of organizational behavior

Employees view the organization as the source of many consequences, some desirable and some undesirable. Some common consequences of their organizational behavior include money, security, recognition, social support, formal and informal sanctions, reprimands, and termination. Through instructions, observation of co-workers and supervisors, and, primarily, personal experience with receiving consequences, employees learn which on-the-job behaviors lead to certain desirable consequences and which behaviors result in undesirable consequences. Ideally, the organization obtains the behavior required for organizational goal accomplishment and employees receive personally desirable consequences. Unfortunately, this is not generally true in today's organizations.

While this initial look at the consequences of modern organizational behavior is overly simplistic, it is the description itself that is of particular interest to this discussion. Due to the nature of most of the management literature, management theorists and practitioners encounter few analyses and descriptions of organizational behavior which contain no allusions to internal explanations of behavior. Words such as those found in the test (drives, attitudes, motives, and needs) are frequently used to suggest that they are the real "causes" of the organizational behavior being analyzed and described.

This latter approach suggests that managers can facilitate desirable behavior by somehow getting at the causes of behavior. However, when it is realized that the "causes" of behavior are only hypothetical, then the causal model takes on different meaning. As B. F. Skinner (1969) pointed out:

> ". . . It is not good scientific practice to explain behavior by appealing to independent variables which have been inferred from the behavior thus explained, although this is commonly done, particularly by psychoanalysts, cognitive theorists, and factor analysts" (p. 264).

Since the behavioral management literature of the past has been predominantly steeped in the jargon of the psychoanalytic and cognitive schools of thought, Skinner's observation seems particularly relevant to this discussion.

Elusive causes of behavior

In the description of organizational behavior in the last section, reference to causes of behavior was noticeably absent. The focus was on the relationship between behavior and its consequences, hence giving it an external orientation. Are we saying, then, that the real causes of behavior are nonexistent or unimportant? No, not at all. We are simply making the point that management theorists and practitioners have often gotten sidetracked while pursuing the elusive causes of organizational behavior. We are proposing the alternative external approach. It involves identifying and managing the external environment which maintains, strengthens, and weakens observable behavior. The external approach suggests that managers should concentrate on the environment rather than looking "inside" the individual for the complex causes of the behavior.

The difference between the internal, causal model of behavior and the external, environmental model is again best illustrated from the perspective of science. The principal goals of science are to understand, predict, and control the phenomena in question. Reliance upon the internal model has definitely contributed to the understanding of organizational behavior but has generally failed to help *predict* and *control* it. When one considers that the very essence of human resource management is to predict and control the attainment of organizational objectives, the importance of looking toward an alternate model becomes clear.

MOTIVATION: THE TRADITIONAL
INTERNAL EXPLANATION

Traditionally, motivation theories have been particularly appealing as explanations of organizational behavior for two major reasons. First, they have helped explain why employees are productive or active or, in other words, what energizes their behavior. Second, motivation theories have attempted to explain the direction organizational behavior takes once it is energized. Generally, two motivational approaches have emerged which are commonly labeled the *content theories* and the *process theories* (Luthans and Ottemann, 1973).

The content theories of motivation attempt to specify what the energizers of behavior are. In a more sophisticated and comprehensive manner, the process theories of motivation attempt to identify the cognitive processes which give behavior purposeful direction. However, both approaches can be traced back to the concept of hedonism, the seeking of pleasure and avoidance of pain. Hedonism was originally proposed by the ancient Greek philosophers and later was popularized by the English utilitarian Jeremy Bentham. As the dichotomization of events into either pleasurable or painful proved increasingly difficult, more sophisticated extensions and refinements were proposed. Hedonism eventually evolved into the modern content and process theories of motivation.

Content theories

In the content approach, Maslow's hierarchy of needs and Herzberg's motivation/hygiene theories have gained the most popularity. They identify the energizers of organizational behavior. According to Maslow, behavior is energized by a hierarchy starting with physiological needs and then moving, in turn, from a need for safety or security, to love or belonging, to esteem, and, finally, to a need for self-actualization (Maslow, 1943). Herzberg, on the other hand, proposes two, as opposed to Maslow's five, levels of needs (Herzberg, et al., 1959). Herzberg's hygiene factors (those that prevent dissatisfaction but do not motivate) include company policy and administration, supervision, salary, interpersonal relations, and working conditions. The motivators include achievement, recognition, responsibility, advancement, and the work itself. The need format of both the Maslow and Herzberg theories is particularly appealing because of its relative simplicity and ease of application. Their contributions play a major role in both the theory and application of the modern behavioral approach to management.

However, it is important to note that neither theory has stood the test of empirical research. Maslow himself never provided any supporting research for his theory and the few studies that have attempted to test it have produced, at best, inconclusive results (Beer, 1966). Herzberg's theory is even more questionable. Herzberg himself does provide a great deal of support for his theory by using a critical-incident method of research (subjects recall incidents when they were satisfied and dissatisfied). However, when other research methodologies are used, the theory is generally not supported. Some researchers claim that even the critical-incident method, if properly used, does not support the two-factor theory (Schneider and Locke, 1971). At best, based upon the available research evidence, the content theories are explanations of satisfaction and not of motivation and causes of behavior.

Process theories

Academicians have generally turned away from the content theories and use process theory approaches (e.g., drive and expectancy theories) to explain motivation. The drive theories take prior experience into account when explaining behavior. For example, a key concept in Clark Hull's historically important drive-reduction theory was habit strength. According to Hull, habit strength was the result of the number of previously reinforced training trials. Previous reinforcement enabled an organism to learn to satisfy fundamental drives. A major problem with this theory was Hull's failure to distinguish between learned and unlearned responses. He implied that all behavior was a function of drive states. However, getting a drink of water and making a complex management decision are quite different behaviors and require different explanations. The water-drinking behavior usually results from physiological deprivation while the decision-making behavior is learned. A modern manager is not driven to make a decision in the same manner that a thirsty organism is driven to get a drink of water.

Another process approach to motivation, but considerably more complex and sophisticated than the drive theories, are the expectancy theories. Whereas the drive theories are past-oriented, the expectancy theories are future-oriented. Vroom (1964) and Porter and Lawler (1968) have developed major contemporary expectancy theories of motivation. Both theories rely heavily upon cognitive processes. Vroom suggests that motivation (force) is a function of the interactions among the value of particular outcomes (valence), subjective behavior-outcome probabilities (expectancy), and beliefs that first-level outcomes (e.g., working at company standards) will lead to second-level outcomes (e.g., a promotion).

Vroom called the relationship of a first-level outcome leading to a second-level outcome *instrumentality*. Figure 1-2 shows the Vroom expectancy model.

FIGURE 1–2.   The Vroom Expectancy Model of Motivation.

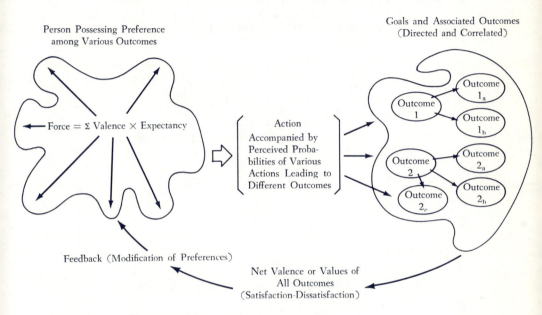

Source: Dunnette, M. D., "The Motives of Industrial Managers," Organizational Behavior and Human Performance *(May 1967), p. 178. Adapted from Vroom, V. H.,* Work and Motivation, *John Wiley & Sons, 1964. Reprinted with permission.*

Porter and Lawler extend the Vroom model. The nine-element model shown in Figure 1-3 is even more future-oriented than the Vroom model. The model shows that Porter and Lawler do not equate effort with performance. The person's abilities and traits and his/her role perceptions intervene between effort and performance. In other words, even though a person places a high value on the reward (1) and expects a high probability between the effort and reward (2) and thus puts out a lot of effort (3), this still may not lead to high performance (6). The reason may be that the person just does not have the necessary ability or traits (4) to perform well or perceives his/her role wrongly (5) and thus performs poorly.

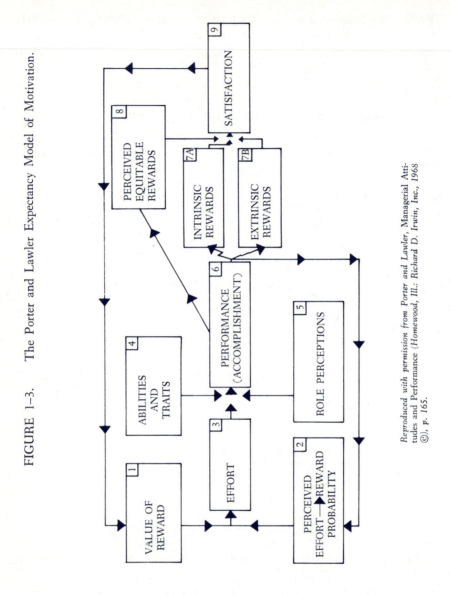

FIGURE 1–3.   The Porter and Lawler Expectancy Model of Motivation.

Reproduced with permission from Porter and Lawler, Managerial Attitudes and Performance (Homewood, Ill.: Richard D. Irwin, Inc., 1968 ©), p. 165.

Even more important, Porter and Lawler reverse the traditional human-relations assumption that satisfaction causes performance. The model shows that performance, if equitably rewarded, will lead to satisfaction. Although there has been some supportive research evidence provided by Porter and Lawler and others (Kuhn, Slocum, and Chase, 1971; Lawler, 1971; Porter and Lawler, 1968; Schuster, Clark, and Rogers,

1971), the model's reliance on unobservable internal psychological processes such as perception make isolating and experimentally testing the cause-effect relationships difficult.

Both the content and process theories of motivation depend upon internal states and processes to explain behavior. They do help to understand behavior, and the more recent expectancy models are beginning to show how expectancies and instrumentalities are acquired and modified (Graen, 1969). In addition, some theorists would argue that the expectancy model help understand the role that consequences play in organizational behavior. However, in dealing with the human problems facing today's management, understanding is not enough. Something must also be done about changing behavior in organizations. Behavioral change requires scientifically proven techniques which are conspicuously absent in the motivational approach.

LEARNING: AN ALTERNATIVE APPROACH

The external or learning approach to the understanding, prediction, and control of organizational behavior is offered as an alternative (but not as a complete replacement) to the motivational approach (Aldis, 1961; Luthans, 1973a; Luthans and White, 1971; Nord, 1969). In the external approach, *observable* behavior in organizations, and its consequences, is the key. This external or environmental model of organizational behavior is based primarily on the pioneering work of B. F. Skinner. Among Skinner's vast number of contributions, his distinction between *respondent* (unlearned) and *operant* (learned) behavior is the most important. On the basis of scientific research, he concluded that operant behavior is a function of its consequences.

Surprisingly, management scholars and practitioners became so preoccupied with the internal explanations embodied in motivation theory that they overlooked Skinners' possible contribution. This oversight was noted by Nord (1969) as follows:

> "Since the major concern of managers of human resources is the prediction and control of behavior of organizational participants, it is curious to find that people with such a need are extremely conversant with McGregor and Maslow and totally ignorant of Skinner. This condition is not surprising since leading scholars in the field, of what might be termed the applied behavioral sciences, have turned out book after book, article after article, and anthology after anthology with scarcely a mention of Skinner's contributions to the design of social systems."

Only recently have attempts been made to correct the oversight. However, the external approach to organizational behavior has met with some resistance to change, since much of the approach directly counters the more traditional internal approach.

The learning approach to organizational behavior is not designed to be simply another in a long line of panaceas. It does, however, offer a theoretical base and a set of techniques which, if properly applied, promise to be a viable alternative to present theory and practice. To refer to the application of the external, environmental, or learning approach to human behavior in organizations, the term organizational behavior modification, or simply O. B. Mod., has been coined.

ORGANIZATIONAL BEHAVIOR MODIFICATION

The term O. B. Mod. was originally used by Luthans (1973a) and later expanded by Luthans and Kreitner (1973 and 1974), Luthans and Lyman (1973), and Luthans and Ottemann (1973). It attempts to integrate the knowledge embodied in the field of organizational behavior with that called behavior modification. The assumption is that despite the primary use of behavior modification on the relatively controllable behavior of children and the behavior of deviant adults, it can be adaptable to the more complex organizational behavior of normal adults.

Virtually all organizational behavior is learned. Therefore, the extensive knowledge about learned behavior that exists in the behavioral sciences should be readily adaptable to organizational behavior. Instead of providing the practicing manager with a general understanding of organizational behavior, which the internal approaches have supplied, the O. B. Mod. approach, when fully formulated, should give the behavioral approach to management both a sound theoretical foundation and a selection of methods for shaping, changing, and directing organizational behavior toward the attainment of objectives.

Control of organizational behavior

Broadly based on behavioral or operant learning theory and more precisely based on the body of theoretical and practical knowledge known as behavior modification, O. B. Mod. attempts to systematically relate the impact that the environment has on organizational behavior. The overriding assumption is that organizational behavior depends on its consequences. The succeeding chapters will chart the historical development and contemporary state of some of the more important and relevant concepts of learning. These concepts describe how the environment actually controls learned behavior. The key word here is *controls,* not causes. Conceivably, behavior traced to its ultimate beginning must have some specific cause or causes and it may be important to isolate the causes of behavior. But the point is, that, thus far at least, years of trying have produced only hypothetical constructs in the search for causes. While the search continues, much more practical utility for human resource management can be gained by recognizing the impact that environmental consequences have on behavior. This latter approach can be graphically illustrated in Figure 1-4.

FIGURE 1–4.   Basic Behavioral Contingency.

Whereas the causes of behavior, as we know them today, are principally hypothetical, the controlling environmental mechanisms and the behavior itself are readily observable. In the terminology of Figure 1-4, cues set the occasion for organizational behavior which, when subsequently emitted by the organizational participant, is followed by various consequences. The consequences, in turn, increase, decrease, or maintain the probability that the behavior will occur again. The key to understanding this model centers on determining how and why various cues signal the individual that certain consequences will follow specific behavior or behavior patterns. To facilitate a better understanding of the simple model in Figure 1-4, we must take a closer look at the relationships between cues, behavior, and consequences.

Cues, behavior, and consequences

Cues, as the term is used in the model, represent environmental conditions or specific stimuli. Cues eventually become paired, through personal or vicarious experience, with various consequences of behavior. Cues take many forms—the behavior of supervisors, co-workers, and subordinates, as well as physical objects, rules, information, formal and informal communications, instructions, schedules, commands, time, and technological instrumentation. Singly or collectively, these behaviors or objects serve to cue organizational behavior. Cued behavior, in turn, may have many consequences. Money is a common consequence of organizational behavior but, perhaps more importantly, social approval, attention, status, privileges, and feedback about performance are also consequences. Many adverse consequences such as social sanctions, ostracism, reprimands, demotions, transfers, pay docks, and terminations are also common in modern organizations.

Despite the apparent weakening of the link between performance and rewards in contemporary organizations, both the positive and negative consequences supposedly come as a result of performance or lack of performance. Management's intent notwithstanding, these consequences concurrently become associated with environmental conditions (cues) and control the probability of the related behavior's reoccurrence. In terms of the predictability of ongoing behavior, it makes a great deal of difference if the cue-behavior-consequence relationship is systematically managed or simply left to random chance. An O. B. Mod. approach does not leave it up to chance; it makes a systematic analysis and application of all three elements: cues, behaviors, and consequences.

Reactions to the foregoing discussion may be: (1) Isn't all this about cues, behavior, and consequences common-sense knowledge? or (2) Why confuse the issue of organizational behavior with cues and consequences? These questions can be answered by noting that all organizational behavior has cues and consequences regardless of the knowledge or intent of the organizational participants (supervisors or subordinates).

All too often, the relationships between cues, behavior, and consequences are unsystematic, inconsistent, and *noncontingent*. In a noncontingent work situation the supervisor may see a subordinate's particular behavior as related to a certain cue and under the control of a certain consequence. The subordinate, on the other hand, has learned to associate a completely different cue and consequence with the behavior desired by the supervisor. For example, an office manager may feel that a threat will stimulate a clerk's performance when, in fact, the manager's action restricts output. In other words, the manager has failed to consider the dynamic relationship between cues, behavior, and consequences.

In a *contingent* work situation the cue-behavior-consequence relationships are understood by both supervisors and subordinates because they are systematically and consistently identified and managed. Subordinates learn to associate certain cues with certain consequences which are contingent upon or only come as a direct result of desirable performance. Managers, as the direct or indirect controllers of many environmental consequences, must be systematic and consistent in the management of cue-behavior-consequence relationships. The practicing manager must become aware of the importance of cues and consequences and hence *manage contingently*.

O. B. Mod. has been formulated to help the practicing manager learn to systematically and consistently manage cue-behavior-consequence relationships. The technical term for this three-element relationship is *behavioral contingency*. Behavioral contingencies are discussed in detail in Chapter 3. The specific technique of *behavioral contingency management* is discussed in Chapter 4. Once management theorists and practitioners understand how organizational behavior is maintained, strengthened, or weakened by the environment, they can begin to develop effective intervention strategies to facilitate the learning of organizational behavior that leads to goal attainment.

A PRELIMINARY WORD
ON BEHAVIOR CONTROL

Because the terms "control," "behavior modification," and, to a lesser extent, "human resource management" are value loaded, an entire chapter (Chapter 9) is devoted to the ethical implications of the organizational behavior change theories and techniques described in this book. In spite of the specific treatment given in Chapter 9, a few preliminary comments seem appropriate at this point. Questions such as the following are frequently heard when the subject of behavioral control arises: "What right does one person have to control the behavior of another?" "Who will control the controllers?" "Aren't behavior modification and its derivative, O. B. Mod., manipulative?" Instead of dealing the subject matter of this book a death blow at the beginning, such questions should actually spur the reader on to examine what O. B. Mod. is all about.

The following represent the authors' point of view for applying O. B. Mod. and its related techniques to organizational behavior problems:

1) Many *behavior problems* (theorists and practitioners may call them attitudinal, mental, or socially rooted problems) do

plague today's managers. In short, many organizational participants simply do not behave in a manner consistent with effective management and organizational goal attainment. It is important to note, however, that the authors do not make the assumption that all organizational goals as they presently exist are correct (from a moral or effectiveness standpoint).

2) The goal of predicting and controlling organizational behavior is implicit in management theory and practice.

3) Behavior is a function of its consequences and can be changed through the management of those consequences. Behavior modification techniques derived from operant learning theory have already been successfully applied in a variety of settings. The fact is that behavior can be effectively controlled via the systematic management of the environment.

4) Through the behavioral phenomenon of *countercontrol*, the supposed controller of behavior is being controlled as much as the person whose behavior is supposedly being controlled. Each is a significant part of the other's consequating environment. Self-control also plays an important role in O. B. Mod.

5) The behavior of organizational participants is already subject to cue-behavior-consequence relationships (or contingencies). Organizational participants are constantly attempting to control the contingencies of others. Unfortunately, they do it without the benefit of a working knowledge of O. B. Mod. Unsystematic contingency management may be very capricious, unpredictable, and detrimental. Basic principles of learning cannot be ignored in the behavioral approach to management as long as rewards and punishments continue to be used to induce performance in organizations.

6) In most cases the organizational environment is very aversive. Punishment is probably the most used and least understood behavior change strategy. O. B. Mod. helps to understand punishment, appreciate its often overlooked side effects, and learn to apply it appropriately and effectively when absolutely necessary. However, O. B. Mod. stresses the more effective use of positive reinforcement in changing organizational behavior.

The above points are only intended to demonstrate why a learning-based approach to human resource management is needed and how such an approach proposes to operate. These points, terms, and concepts are given detailed attention in subsequent chapters.

Learning Theory Background 2

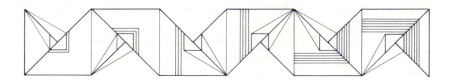

An important variant of the question "What makes people behave?" is the question "How do people learn?" Probably everyone, in varying degrees of sophistication, has their own personal learning theory. Then again, some of us may simply admit to knowing some things and not knowing others without any real idea of how we learned the things we know.

Numerous learning theories have been proposed by behavioral scientists and philosophers as well. There is little agreement among them; there is no single, universally accepted theory of learning. However, one common thread running through the behavioral science definitions of learning is the observation that a change in behavior takes place. After concurring on behavioral change, agreeing upon other aspects of learning becomes more difficult.

This chapter first defines what is meant by learning. The rest of the chapter is devoted to the historical background of learning theory. Such a historical discussion is important to O. B. Mod. because it indicates how the external approach can make a significant contribution. Without a working knowledge of learning theory, the reader and ultimately the user of O. B. Mod. would be left with a seemingly disjointed array of terms and techniques. A sense of history also enhances the credibility of any "new" subject, although the newness of behavioral learning theory as applied to human resource management is simply a function of its lack of adequate exposure.

DEFINITION OF LEARNING

One of the most heated controversies about learning stems from the same internal versus external approaches discussed in the last chapter. The internal approach or *cognitive* learning theories explain the acquisition of knowledge, but not necessarily behavior, through perception, thinking, judgment, and reason. The external approach or *behavioral* learning theories deal only with behavioral change, not cognitive, unobservable knowledge acquisition.

The behavioral learning theorists or behaviorists first make a careful distinction between *respondent* (reflexive, unlearned) behavior and *operant* (voluntary, learned) behavior. By definition, operant behavior is of major concern in learning. After giving examples of respondent behavior such as the shedding of tears while peeling onions, Keller (1954) offers a profound statement of what is meant by learned (operant) behavior:

> "Operant (voluntary) behavior includes an even greater amount of human activity—from the wrigglings and squirmings and crowings of an infant in its crib to the highest perfection and complication of adult skills and reasoning power. It takes in all those movements of an organism that may at some time be said to *have an effect upon* or *do something to* his outside world. Operant behavior *operates* on this world, so to speak, either directly or indirectly" (p. 2).

This behavior which operates on and changes the environment is what learning is all about. Thus, learning is defined and used in this book as *any change in behavior that results in a change in the environment.*

As Keller (1954) notes, it isn't always easy to determine just how the environment is changed by the operant behavior. "Only when you look into the history of such behavior will you find that, at some time or other, some form of the response in question really did make things happen" (p. 2).

Because learned behavior is defined as having some effect on the environment, behaviorists deal primarily with objective or observable behavior. The cry of a child, the depressing of typewriter keys by a secretary, and the pushing of a turret lathe start button by a machinist are all objective, observable behaviors which have an effect on the environment. On the other hand, the child's need for attention, the secretary's attitude toward work, and the machinist's drive for self-actualization are subjective and unobservable. However, a broad interpretation of learning could deal with learned needs, attitudes, and drives because they can also affect the environment.

WATSONIAN BEHAVIORISM

In 1913, an outspoken young American psychologist, John B. Watson, opened up a whole new area of thought in the study of human behavior in this country. His article, entitled "Psychology as the Behaviorist Views It," became known as "The Behaviorist Manifesto." He picked up the conditioned reflex or stimulus-response (S-R) approach to behavior where the Russian physiologists, Sechenov and, more notably, Ivan Pavlov, left off. Although the article started a revolution in American psychology, it was not entirely original (Razran, 1965). Watsonian behaviorism and Russian physiology had some features in common, such as using objective behavior as a dependent variable and conditioned reflexes as the explanatory mechanism of the objective behavior.

The classic stimulus-response mechanism

The Watsonian doctrine held that consciousness (e.g., thoughts or feelings) belonged in the realm of fantasy; human behavior could best be understood by studying observable, objective, and practical facts. In other words, Watson wanted to approach the study of behavior from the perspective of science rather than conscious experience and introspection. The latter approach had dominated psychology up to that time, but the European structuralists and American philosophers who espoused that approach were now being challenged by Watson to be more scientific.

Watson believed that all learned behavior consisted of responses elicited by prior stimuli. The stimuli supposedly came from within the organism as well as from the outside environment and continually bombarded the organism. In Watson's words (1924), "Now the organism does something when it is assailed by stimuli. It responds. It moves. The response may be so slight that it can be observed only by the use of instruments" (p. 13). Typical human responses ranged from gross motor activity to minute changes in respiration or blood pressure, and each response could be observed under the proper conditions.

Since Watson felt that most human behavior was learned, he abandoned the concept of instinct (inborn tendencies to behave in certain ways), the then popular explanation for behavior. He substituted habit for instinct. A habit was simply a learned response which eventually became paired with stimuli capable of evoking it. Hence, a trained behaviorist, according to Watson, was capable of predicting and controlling behavior by identifying the appropriate stimulus-response (S-R) pairings. Watson's intentions were clear when he stated: "The interest of the behaviorist in man's doings is more than the interest of the spectator—he wants to control man's reactions as physical scientists want to control and manipulate other natural phenomena" (Watson, 1924, p. 11).

Classic stimulus-response experiments

A frequently cited experiment by Watson and Rayner (1920) probably best illustrates Watsonian behaviorism. The object of the classic experiment was to produce a conditioned emotional response in an eleven-month-old subject named Albert. In proper Watsonian fashion, the subject's behavior was carefully and systematically observed prior to the experiment. Albert was seen as sluggish but healthy. He responded with no fear to successive presentations of unfamiliar neutral stimuli such as a monkey, a dog, a white rat, a rabbit, cotton, wool, masks with and without hair, and burning newspapers. This alone tended to refute or at least question some of the popularly held notions about instinctive fear. However, the experimenters did discover an unconditioned aversive stimulus when they struck an iron bar with a hammer above and behind the subject's head. The usually quiet Albert broke into a crying fit after three such stimulations.

With this background, Watson and Rayner (1920) asked the hypothetical question: "Can we condition fear of an animal, e.g., a white rat, by visually presenting it and simultaneously striking a steel bar?" The experimenters proceeded to present the subject with the paired stimuli, one naturally aversive and one neutral. After several pairings, Albert cried at the sight of the white rat alone. He had learned to associate the white rat with the naturally fearful noise of the hammer hitting the iron bar. In Watsonian terminology, an emotional response of fear had been conditioned through the systematic manipulation of environmental stimuli. Moreover, his conditioned fear of the white rat generalized to other furry things such as a rabbit, a dog, and a hairy Santa Claus mask.

In terms of a conditioning or learning paradigm (an ideal model), Watson and Rayner conditioned an emotional response in Albert in much the same manner that Pavlov (1927) had conditioned dogs to salivate at the sight of a luminous circle on a screen. Initially, Albert's crying in the presence of the white rat was as unnatural as a dog salivating at the sight of a lighted circle. But through the systematic presentation of paired stimuli, the child learned to associate the rat with a fearful noise and Pavlov's dogs learned to associate the sight of a luminous circle with food. Figure 2–1 outlines the conditioning paradigm which was operative during Watson's and Rayner's experiment with Albert.

Following the Pavlovian tradition, Figure 2–1 shows that a neutral stimulus (N.S.), the white rat, was paired with an unconditioned aversive stimulus (U.A.S.), which was the sound of a hammer hitting an iron bar. After a number of stimulus pairings, the previously neutral stimulus (white rat), when presented alone, elicited a conditioned emotional response (C.E.R.), which was crying. The conditioning (indicated by broken lines in Figure 2–1) gave a previously neutral stimulus aversive properties. As hypothesized, the experimenters were able to condition a fear response in Albert.

FIGURE 2–1.   The Reflex or Classical Conditioning Paradigm.

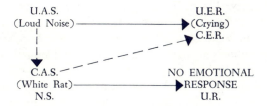

Watson's contributions

In spite of the legitimate criticism of Watson's somewhat thoughtless choice of subjects, his relatively crude research designs, and his overzealous generalizations, there can be little argument that he made some valuable contributions to the study of human behavior. As Watson's work became known, many American psychologists jumped on the Watsonian bandwagon. The popularity was a result of the confident and forceful simplicity with which Watson presented the behavioral constructs. Watson's approach especially appealed to those who had become disenchanted with the structural and functional approaches which were preoccupied with the study of the mind. As is often stated with tongue in cheek, Watson caused psychology to lose its mind.

In retrospect, Watsonian behaviorism became almost a fad and, like all fads, went out of style about as fast as it came in. According to Hilgard (1962):

"As enthusiastic supporters of such systems tend to do, they [the behaviorists] went to extremes, but gradually the excitement about behaviorism has subsided. There are still a few ardent behaviorists, but most contemporary psychologists are not extreme about it" (p. 17).

In spite of the fact that modern psychologists are generally not Watsonian behaviorists, the field of psychology has been greatly influenced by his work. Probably the single greatest impact comes from his recognition of the scientific value of studying observable behavior. Instead of taking hypothetical trips into the mind, Watson offered a viable, scientific alternative. He challenged the field of psychology to be scientific in the following words:

"Why don't we make what we can observe the real field of psychology? Let us limit ourselves to things that can be observed, and formulate laws concerning only the observed things. Now what can we observe? Well, we can observe *behavior—what the organism does or says*" (Watson and MacDougall, 1929, p. 18).

His challenge to deal only with observable behavior has been heeded by many modern psychologists. On the other hand, his preoccupation with S-R connections has been questioned. Contemporary behaviorists do not go along with Watson's S-R explanation for all learned behavior. Today, more attention is focused on the effect of subsequent stimuli on objective behavior than on causal prior stimuli. The reinforcement learning theorists are largely responsible for this shift in focus.

REINFORCEMENT LEARNING THEORIES

Like Watsonian behaviorism, the reinforcement theories deal with objective behavior rather than consciousness or cognitive processes. However, with the exception of Edwin R. Guthrie, who, like Watson, believed that learning resulted from the pairing of stimuli and responses, Watson's behaviorist successors placed increasing emphasis on the use of *reinforcement* or rewards in learning. This marked a significant departure from Watson's S-R paradigm in which prior stimuli evoked or elicited a response.

Generally interpreted, reinforcement can only have an effect if the response comes first. This has meant a reversal of the traditional S-R paradigm. Since a reinforcing event in the environment could be interpreted as a stimulus, an R-S pairing actually replaced S-R as the dominant theme of behaviorism. Among the learning theorists most often associated with this R-S orientation are Edward L. Thorndike, Clark Hull, Neal Miller, and most notably B. F. Skinner.

The reinforcement theorists were convinced that Watsonian behaviorism was not an adequate explanation of complex behavior. They saw learned behavior as strengthened or reinforced by rewards. The effect of reinforcement on behavior was initially proposed in the concept of hedonism. However, the reinforcement learning theorists went beyond simple hedonism.

Law of effect

The first comprehensive reinforcement theory of learning can be found in Edward L. Thorndike's law of effect. Through years of scientific animal research he discovered the impact of behavioral consequences. Rather than depending exclusively upon prior eliciting stimuli as the causal factor in learned behavior, as Watson had done, Thorndike turned to consequences for explaining behavior. The resulting law of effect is described by Thorndike (1913) as follows:

"When a modifiable connection between a situation and a response is made and is accompanied or followed by a satisfying state of affairs, that connection's strength is increased: when made and accompanied or followed by an annoying state of affairs, its strength is decreased" (p. 4).

Stimulus-response connections, according to Thorndike's interpretation, are reinforced or strengthened by satisfying consequences. His law has had a lasting impact on the understanding, prediction, and control of behavior. For example, Millenson (1967) claims that the law of effect ". . . survives today as a fundamental principle in the analysis and control of adaptive behavior" (p. 10) and Vroom (1964), after reviewing the motivation literature, concluded:

"Without a doubt the law of effect or principle of reinforcement must be included among the most substantiated findings of experimental psychology and is at the same time among the most useful findings for an applied psychology concerned with the control of human behavior" (p. 13).

Drive-reduction theory

Another pioneering reinforcement theorist was Clark L. Hull. A Yale psychologist with an engineering background, Hull formulated a complex scientific theory of psychology, complete with mathematical postulates, logic, and theorems. Hill (1963) notes that "Hull did not regard his theory as a final statement about the nature of learning. Rather, it was intended as a tentative formulation, always subject to revision to bring it in line with new data or new ideas" (p. 132).

Hull proposed a drive-reduction theory characterizing behavior as caused by the independent variables of deprivation, painful stimulation, magnitude of reward, and number of previously reinforced training trials. He felt that these four independent variables led to three intervening variables: drive, resulting from deprivation and pain; incentive motivation, tied to the magnitude of reward; and habit strength, derived from the number of previously reinforced training trials. Finally, a combination of drive, incentive motivation, and habit strength generate an excitatory potential, i.e., a tendency to respond in a given manner in the presence of an appropriate stimulus.

Despite the fact that it was more sophisticated than Watson's mechanistic interpretation, Hull's theory largely followed Watson's lead by contending that all behavior involves stimulus-response connections. Hull simply considered the effect of reinforcement while Watson did not. It is the habit-strength variable, based upon the number of previously reinforced training trials, that qualifies Hull as a reinforcement learning theorist. Otherwise, he could be considered a motivation theorist.

Neal Miller, another Yale psychologist, extended Hull's theory. Miller divided learning into four basic elements: drive, cue, response, and reward. Like Thorndike and Hull, Miller considered the effects of both prior and subsequent stimuli on behavior. According to Miller, subsequent stimuli in the form of rewarding events have the capacity to strengthen behavior. For example, a small boy may learn to run to his father when he comes home from a trip. Broken down into Miller's elements, the boy likes candy (drive), so when he hears the garage door slam (cue), he runs (response) to his dad to get some candy (reward). If the boy in fact does receive the candy, this will strengthen the probability of running to his father in the future. Miller believed that all learned behavior could be broken down this way.

SKINNERIAN BEHAVIORISM

Like the others discussed above, the Harvard psychologist B. F. Skinner could also be considered a reinforcement theorist. But in terms of empirical research, written literature, conceptual formulations, or contro- versy, Skinner certainly deserves special attention. He is so important that a few years ago the American Psychological Association voted him the most influential living psychologist. In an articulate and logical fashion, Skinner has merged his predecessors' and his own work into a practical technology of learned behavior (see: Skinner, 1969; Skinner, 1971).

Watson and Thorndike laid the primary historical foundation for Skinner's work. Conceptually, Skinner's approach can be traced to Wat- son's preoccupation with objective, observable behavior and Thorndike's emphasis on the effect of the consequences of behavior. Over forty years of exacting laboratory and field research by Skinner, his students, and conceptual adherents have produced an impressive theoretical and empirical base for a comprehensive behavioral learning theory.

At the very heart of Skinnerian behaviorism is a single contention. *Behavior is a function of its consequences.* The Skinnerian explana- tion is based on the external approach; it emphasizes the effect of en- vironmental consequences on objective, observable behavior. In Skinner's words (1953):

> "The practice of looking inside the organism for an explanation of behavior has tended to obscure the variables which are im- mediately available for a scientific analysis. These variables lie outside the organism, in its immediate environment and in its environmental history" (p. 31).

The collective influence of both Watson and Thorndike are ap- parent in this statement. Before discussing the more technical aspects of Skinnerian behaviorism, however, it may be interesting to analyze why Skinner and his works are so controversial.

The controversy surrounding Skinner

Find a dozen people who have heard of B. F. Skinner and quite probably a surprising number of them will be critical of him and his work. If the matter is pursued and the critics are asked exactly how familiar they are with Skinner's work, typically the answer will be that they have read excerpts from *Beyond Freedom and Dignity* (1971), Skinner's most recent and controversial work. When one considers the logical sequence of a scientist's career (basic research, formulation, application, publication, and extrapolation), it appears that critics who are familiar with Skinner's work only through a quick reading or a second-hand account of *Beyond Freedom and Dignity* have overlooked the other crucial steps of Skinner's extensive career (see: Skinner, 1938; Skinner, 1953; Skinner, 1969).

Too often, the criticisms of Skinner and his works are based upon misinformation and misunderstanding. The general public and particularly many management scholars and practitioners have not been exposed to Skinner's basic premises and the many valuable contributions he has made to the study of human behavior. Instead, most people are familiar only with the extrapolation stage of Skinner's career. All they know of him is that he suggested behavioral control and manipulation of people as ways to change our culture. This, of course, collides with the cherished American concepts of freedom, dignity, and democracy. The desirability or lack of desirability of Skinner's extrapolation should not be allowed to depreciate the quality, importance, or relevance of his other work. It is his basic research findings and theoretical formulations that are of particular interest to the development of O. B. Mod.

Management scholars or practitioners who take the time to carefully study Skinner's fundamental concepts of behavior control should see the potential application to managing people. Many of Skinner's concepts and principles have been empirically validated both in the laboratory and in field settings. Even his most ardent critics admit that his behavior principles work. The position taken by this book is that the behavioral approach to management should study Skinnerian behaviorism and apply its techniques as the situation warrants. Skinnerian behaviorism certainly does not represent the final answer to the behavioral approach to management, but it does represent a badly neglected area that needs study and application.

The essence of Skinnerian behaviorism

In 1938, B. F. Skinner, then an assistant professor of psychology at the University of Minnesota, wrote a book, entitled *The Behavior of Organisms,* which permanently altered the course of twentieth-century behaviorism and the entire field of psychology. While citing the significance of this book, Skinner (1938) noted: "One outstanding aspect of the present book, which can hardly be overlooked, is the shift in emphasis from respondent to operant behavior" (p. 438). With the publication of this book, Skinner made a break with his behaviorist predecessors by relegating stimulus-response connections to a comparatively minor role in the explanation of behavior.

While Pavlov, Watson, Thorndike, Hull, and Miller each to a greater or lesser degree characterized all behavior as chains of S-R connections, Skinner looked beyond reflexes to environmental consequences as the controlling mechanisms of learned behavior. He attached the label *operant* to learned behavior because it operates on the environment to produce a consequence. He called unlearned or reflexive behavior *respondent* behavior.

Skinner was the first to make the important distinction between operant and respondent behavior. Had he not done so, behaviorists might have spent years developing patchwork formulations intended to explain all behavior in terms of S-R connections. The respondent/operant distinction has permitted learning theorists to accurately portray the environment as a source of both prior and consequent stimuli relative to objective behavior. The traditional S-R paradigm has been found acceptable for explaining respondent behavior but unacceptable for explaining operant behavior. Operant behavior, as initially conceived by Skinner, is seen as that behavior which is shaped, strengthened, maintained, or weakened by its consequences.

Respondent and operant behavior

Respondent behavior is that behavior which is *elicited* by a prior stimulus. It most commonly occurs in the form of reflexes. To the extent that reflexive behavior comes naturally, it is unlearned. Healthy human beings do not have to learn to jerk their knee in response to a doctor's tap with a hammer or learn to shed tears while peeling onions. Respondent behavior is a function of our genetic history or endowment. It was this type of S-R scheme that the early behaviorists generalized to all behavior. Operant behavior, on the other hand, is *emitted* by the organism rather than elicited by a definite prior stimulus; operant behavior must be learned. Most complex human behavior falls into this operant category.

Operant behavior, although it may become paired with prior stimuli, is not caused by the prior stimuli in the sense that the doctor's tap causes the knee-jerk response. For example, if an individual emits behavior appropriate to the successful driving of an automobile only when sitting behind the steering wheel, the steering wheel cannot be called a stimulus which elicits or causes the driving behavior. The driving responses are said to be emitted because of the effects they will produce in the environmnt, namely, getting quickly and safely from one location to another.

The fundamental difference between respondent and operant behavior may be further illustrated by the functional relationship between a response and the environment. With respondent behavior the environment acts on the organism in the form of a stimulus-response connection. The reverse functional relationship is true in operant behavior. The organism must act on the environment to produce a consequence. The doctor must tap the knee in respondent behavior but the individual must drive the automobile in operant behavior. This difference is very important in understanding learned behavior.

Operant conditioning

With the distinction between respondent and operant behavior clarified, it is now possible to examine a procedure Skinner called *operant conditioning*. Skinner (1953) makes the distinction between operant conditioning and respondent or classical conditioning as follows:

> "Pavlov . . . called all events which strengthened behavior 'reinforcement' and all the resulting changes 'conditioning.' In the Pavlovian experiment, however, a reinforcer is paired with a *stimulus;* whereas in operant behavior it is contingent upon a response. Operant reinforcement is therefore a separate process and requires a separate analysis" (p. 65).

The influence of Thorndike's law of effect on operant conditioning is obvious. Essentially, an operant, once emitted by an organism, may be effectively controlled or conditioned (strengthened, maintained, or eliminated) through the systematic management of the consequences of that behavior. It is important to emphasize that this can only occur with operant or learned behavior.

Recent experiments indicate there is more accurately a gray rather than a black and white distinction between respondent and operant behavior. Further experimentation will eventually make this important distinction more operational. However, relative to the use of operant conditioning in management, there is no question that virtually all organizational behavior falls into the operant category. Organizational behavior is largely learned. It follows that the mechanism of learning brought out by Skinner may be managed and applied to organizational behavior.

The concept of contingency

The final Skinnerian contribution to be discussed is the concept of contingency. Contingencies are specific formulations of the interaction between an organism's operant behavior and its environment (Skinner, 1969, p. 7). A contingent relationship could be simply thought of as an if-then relationship. Learned behavior operates on the environment to produce a change in the environment. Therefore, if the behavior causes the environmental change, then the environmental change can be said to be contingent upon the behavior. In other words, the specific environmental change only comes when the behavior has been emitted. For example, getting coffee from the office coffee machine is contingent upon inserting the proper coinage in the slot. *If* the proper coin is inserted, *then* coffee will come out. In this particular contingency we see an obvious behavior (putting in the coin) and an equally obvious consequence (coffee).

Technically, prior environmental conditions or cues also play an important role in contingencies. The Skinnerian concept of contingency involves three major elements: (1) a prior environmental state or cue; (2) a behavior; and (3) a consequence. The process of reducing complex behavior into these three elements of the contingency is termed *functional analysis*. Functional analysis attempts to systematically determine what cues are present when a specific response is emitted and, more importantly, what consequences are supporting that response.

Skinner (1969) contrasted the contingency concept (cue-behavior-consequence) with the more traditional S-R scheme in the following way:

"The relationships are much more complex than those between a stimulus and a response, and they are much more productive in both theoretical and experimental analyses. The behavior generated by a given set of contingencies can be accounted for without appealing to hypothetical inner states or processes. If a conspicuous stimulus does not have an effect, it is not because the organism has not attended to it or because some central gatekeeper has screened it out, but because the stimulus plays no important role in the prevailing contingencies" (pp. 7–8).

By viewing all learned behavior in the context of contingencies, Skinnerian behaviorists have been able to study how behavior is learned by systematically managing the contingencies of animals in highly controlled experimental settings and studying humans in less controlled environments. The result of this research has been a reliable technology of learned behavior. Much of the material in the succeeding chapters can be attributed directly or indirectly to the work of B. F. Skinner.

BEHAVIOR MODIFICATION

Watsonian and Skinnerian behaviorism serve as the theoretical and research base for the actual techniques of behavioral change commonly called behavior modification. The precise meaning of behavior modification, like learning itself, is difficult to pin down. Goodall (1972) points out that in its short lifetime, the term behavior modification has come to mean so many things to so many people that it is fast losing whatever meaning it once had. However, in its broadest interpretation, behavior modification refers to the application of techniques derived from the two schools of behaviorism with their accompanying classical and operant conditioning theories and procedures.

An approach called *behavior therapy* is most closely associated with Watsonian behaviorism and classical conditioning. Behavior therapy, based on the work of Wolpe (1958) and others, is used in the clinical psychotherapeutic treatment of maladaptive behavior (for example, see: Sherman, 1973). Skinnerian behaviorism and its operant conditioning paradigm, meanwhile, has been widely applied in an approach commonly referred to as *applied behavior analysis*. It is carried on in natural, real-life settings. The emphasis is upon changing behavior through the management of consequences. Most of the specific behavioral change techniques presented as O. B. Mod. could collectively fall under applied behavior analysis.

Specifically, behavior modification (popularly known as B. Mod.) is the practical application of Skinnerian operant conditioning and related techniques. The word "practical" is particularly significant because behavior modification is most frequently used with actual human behavior problems as opposed to experimentally arranged laboratory problems. While citing examples of trends toward the study of behavior in natural settings, Brandt (1972) has noted the following about behavior modification:

> ". . . [An] important trend is the activity of change agents, especially those practicing behavior modification or operant conditioning techniques in everyday settings. Here is an instance in which techniques originally developed in the laboratory are now being applied widely in naturalistic settings. Classical conditioning techniques, on the other hand, have not yet been transferred from the laboratory to the field to any great extent" (p. 13).

Change agents using behavior modification in the natural environment attempt to identify and rearrange the consequences of which behavior is a function. Simply stated, behavior modifiers systematically manage the contingencies they isolate, thereby effecting changes in behavior. In general use for less than a decade (for examples of early applications, see: Krasner and Ullmann, 1965; Ullmann and Krasner, 1965), behavior modification, in one form or another, has been used successfully in clinics, hospitals, schools, factories, and homes.

Unfortunately, like its founding father B. F. Skinner, behavior modification has been marked by much recent controversy. Also like Skinner, much of the controversy surrounding behavior modification is based on misinformation and misunderstanding. The next chapter, which gives specific attention to the principles of behavior modification, will hopefully settle this problem, at least in its application to human resource management.

FIGURE 2–2.   Historical Development of Organizational Behavior
                Modification.

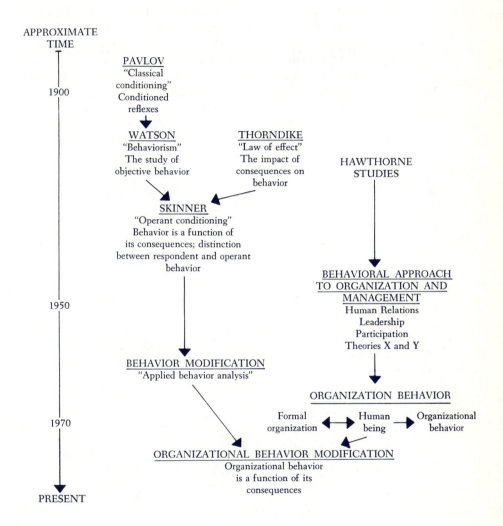

O. B. MOD: HISTORICAL INTEGRATION

Figure 2–2 graphically and chronologically traces the historical contributions to O. B. Mod. As the graph shows, O. B. Mod. is an integration of operant learning theory/behavior modification and behavioral management theory/organizational behavior.

The most significant point of departure for O. B. Mod. is the Skinnerian assumption, based upon many years of empirical research, that *organizational behavior is a function of its consequences.*

Principles of   3
Behavior Modification

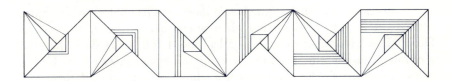

Behavior modification is a scientifically derived set of principles and techniques which can be used to effectively change behavior. Behavior modification principles and techniques have largely evolved from the work of the behavioral learning theorists discussed in the last chapter. Contrary to the mistaken notion of some people, behavior modification is not mystical psychological manipulation of people. Instead, it is a straightforward technology of learned behavior and, like any technology, has underlying principles and procedural methodology. A working knowledge of the principles and techniques will facilitate the development of the technical skills necessary for the successful application of the O. B. Mod. approach to human resource management. This chapter translates the vast amount of theoretical, technical, and empirical behavior modification literature into workable form and language for human resource management.

At this point, the reader is asked to examine the following critical incidents which represent fairly typical human resource management situations. A surface analysis will suffice for now but it would be helpful if the reader made some notes to himself/herself on each incident. The purpose of this exercise is to initially consider three typical situations, read the "what" and "how" of behavior modification (keeping the incidents in mind as practical references), and then reconsider each of the situations in a behavior modification framework. The reader's self-comparison of his/her analyses of the incidents before and after reading about behavior modification should prove interesting.

Incident 1: During an annual performance appraisal meeting, a section chief in a heavy manufacturing firm warns one of his first-line supervisors that he may be terminated after six weeks if his general attitude doesn't improve. Six weeks later the supervisor is terminated and complains of not knowing why.

Incident 2: A head nurse in a general hospital feels she should stay one step ahead of her subordinates by keeping them guessing. She feels that her practice of really raising hell with her entire staff once or twice a month helps keep them in line. While talking with a management consultant, she confides that her staff's overall performance and satisfaction are not what she would like them to be or thinks they could be.

Incident 3: During lunch one day, a secretary for an insurance company relates to a friend her observation that whenever the Claims Department boss comes to work in a bad mood and comes down hard on a couple of people, the mood of the entire office staff takes a turn for the worse. Everyone in the office becomes edgy and nervous and there is a lot of griping about the company.

FUNDAMENTAL PRINCIPLES

Three fundamental principles seem to emerge from the extensive literature on behavior modification. They include: (1) the necessity of dealing exclusively with observable behavioral events; (2) the use of frequency of behavioral events as the basic datum; and (3) the importance of viewing behavior within a contingency context. An understanding of these principles is the first step toward applying O. B. Mod to the practice of more effective human resource management.

Behavioral events

DEAL IN TERMS OF SPECIFIC, OBSERVABLE BEHAVIORAL EVENTS OR RESPONSES WHICH HAVE AN OBSERVABLE EFFECT ON THE ENVIRONMENT.

Following the tradition of Watsonian behaviorism, behavior modification takes a scientific view of human behavior. To satisfy the scientific goals of understanding, prediction, and control, the study of human behavior only deals with observable behavior. In experimental terms, the dependent (effect) variable in behavior modification is always observable behavior or behavior which has an observable effect on the environment. The major independent (cause) variables include reinforcement, stimulus control, deprivation-satiation, and aversive stimuli (Wenrich, 1970, p. 7).

Deprivation-satiation, in contrast to the other three independent variables, is of little utility to the study of organizational behavior. As Luthans and Otteman (1973) point out:

> "The deprivation-satiation of primary reinforcers (food, water, sex, and sleep) have been a central concern of traditional motivation theorists in psychology. However, in organizations these primary needs and drives have little relevance to more complex human behavior. Of greater importance to organizational behavior are the conditioned or secondary reinforcers."

Deprivation-satiation mainly applies to unlearned, not learned, behaviors. Thus, reinforcement, stimulus control, and aversive stimuli are the independent variables most applicable to the prediction and control of the sole dependent variable, observable organizational behavior.

The independent variables are given attention later. The dependent variable is the focus of the first principle. However, just noting the importance of observable behavior is not enough. Realizing that the measurement of a dependent variable is a vital characteristic of a scientific approach, we must reduce behavior down into workable units. The working unit for behavior modification is the *behavioral event*. Skinner (1969), referring to such behavioral events as responses, pointed out:

> "To be observed, a response must affect the environment—it must have an effect upon an observer or upon an instrument which in turn can affect an observer. This is as true of the contraction of a small group of muscle fibers as of pressing a lever or pacing a figure 8. If we can see a response, we can make reinforcement contingent upon it; if we are to make a reinforcer contingent upon a response, we must be able to see it or at least its effects" (p. 130).

The terms behavioral event and response are used interchangeably; they are the basic, measurable building blocks of behavior.

Figure 3–1 offers some examples of the difference between behavior and related behavioral events or responses. The behavior modifier's basic building blocks are the behavioral events or responses, not overall behavior. The figure shows that the behavioral events are much more specific and represent only one instance of a larger class of behavior. Although the identification of overall behavior gets the behavior modifier headed in the right direction, it lacks the specificity necessary for a meaningful functional analysis (cue-behavior-consequence). An effective functional analysis can come only from the identification, observation, and measurement of specific behavioral events.

FIGURE 3–1.   Identifying Behavioral Events.

Behavior	General Effect on the Environment	Specific Response or Behavioral Event
1. Approving behavior (nonverbal)	Increases the strength of the approved behavior	A floor manager of a department store gives a subordinate a smile and a nod of approval.
2. Approving behavior (verbal)	Increases the strength of the approved behavior	An Army sergeant tells a private to "keep up the good work."
3. Disapproving behavior (nonverbal)	Decreases the strength of the disapproved behavior	An office manager shakes her head and frowns in disapproval of a clerk's action.
4. Disapproving behavior (verbal)	Decreases the strength of the disapproved behavior	After a rough landing a flight instructor tells his student pilot to make a slower approach next time.
5. Punctual behavior	Increases the probability of getting to designated places on time	An industrial-products salesman arrives at the outer office of a potential customer five minutes early for an appointment.
6. Tardy behavior	Increases the probability of getting to designated places late	An assembly-line worker in an automobile plant punches in twenty-five minutes after start-up time.
7. Disruptive behavior	Disrupts or otherwise interrupts the productive behavior of others	An electrician taps a busy welder on the shoulder and tells him a joke.
8. Productive behavior (in a work context)	Facilitates the achievement of organizational goals	A secretary rapidly types an error-free letter.
9. Unproductive behavior (in a work context)	Hinders the achievement of organizational goals	An assistant personnel administrator in a hospital calls in sick and goes golfing.
10. Instructive behavior	Increases the probability of another's productive behavior	A head bank teller takes time to suggest a more efficient way of handling a transaction to an assistant.

Using the illustrations in Figure 3–1 as a general guide, the reader may want to construct similar examples. Behavior other than that listed may be identified or those in the figure may be reused to identify other possible behavioral events. The behavior listed represents a whole class of typical organizational behavior events. To do the exercise, simply identify a behavior, note its general effect on the environment, and observe and record related behavioral events as emitted by yourself or anyone around you. Then check back to Figure 3–1 and see if each of your listings of the behavior, the general effect, and the behavioral event is somewhat equivalent to those listed in Figure 3–1. You may find that this is not as simple as you thought it would be. Yet, in order to change behavior, the specific behavioral event must first be identified.

Frequency of behavioral events

MEASURE BEHAVIOR IN TERMS OF RESPONSE FREQUENCY.

Measurement lies at the very heart of any scientific analysis. The dependent variable (observable behavior events, in this case) must be quantifiable so that the effect the independent variable has on it can be measured. The measurement of behavior has taken many forms in the past. Hilgard's and Marquis' (1940) classic review of conditioning states: "Among the measures of strength of response used in inferring strength of conditioning may be mentioned magnitude, latency, percentage frequency, total number of responses, and rate of responding" (pp. 136–37).

Importantly, it was not until behavioral scientists started using rate of responding or *frequency* of behavioral events as a dependent variable that a science of behavior became a distinct possibility (Skinner, 1966, p. 16). An important change in emphasis accompanied the shift in focus. What the organism did or how it behaved was relegated to a position of secondary importance; the key lay in *how often* it emitted the response in question. In modern analysis, responses occurring frequently are said to be relatively strong whereas responses with low frequency are considered relatively weak. The important point is not the size or intensity of the behavioral event, but how often it is emitted. For example, it is not how fast the shipping clerk runs from the plant gate to the punchclock, but the frequency of his punching in on time or not that is important to behavior modification.

The past dimension of response frequency • There are two important dimensions of response frequency which relate to time. As noted, a record of the frequency with which a given response has occurred during a specified time period indicates its strength. In this case, the time focus is historical or past-oriented. The behavioral events have happened and they are a matter of historical record. Records of such response frequency may be formally recorded on paper or recorded in a person's memory. For example, an employee with a reputation for prompt task completion may have that reputation because his personnel folder contains several performance appraisal sheets noting prompt task completions in the past. However, much less formal response records generally are kept.

Whether aware of it or not, most people carry countless response records in their memory. The common practice of labeling people shows this to be true. For example, Mr. A is the office flirt, Ms. B is a hard worker, Mr. C is a golf nut, Mr. D is honest because he pays all his personal debts promptly, and Mr. E is a bug on keeping the shop floor clean. Upon close inspection, each of these statements or labels reflects the strength of a particular response. Response strength is a function of observed response frequency, and response frequency is the basic datum for measurement of behavioral events.

The future dimension of response frequency • The other key dimension of response frequency deals with future time and the prediction of behavior. Probability goes hand in hand with the prediction of the future. Applied to frequency of response, probability is an extrapolation of the past; it is an inference based upon past rate of responding (Skinner, 1969, p. 118). The stronger a response, as indicated by its frequency of occurrence, the greater its probability of reoccurrence. By the same token, the weaker a response, the lower its probability of reoccurrence.

Although the concept of response probability may appear complex, we commonly make use of it. For instance, when a regional sales manager commends a salesman for making an important sale, he is not attempting to alter the complex chain of behavior just emitted. That behavior has passed inalterably into history. The sales manager hopes that his commendation will increase the probability of similar behavior on the part of the salesman in the future.

The relationship between the past and future dimensions of response frequency is subtle, but important. With regard to behavior prediction and control (the future), the behavior modifier attempts to alter the probability of response by systematically and consistently managing the consequences of observable behavioral events. Unavoidably, the success or failure of such behavior modification efforts is revealed in a carefully kept record of response frequency (the past). In this manner, both dimensions of response frequency are appropriate to a science of learned behavior.

Mechanics of measuring frequency • There are certain mechanics of formally recording response frequency. The word *frequency* denotes a link between number of occurrences and time. More specifically, frequency measures the number of times a phenomenon has occurred during a specified period. We often speak in terms of such frequency when describing our daily lives. Some examples include: "I've been to eight conventions in two years"; "My golf game was really on today; I birdied four holes"; and "This punchpress has jamed twelve times today." Each of these statements identifies the frequency of some event over time. In each case something happened a given number of times during a specified time period. The application of frequency to behavior modification is similar except that more attention is given to specific responses as they occur over time.

Once a behavioral event has been identified and is under observation, the recording of its frequency of occurrence is made relatively simple through the use of a two-dimensional chart similar to the one shown in Figure 3–2. This procedure is called *charting*. The vertical axis represents number of occurrences and the horizontal axis represents elapsed time.

FIGURE 3–2.   Charting Response Frequencies.

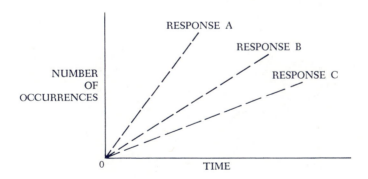

Inspection of the response frequency chart quickly shows the relative strength of the charted responses. By comparing the slopes or steepness of the three response frequencies charted in Figure 3–2, the reader can see that A is relatively stronger than B and B, in turn, is relatively stronger than C.

When response frequency is measured prior to attempts to change the behavior, the measurement is called a *baseline*. A baseline measure can tell an observer the natural or unmanaged strength of responses. In experimental terms, the baseline is essentially the control condition. The baseline data plays an important role in any systematic approach to changing behavior.

A practical example of charting • Figure 3–3 shows how an on-the-job response such as unauthorized absences from the work area can be charted. Changes in the frequency of a single response such as the one shown in the figure reveal past consequences of that response. During the first month of observation, the response grew steadily stronger which sug-

FIGURE 3–3.   Hypothetical Response Frequency Chart.

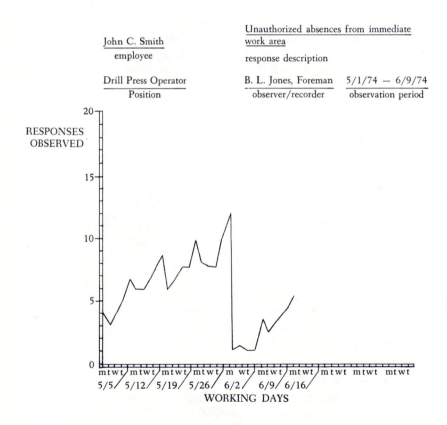

gests the presence of a favorable environment for such behavior. Also during the first month a trend in responding seemed to be developing. Smith's unauthorized absences were less frequent on Mondays but advanced during the week. Each Friday shows a new high. Evidently, the environment became progressively supportive as each weekday passed. Then suddenly on Monday, May 29, the employee did not emit the response once.

Since other relevant information is missing, one can only make an educated guess as to what caused the reversal. Considering the dramatic drop in frequency, it is very likely that Smith was contingently punished for wandering away from his job. Unfortunately, as is frequently the case with punishment, the response dramatically dropped off but only temporarily. The behavior subsequently reestablished itself. The purpose of this example is not to get into all the dynamics of behavioral change (an entire later chapter is devoted to punishment), but the illustration does point out the importance of charting response frequencies in making a systematic analysis of behavior.

The foregoing discussion of the response frequency chart had a noted absence of any reference to terms such as "attitudes," "motives," "drives," "desires," "needs," or "purposes." These inner states simply have no place in an objective, scientific analysis of behavior. Only the frequency of observable behavior serves as a useful datum. Finally, when placed in the context of a behavioral contingency, frequency of response not only tells us how strong a particular response is, but it also tells us what environmental conditions are responsible for its strength.

Behavioral contingencies

BECAUSE BEHAVIOR IS A FUNCTION OF ITS CONSEQUENCES, THE CONTINGENCY RELATIONSHIP MUST BE IDENTIFIED.

The third and final principle of behavior modification is a basic premise in O. B. Mod. and has been mentioned frequently: *Behavior is a function of its consequences.* The importance of this principle is derived from the vital connection between behavior and its consequences. Stated another way, behavior is strengthened, maintained, and weakened by its consequences. Consistent with the second principle, the strength of behavior is always measured in terms of response frequency. At the heart of this third principle is a concept that ties behavior modification together, *behavioral contingency.*

Modern behaviorists use the term contingency to identify a dependent relationship between an organism and its immediate environment. Consistent with Watson's preoccupation with objective behavior and Thorndike's law of effect, this contingent relationship describes how objective behavior is determined (i.e., controlled in response frequency) by its consequences. Thus, contingencies help isolate the effects of consequences on response frequency. Skinner (1969) identified the three major elements of a behavioral contingency, sometimes referred to as a three-term contingency, as follows:

> "An adequate formulation of the interaction between an organism and its environment must always specify three things: (1) the occasion upon which a response occurs, (2) the response itself, and (3) the . . . consequences. The interrelationships among them are the contingencies . . ." (p. 7).

In response/consequence pairings, where the response must first be emitted before the consequence occurs, the consequence is contingent upon the response. In other words, an if-then sequence exists. *If* the response is emitted by the person, *then* the consequence occurs. Socially shy employees, for example, may be contingent in their greeting behavior of co-workers; if someone says hello to them first, then they will reciprocate.

Importantly, as individuals learn to associate certain consequences with certain environmental occasions or situations (cues), other sets of if-then contingencies evolve. In this case, the "if" becomes a particular situation in the immediate environment such as physical location, commands, instructions, or proximity of certain other people, and the "then" becomes a response. As an example, if an enlisted man walks past an officer, then he will salute. Either by following rules or by actually learning through personal or vicarious experience which consequences are paired with which situations, the behavior of people may actually come to be controlled by environmental situations or cues.

Such so-called *stimulus control*, however, is not functionally equivalent to the traditional behaviorism S-R connection in spite of the surface similarity. Cues in the contingent relationship do not elicit (cause) learned responses in the manner that onion juice elicits tears; cues only *set the occasion* for the person to emit a response which is, in turn, followed by a consequence. Cues do not *cause* the response.

The three-term contingency was depicted in Chapter 1 as cue-behavior-consequence. Since cues represent antecedent events or events

FIGURE 3-4. Organizational Behavior Contingencies.

	Antecedent	⟶	Behavioral Event	⟶	Consequence
1.	Payday		Opening the mailbox for a paycheck		Receiving a paycheck
2.	A manager enters the work area		Telling the manager how well the work is progressing		Receiving a compliment from the manager
3.	Proximity of the office clown		Asking if he's heard any good ones lately		Hearing a joke
4.	A messy work area		Ordering all machine operators to clean around their machines		A clean work area
5.	A letter in the "In" basket		Answering the letter		An empty "In" basket
6.	A pressure gauge needle nears the danger point		Making an appropriate mechanical adjustment		The pressure gauge needle returns to normal
7.	A computer program fails to run		Rewriting a format statement		The program runs
8.	An exceptionally hectic day at the office		Berating the secretary		The secretary's performance drops
9.	An overhead job needs to be quickly finished before quitting time		Climbing an unsafe ladder		Falling through a broken rung
10.	A position description posted on the luncheon bulletin board		Applying for the position in the personnel office		Getting the position

occurring prior to a response being emitted, an ANTECEDENT $\longrightarrow$ BE-HAVIOR $\longrightarrow$ CONSEQUENCE, or simply an A→B→C model, can be used to identify each term and its relationship to the other two terms in the three-term contingency. Some common organizational contingencies are listed in Figure 3–4. At this point the reader may want to pick up where he/she left off in identifying behaviors and related behavioral events derived from Figure 3–1 and observe and record some behavioral contingencies. Figure 3–4 should be used as a guide while the reader works on the "A→B→C's" of behavior modification.

The A→B→C model is used throughout the rest of the book to represent the important three-term contingency. Functional analysis reduces complex learned or operant behavior to A→B→C terms. Once reduced, behavioral events become manageable through the systematic and consistent control of consequences and consequence/antecedent pairings.

SPECIFIC PROCEDURES AND TECHNIQUES

The basic procedures and techniques of behavior modification are derived from the collective principles of behavior modification just discussed. Behavioral events are the common denominator, frequency of response permits objective quantification and measurement of behavior, and contingencies reveal the person/environment interaction. Each of the three principles was abstracted out of context for the purposes of description and analysis. Now they are placed back into a whole context for a discussion of the "hows" of behavior modification. Some of the more important hows include intervention strategies, schedules of reinforcement, discrimination and generalization, chained behavior, shaping, and modeling. Each of these should be considered in light of the three principles of behavior modification.

Intervention strategies

Behavioral control basically involves the management of contingencies. However, before contingencies can be managed, the manager must possess a working knowledge of the effects that various consequences have on response frequency. While the principle "behavior is a function of its consequences" speaks of a person/environment interaction, it is not specific enough for a technology of behavioral change. It fails to describe exactly how consequences come to effect changes in response frequency.

Earlier it was suggested that behavior, in terms of the principle of response frequency, may be strengthened, maintained, or weakened. Yet, like the other principles, this one fails to describe how consequences affect frequency of responding.

Fortunately, there are some answers to the questions raised by the principles of behavior modification. Years of scientific experimentation have produced precise information needed for the control of response frequency with contingent consequences. Four general behavior modification strategies have emerged. The four strategies are positive reinforcement, negative reinforcement, punishment, and extinction. These strategies for behavioral change may be used singly or in various combinations. Each strategy defines a class of consequences which has a particular effect on response frequency. However, it should be remembered that the consequences must be contingent upon a specific behavioral event.

Positive and negative reinforcement, punishment, and extinction may be called strategies if they are systematically applied as consequences to bring about changes in response frequency. However, it is important to note that the four approaches work equally well when applied in an unwitting, accidental, and unsystematic way. The point is, to varying degrees everybody is already a behavior modifier, struggling to control behavior with consequences, without specific knowledge of the principles and techniques of behavior modification. Hopefully, this book will allow the practicing manager of human resources to turn unsystematic and accidental control of organizational behavior into planned and carefully implemented strategies for more effective goal attainment.

Figure 3–5 shows the four basic behavior modification strategies and their combinations and indicates the various effects each strategy has on response frequency. All four strategies share three common characteristics: (1) they are used to change the frequencies of objective behavioral events or responses; (2) in each strategy the consequence must be contingent upon the specified response, so that immediacy is normally required to ensure a contingent relationship; and (3) the type of effect a particular form of consequence has on a response's subsequent frequency of occurrence determines its strategy category.

To clarify the last point, consequence strategies cannot be labeled subjectively or in an a priori manner. Consequences are named for their strategy category, i.e., if the presentation of a contingent consequence weakens a response by decreasing its frequency of occurrence, the strategy is called punishment and the consequence is labeled a punisher. Thus, consequences are not arbitrarily labeled, but are labeled in terms of what impact they actually have on response frequency.

The successful use of the intervention strategies depends on the ability of the behavior modifier to efficiently present and withdraw en-

FIGURE 3–5.   Behavior Modification Strategies.

Strategy	Antecedent	Behavioral Events	Consequence	Behavior Outcome
Positive reinforcement	A given environmental setting	⟶ B ⟶	Contingent presentation of an environmental condition	Increase in the frequency of response B
Negative reinforcement	"	⟶ B ⟶	Contingent termination or withdrawal of an environmental condition	Increase in the frequency of response B
Punishment	"	⟶ B ⟶	Contingent presentation of an environmental condition	Decrease in the frequency of response B
Extinction	"	⟶ B ⟶	None	Decrease in the frequency of response B
Combination strategies Extinction/positive reinforcement Punishment/positive reinforcement Punishment/negative reinforcement	"	⟶ Incompatible responses B & C	Combinations of consequences listed above	Decrease in the frequency of response B; increase in the frequency of response C

vironmental conditions in a contingent manner. These environmental conditions may include almost any changes in the environment but many are very subtle or not recognizable to the casual observer. Organizational examples include, but are not limited to, payment of money, the withdrawal or termination of affection, a handshake, a pat on the back, a criticism, a compliment, a layoff, a threat, a promotion, an invitation to dinner, an offer to buy a cup of coffee, information about performance, a new typewriter, extra work, and permission to leave work early. The following spell out in more detail what is involved in each specific strategy.

Positive reinforcement • Positive reinforcement is one of the most firmly established laws of learning (Vroom, 1964, p. 13). As the term suggests, positive reinforcement strengthens behavior.

A positively reinforced response has a greater probability of reoccurrence simply because it pays off. For example, we repeatedly return to a favorite bookstore because we consistently get good books there. (In this example, the determination of what constitutes a good book is irrelevant.) Since the response of going to the same bookstore is strong some consequence must be reinforcing it. In this case, a good book is a positive reinforcer which maintains or strengthens the frequency of our visits to the bookstore. This entire process is called positive reinforcement and a positive reinforcement strategy is being used by the bookstore owner to attain his organizational goals of sales and profits. The more frequently customers are positively reinforced by locating books they desire, the more successful the bookstore can be.

Negative reinforcement • Negative reinforcement is both like and unlike positive reinforcement and is often confused with punishment. It is like positive reinforcement in that it increases the frequency of a response but unlike positive reinforcement in that its reinforcing properties come through the contingent termination or withdrawal of some condition.

A very simple example of negative reinforcement would be to close the window in a very cold room. Terminating the cold air from entering the room should increase the subsequent frequency of closing-window responses. An organizational example would be the draftsman who works harder (emits more productive responses) to get a nagging chief engineer off his back. If, by working harder, the draftsman actually causes the chief engineer to stop nagging, then the working response is said to be negatively reinforced. The removal of the aversive chief engineer resulted in an increase in productive responses. The chief engineer's nagging is labeled a negative reinforcement strategy.

The important point to remember is that negative reinforcement increases the frequency of the behavioral event upon which it is contingent and thus is not the same as a punishment strategy. The term "negative" has the mistaken connotation of punishment to most people.

Punishment • A response is punished when the contingent presentation of an environmental condition decreases its frequency of occurrence. A bright young stock analyst who stops telling his boss about the new technique he has developed because every time he has done so in the past the boss admonished him for wasting precious company time has been punished. The actions of the boss are called punishers because of the effect they had on the strength of the analyst's response. A punishment strategy is designed to decrease the response frequency. Like the other strategies, it must be systematically applied to have the intended results on behavior.

Punishment is both widely used and abused. There are many undesirable side effects. As a result, most behavior modification experts rely less on punishment and more on positive reinforcement for changing behavior. However, because of its widespread use in attempts to control organizational behavior, it is given specific attention in Chapter 6.

Extinction • It may seem strange to call extinction a strategy because nothing happens. But the very fact that nothing happens makes extinction a very potent behavior modification intervention strategy. Since learned responses must be reinforced to reoccur, it is easy to see why responses that are no longer reinforced decrease in frequency and eventually disappear. Extinguished responses are replaced by responses that pay off.

If a door-to-door salesperson stops calling on a house after three different tries because he/she consistently finds no one at home, the response of calling on that particular house has been extinguished. The response has disappeared due to a lack of reinforcement (the reinforcer in this case is the answering of the door by a potential customer). If a housewife inside the house has been ignoring the salesperson's knock for whatever reason, she has used a strategy of extinction to decrease the salesperson's response frequency.

Extinction/positive reinforcement • Combination strategies are normally used when there are two incompatible responses, one undesirable and one desirable. Punctuality is incompatible with being late, productive work is incompatible with loafing, and being courteous to customers is incompatible with being discourteous. In each of these instances, the two responses cannot be emitted simultaneously; they represent an either-or situation.

A combination behavior modification strategy such as extinction/positive reinforcement can weaken the undesirable response and strengthen a desirable, incompatible response. Consider, for example, the common situation of the overly dependent subordinate. Sometimes subordinates who have been around for a long time still behave like new employees and continually ask superiors for answers to problems they should be solving on their own. Consistent with the strengthening effect of positive reinforcement, the subordinate becomes dependent on the boss because such behavior has led to the speedy solution of his/her problems in the past. In short, dependent behavior has been positively reinforced and therefore increases in frequency.

Several strategies are open to the boss once he/she observes what is happening and resolves to bring about a change. The practical solution would be to use a strategy of extinction for the dependent responses (stop positively reinforcing them) and, in turn, positively reinforce independent problem-solving behavior. This approach can and should be open and aboveboard. Instructions from the superior may fully prepare the subordinate for a change in contingencies. If effective, the combination extinction/positive reinforcement strategy should weaken dependence and strengthen independence.

Punishment/positive reinforcement • This combination is designed to accomplish the same end as the extinction/positive reinforcement strategy, but the means are different. Undesirable responses (for example, those that detract from goal attainment in an organization) are followed by conditions which weaken them. In other words, they are punished. At the same time, desirable, incompatible responses are positively reinforced and hence strengthened. Punishment may be chosen over extinction to weaken the undesirable response because that response is so unsafe or disruptive that the time required for extinction to take effect cannot be spared. For example, horseplay by a worker on a dangerous job may require an immediate reprimand. Positive reinforcement of an incompatible attentive work response would constitute the other half of the punishment/positive reinforcement strategy in this case.

Punishment/negative reinforcement • This is a relatively complex combination strategy. A particularly troublesome response is punished until a desirable, incompatible response is emitted. Because the contingent presentation of an environmental condition weakens an undesirable response, the undesirable response is said to have been punished. Negative reinforcement enters the picture when the punisher is not withdrawn until the undesirable response is replaced by a desirable, incompatible response. The company comptroller who nags one of his idle accountants until he gets back to work is using a combination punishment/negative reinforcement strategy. The accountant's idleness is punished while his resumption of work is negatively reinforced.

Schedules of reinforcement

In analyzing a specific behavioral contingency, a behavior modifier must know more than simply "what" a contingent consequence is. "When" or "how often" the consequence follows the response in question is also important. Eventual success or failure of a particular behavior modification strategy frequently depends on the *scheduling* and *timing* of contingent consequences. The administration of reinforcement is as important to behavioral control as what the reinforcer is. For example, in terms of response strength it matters if a consequence is made contingent upon every instance of a particular response or every tenth instance. Similarly, contingent consequences tied to the passage of time have their own distinctive effects on response strength.

Empirical research on the effects that various schedules of reinforcement have on response strength has been carried out with nonhuman and human subjects (Ferster and Skinner, 1957; Yukl, Wexley, and Seymore, 1972). This extensive research has uncovered some very consistent results on what impact various schedules of reinforcement have on frequency of responding. In short, the timing of positive reinforcement has been found to be a fairly reliable causal variable in behavior. In fact, the schedule of reinforcement often has a greater effect on frequency of responding than the size or magnitude of the reinforcer.

For example, Yukl, Wexley, and Seymore (1972) experimentally demonstrated that a group of subjects performing routine tasks who were given the opportunity to earn $1.50 per hour plus the 50/50 chance to earn a 25¢ incentive (determined by a coin flip after the completion of each piece) outperformed an identical group earning $1.50 per hour plus an automatic incentive of 25¢ for each piece. Such interesting results point to the significance of how reinforcements are scheduled as opposed to the amount or size of the reinforcer. Results such as this emphasize the importance of administering wage-incentive systems in modern organizations.

As the term schedules of reinforcement suggests, virtually all of the research on the effects of various consequence schedules has almost solely depended upon positive reinforcement. This is due to the tendency of modern behaviorists to prefer positive reinforcement to the other more unpredictable strategies such as punishment, which has so many undesirable and unpredictable side effects.

Like the other areas of behavior modification, research on schedules of reinforcement has led to highly specialized terminology. Continuous, intermittent, fixed ratio, variable ratio, fixed interval, and variable interval are all terms associated with scheduling reinforcements. Significantly, each method produces an identifiable pattern of responding. Figure 3–6 lists the two major types of reinforcement schedules, *continuous* and *intermittent,* and four intermittent subtypes: fixed and variable ratio, and fixed and variable interval.

If a secretary is warmly thanked every time she voluntarily gets her boss a cup of coffee, that response is being continuously reinforced. However, because of the nature of a continuous schedule, the secretary's

FIGURE 3–6.   Schedules of Reinforcement.

Schedule	Description	Effects on Responding
Continuous (CRF)	Reinforcer follows every response.	(1) Steady high rate of performance as long as reinforcement continues to follow every response. (2) High frequency of reinforcement may lead to early satiation. (3) Behavior weakens rapidly (undergoes extinction) when reinforcers are withheld. (4) Appropriate for newly emitted, unstable, or low-frequency responses.
Intermittent	Reinforcer does not follow every response.	(1) Capable of producing high frequencies of responding. (2) Low frequency of reinforcement precludes early satiation. (3) Appropriate for stable or high-frequency responses.
Fixed ratio (FR)	A fixed number of responses must be emitted before reinforcement occurs.	(1) A fixed ratio of 1:1 (reinforcement occurs after every response) is the same as a continuous schedule. (2) Tends to produce a high rate of response which is vigorous and steady.
Variable ratio (VR)	A varying or random number of responses must be emitted before reinforcement occurs.	(1) Capable of producing a high rate of response which is vigorous, steady, and resistant to extinction.
Fixed interval (FI)	The first response after a specific period of time has elapsed is reinforced.	(1) Produces an uneven response pattern varying from a very slow, unenergetic response immediately following reinforcement to a very fast, vigorous response immediately preceding reinforcement.
Variable interval (VI)	The first response after varying or random periods of time have elapsed is reinforced.	(1) Tends to produce a high rate of response which is vigorous, steady, and resistant to extinction.

courteous service may stop (undergo extinction) if he either deliberately or nondeliberately fails to thank her two or three times in a row. A continuous reinforcement schedule, simply known as CRF, is effective at maintaining response strength as long as reinforcement follows every time. Unreinforced responses, whether due to accidental oversight or deliberate plan, stand out in contrast to a continuous stream of reinforcement. Responses on CRF undergo extinction quite easily. In other words, the response stops being emitted shortly after the contingent reinforcement ceases.

Surprisingly, an intermittent reinforcement schedule which does not reinforce every response tends to promote stronger behavior than does CRF. As Figure 3–6 indicates, intermittent reinforcement leads to stable and high-frequency responding. The common slot machine serves as a testimony of the tremendous power that intermittent schedules of reinforcement have on behavior. Its potential of a payoff on the next lever pull promotes coin-insertion and lever-pulling responses. The gambling devices pay off after a varying number of lever pulls and thus reinforce lever pulling on a variable ratio schedule.

When the reinforcement criterion becomes a fixed number of responses, a fixed ratio schedule is in effect. As Ferster and Perrott (1968) point out: "The term *ratio* refers to the ratio of performances to reinforcement" (p. 200). A piece-rate incentive system in industry is a form of fixed ratio schedule. Employees are given an incentive payment after producing a specified number of pieces.

Interval schedule reinforcement criteria are tied to the passage of time. The first response after the stated time interval has elapsed is reinforced. Although many responses may be emitted before the stated interval elapses, they go unreinforced. A common example of administering reinforcement on a fixed interval schedule is the hourly, weekly, or monthly payment of organizational participants. An example of a variable interval schedule would be the regional sales manager who randomly drops by a local sales office without prior notice to formally recognize outstanding performance.

The various schedules of reinforcement have been largely either taken for granted or unsystematically administered by management. However, with an O. B. Mod. approach, schedules are given a great deal of attention and their vital contribution to more effective human resource management is recognized.

Discrimination and generalization

As discussed earlier, one of the if-then relationships in a behavioral contingency occurs between the antecedent cue and the behavioral event.

Technically, antecedent conditions set the occasion for responses to be emitted. By receiving different consequences in different situations, people learn to associate certain response/consequence if-then relationships with certain antecedent situations. While both discrimination and generalization relate to the $A \rightarrow B$ portion of the contingency, the mechanics of each are different.

As the word *discrimination* implies, people learn that certain responses are appropriate only in specific environmental settings. This simply amounts to discriminating between various environmental cues in order for certain behaviors to be emitted. We say hello to people we like because they will say hello back. Putting this example into functional terms, seeing someone we like sets the occasion for our response of saying hello, which has the consequence of a reinforcing greeting in return.

In a negative light, discrimination also enables a production worker or a clerical worker to look busy when a stern supervisor is in the area. The association between the antecedent cue of seeing the supervisor and the response of looking busy is a function of the worker's past experience. Perhaps, at an earlier time, the supervisor punished the worker or punished someone the worker identified with for not being busy. Because discrimination is learned, people can be taught through managed contingencies to respond in appropriate ways in various environmental settings.

In other words, $A \rightarrow B$ connections can be taught. Specific environmental settings eventually come to serve as direct cues telling the individual which responses are appropriate and probable. By discriminating between environmental cues, an organizational participant can learn such things as who can be trusted with privileged information, who is good at providing answers to difficult problems, where to eat lunch, how to get to work, where and when to look busy, and where and when it is safe to loaf.

It is also possible for a particular response to *generalize* to more than a single environmental setting or cue. To the extent that cues and the consequences with which they are associated are similar, a person may come to emit the same response in a number of different situations. As with discrimination, the key relationship in generalization is still the $A \rightarrow B$ connection. Generalization, however, broadens rather than narrows the antecedent control of behavior. For example, in vestibule training (duplicating on-the-job situations in a company classroom) trainers count on the trainees' ability to generalize the skills they have learned in the simulated setting to the real work area.

As with discrimination, generalization may be taught through the management of contingencies whereby programmed consequences are systematically and consistently matched with specific antecedents. It would be virtually impossible for people to cope with the everyday world without using the process of generalization.

Chained behavior

Only careful observation, identification of behavioral events, charting of response frequency, and recognition of response/consequence contingencies (in other words, functional analysis) can reduce complex behavior to A→B→C terms. Obviously, this task can be difficult. One of the complicating factors is chained behavior. Through operant conditioning, people build behavioral chains. Linkages occur at the antecedent and consequence portions of the contingencies involved, i.e., a consequence in one contingency may at the same time serve as an antecedent in another. This dual consequence/antecedent relationship can best be illustrated graphically.

Figure 3–7 graphically depicts the chained contingencies of a simple organizational behavior, the typing of a letter. Virtually all organizational behavior consists of such linked contingencies. When functionally analyzing complex organizational behavior, the manager using an O. B. Mod. approach should not overlook the dual roles that both consequences and antecedents can play.

FIGURE 3–7.   Chained Behavior.

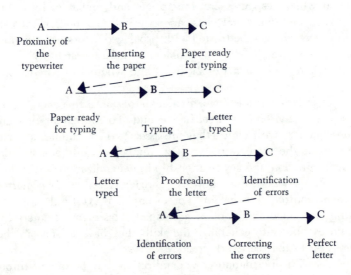

Shaped behavior

The shaping proces is a very vital aspect of behavior modification. A given response may be emitted that does not meet the specifications of a desired response. For example, getting to work five minutes late is almost the same as being on time, but it still is not considered a punctual response. However, by systematically reinforcing successive approximations, a manager may shape a response into its desired form.

The procedure is relatively simple. Closer approximations to the target response are emitted and contingently reinforced. The less desirable approximations, including those reinforced earlier in the shaping process, are put on extinction. In this manner, behavior may actually be shaped into what is desired. Shaping solves the problem of waiting for the opportunity to reinforce a desired response. It is a particularly important technique in behavior modification if a desired response is not currently in a person's behavior repertoire.

Beatty and Schneier (1972) reported an interesting and potentially valuable industrial application of shaping in the training of hard-core unemployed. Since the hard-core unemployed person generally comes from a disadvantaged background, his/her chances of obtaining and holding a regular job are not very good. In behavior modification terminology, the behavior repertoires simply are not developed to the point of being able to quickly and efficiently emit productive on-the-job responses in order to receive the consequences contingent upon successful performance.

Beatty and Schneier developed a three-stage hard-core training model to counter this problem. The model consists of an off-the-job training stage, an on-the-job training stage, and finally, a complete job performance stage. The first two phases are gradual approximations to reach the third. By progressing through the three-stage sequence, a trainee's work responses are being systematically shaped.

Continuous reinforcement is initially used with weak responses or responses roughly approximating the desired productive responses. Positive reinforcement for satisfactory work is experienced, perhaps for many of the hard-core unemployables for the first time. As the work responses grow stronger and more accurate, the reinforcement is switched to a variable ratio basis in order to facilitate stable performance and high rates of responding.

Thus shaped into adequate performance, the trainees are exposed to the full demands of their new job. As the behavior learned during training generalizes to the actual job, it is reinforced with contingent praise and wages. Importantly, the Beatty and Schneier training model can also be used to shape a number of other job behaviors such as punctuality, attendance, speed, accuracy, and even initiative.

A side benefit of the shaping procedure when applied to human resource management is that it forces managers to look for desirable aspects of subordinate performance. Shaping must start with some approximation of the target or goal response, i.e., behavior modification works with *ongoing* behavior; it does not actually create behavior. A contingency manager is not preoccupied with what is wrong with his/her subordinate's performance. Instead, using this approach, the manager strives to identify shapable approximations of desirable on-the-job responses and thus starts to reinforce desirable behavior instead of commenting and focusing only on undesirable behavior. The positive rather than the negative is emphasized.

Modeling

Within an organizational context, much behavior is learned by imitating others. Subordinates, co-workers, and superiors all show one another how to behave, and there are fairly reliable indications of what consequences may be expected when similar responses are emitted. Frequently, behavior does speak much louder than words. For example, a safety engineer who smokes in a no-smoking area cannot reasonably expect other members of the organization to observe the restriction.

Through modeling, organizational participants learn how to behave, learn relevant response/consequence contingencies, and learn when it is appropriate to respond in given ways. The modeling process is important in the O. B. Mod. approach because it can be managed just as contingencies are managed. An understanding of modeling, like the other procedures and techniques discussed in this section, can lead to more effective human resource management.

APPLICATION OF PRINCIPLES AND TECHNIQUES

After reading about the principles, procedures, and techniques of behavior modification, the reader has hopefully gained an appreciation of the *technology of learned behavior*. It has a special language, its own body of theoretical and empirical knowledge, and a sophisticated collection of interrelated procedures and techniques capable of application to human resource management. However, as with any technical tool, behavior modification can also be misapplied by those who have not fully understood its complexities and subtleties.

To put the principles and techniques of behavior modification into a practical organizational behavior context, the reader is urged to reconsider the three incidents presented at the beginning of the chapter. The reader should jot down his/her behavior modification interpretations of the incidents before reading the following interpretations. Post-behavior modification interpretations should prove interesting when compared with preliminary interpretations. Remember, the reader should reduce the incidents to A→B→C terms and analyze *contingently*.

Incident 1 interpretation: "Firing the Supervisor"

A man has been fired from his job, the severest economic sanction an organization can apply. The termination took place directly or at least indirectly because of factors such as a subjective performance appraisal, the unwitting and unsuccessful application of a negative reinforcement strategy, and a failure to formulate specific objective performance goals for the six-week period.

One key question stands out in this incident. Did the first-line supervisor really deserve to be terminated? It is quite possible that the supervisor performed poorly or, in the "internal" terminology of the section chief, had a bad attitude. But was it the man who was at fault or was it the environment which was not conducive to his performing adequately?

The section chief's strategy was simple; he applied pressure on the man in the form of threatened termination, waited six weeks, and carried out his threat. His actions were those of a passive rather than an active manager. Instead of actively applying his human resource management skills by structuring the work environment to weaken the supervisor's undesirable behavior and strengthen desirable behavior, he chose to passively apply pressure and shift the entire responsibility for change to his subordinate. The section chief tried to change the person rather than the environment.

In behavior modification terms, the section chief attempted to use a threat of termination as a negative reinforcer. Removal of the threat was made contingent upon an improvement in the supervisor's general attitude. This action stands as a good example of the unwitting use of behavior modification. Even if the manager was familiar with the principles of behavior modification and possessed the appropriate skills, negative reinforcement would be very difficult to use effectively. In this case the section chief was not aware of or able to utilize an O. B. Mod. approach. He was concerned with "attitude" when he should have been focusing his attention on the supervisor's performance-related behavior. Was the supervisor coming in late, overstaying his breaks, being disrespectful to his superiors, turning in unsatisfactory or false production and quality reports, or mistreating his subordinates? These latter possibilities relate to observable on-the-job behavior, not vague internal states.

A contingent manager would have proceeded in the following manner. After specifically identifying the supervisor's desirable and undesirable behaviors, he would have collected some baseline data and carried out functional analyses to determine what consequences were supporting the behaviors in question.

On the basis of that information, the contingent manager would have met with the supervisor to identify the problem behaviors, mutually determine some realistic behavior improvement goals, and outline the contingencies for the next six weeks. By maintaining response frequency charts on the supervisor's key responses or by having the supervisor monitor his own behavior, the manager, after the six-week period had elapsed, would have sufficient objective behavioral data upon which to base a termination/retention decision.

Incident 2 interpretation: "The Head Nurse's Style"

The head nurse has some behavior problems of her own. On the basis of her arbitrary and vague notion of how to manage human resources, she has chosen to rely heavily on the very potent but unpredictable behavioral control strategy of punishment. Compounding her problems is her noncontingent use of punishment. In other words, she is not making it consistently contingent on specific responses. Contingencies exist regardless of a manager's knowledge, intent, or desire. Even the indiscriminate use of punishers creates accidental contingencies that effectively reduce response frequencies. Unfortunately, many of the resulting weakened responses may have been productive or otherwise desirable goals like patient care in the hospital.

In effect, the head nurse is establishing unplanned contingencies with her unsystematic use of punishment. In a noncontingent environment people do not have the opportunity to learn precisely which responses will lead to which consequences. This is because response/consequence connections are random, unsystematic, and unpredictable. A noncontingent work environment generally has little chance of increasing the probability of productive behavior.

In the final analysis, the head nurse must bring her own behavior under control before she can possibly hope to control the behavior of her subordinates by managing contingently. She should also move to a positive reinforcement strategy to accelerate the desirable behavior of her subordinates.

Incident 3 interpretation: "The Boss's Bad Mood"

Modeling is the key behavior modification procedure in this case, although punishment again enters the picture. Whether the Claims Department head realizes it or not, he is a highly visible behavioral model for his people. His position and status make him a very significant member of the work group. In many respects, as his mood goes, so goes the mood of the office. Aside from the effect of simply imitating the department head's behavior, the behavior of every work group member is affected to varying extents by the consequences of his/her relevant co-workers' behavior. When the department head comes down hard on one member of the work group, other members of the group who identify with the punished person may be vicariously punished (see: Bandura, 1971, pp. 47–51).

In other words, even though someone else has been punished, their behavior may show the signs of punishment—reduced frequency of response. Vicarious punishment may create accidental contingencies that result in the weakening of desirable responses. Punishment often creates unwanted and unpredictable side effects such as anxious or counterproductive responses. Like the head nurse, the Claims Department head must put *himself* under the control of different contingencies and learn how to manage his people in a contingent manner.

Behavioral Contingency Management

4

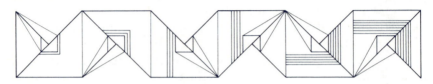

Taken together, the first three chapters of this book serve as the theoretical and technical foundation for O. B. Mod. We have used the term O. B. Mod. (organizational behavior modification) rather than just B. Mod. (behavior modification) to emphasize that the application is to *organizational* behavior and human resource management. Such an application has been almost totally ignored in the past and is just now beginning to emerge as a widely recognized behavioral approach to management. This chapter is the first to focus directly on O. B. Mod. The others, of course, are necessary background information.

THE PRACTICING MANAGER AS A BEHAVIORAL SCIENTIST

Going as far back as the famous Hawthorne studies of the late 1920s and early 1930s, the dialogue between behavioral scientists and those actually responsible for managing human resources has steadily grown in both quantity and quality. At first, the practicing manager, at best, sporadically read reports of behavioral science studies.

However, through the years managers have been exposed to progressively greater amounts of behavioral science theory and research. Knowledge is gained through formal collegiate education, professional organizations, management-development seminars, and numerous professional publications. Still more recently, a burgeoning consulting business, via well-known behavioral science consultants such as Saul Gellerman, Robert Blake, and Rensis Likert, has placed the behavioral scientist and the practicing manager in direct contact with one another.

Generally, this relationship between the behavioral science consultant and the management practitioner has been mutually rewarding. Too often, however, the behavioral scientist, as a management consultant, has prescribed or pushed for one particular approach or technique without the benefit of an adequate diagnosis. This brings to mind the situation of an unsuspecting patient with an earache who retains the services of a doctor who is bent on performing an appendectomy. In an effort to generate more situational sensitivity, full-time applied behavioral scientists or internal change agents, often residing in newly created organization development (O. D.) departments, have become popular. However, as the economy dipped in the early 1970s, the resident behavioral scientist often was the first to go and the activities of O. D. departments were cut back.

With this history, the question becomes, how can behavioral science concepts and techniques be economically and pragmatically applied to improve human resource management? The answer, at least in the long run, is to educate and train the practicing manager himself in the theories and methods of behavioral science.

The internal approach to organizational behavior would suggest that practicing managers be trained in psychiatry or perhaps even parapsychology. Obviously, this would not be realistic or desirable from either a societal or an organizational viewpoint. The external approach is much more realistic for practicing managers, regardless of educational background, experience, or current position. By understanding and applying what is embodied in O. B. Mod., the practicing manager, in a sense, can become a behavioral scientist.

This interpretation of a manager as a behavioral scientist is valid to the extent that the manager collects and interprets behavioral data (diagnosis) and selects and applies appropriate behavioral techniques (prescription). While the practicing manager must continue to depend on the academic behavioral scientist for new theoretical concepts, techniques, and tools, an O. B. Mod. approach allows him/her to collect diagnostic behavioral data on the job. Strict reliance on data collected under highly controlled conditions and analyzed and interpreted by academic behavioral scientists is unnecessary. This does not mean that the behavioral scientist is relegated to a dusty academic shelf; much is needed in the way of rigorous theoretical and empirical research. However, it does imply that the behavioral scientist is best equipped to carry out original research while the practicing manager, given the appropriate perspective, knowledge, and skill development, is in the best position to carry out the practical applications in managing human resources.

To date, virtually all of the diagnostic tools proposed by behavioral scientists have been steeped in academic jargon, tied to the internal approach, or dependent upon sophisticated statistical analyses. On the other hand, O. B. Mod., with frequency of response as its basic datum, can provide a workable behavioral technology for the practicing manager. On-the-job behavior is readily quantifiable when reduced to frequencies of response. O. B. Mod. allows the practicing manager to collect voluminous behavioral data with relative ease. With the practicing manager collecting and interpreting behavioral data and subsequently applying proven intervention strategies and techniques, the diagnostic/prescriptive circle can be neatly closed within the confines of today's organizations.

ORGANIZATIONAL BEHAVIOR VERSUS ORGANIZATIONAL ACTIVITIES

There is not a direct relationship between an employee's responses and common measures of organizational effectiveness such as profitability or service to the community. In O. B. Mod., a careful distinction is made between behavioral events, performance, and organizational consequences. The ramifications of this distinction must be fully understood by the practitioner in order to implement an O. B. Mod. approach to human resource management.

Organizational behavior repertoire

Each employee has a unique set of behaviors or behavior repertoire. The repertoire contains all the responses the organizational participant has learned and is capable of emitting, and it is constantly changing. The left-hand side of Figure 4–1 depicts the employee's behavior repertoire. The figure shows that only part of the repertoire is performance related. The repertoire also contains many potentially disruptive or counterproductive behaviors and behaviors unrelated to performance. In addition, the repertoire does not contain all the necessary behavioral demands of a particular job. Actually, in most cases, there may even be a minority of responses capable of being emitted by an employee that are directly related to his/her performance. As Figure 4–1 indicates, the process of matching the individual employee's behavior repertoire with the behavioral performance demands of the job necessitates some learning and, occasionally, some unlearning. To facilitate effective matching, the connections between specific behavioral events and more conventional measures of organizational activity must be identified.

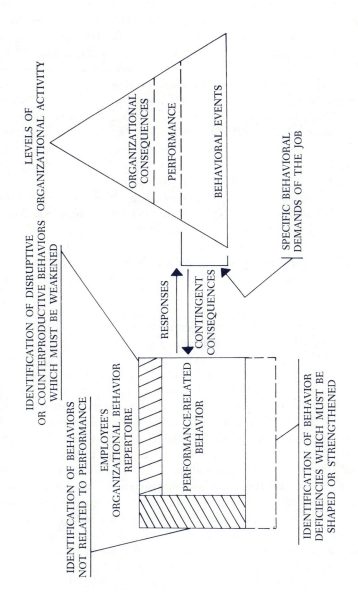

FIGURE 4-1. Matching Organizational Behavior Repertoire with Organizational Activities.

In managing people, most practitioners do not use the behavioral event as a common denominator. Instead, they typically deal in terms of the organizational consequences of behavioral events. Organizational consequences are simply changes in the environment caused by organizational behavior. Terms such as "performance," "effectiveness," "reliability," "efficiency," "profitability" and "service" are commonly heard in descriptions of organizational activity. Performance appraisals are common but behavior appraisals are unheard of. Although performance and other measures of organizational success are certainly important, they are of little value to a functional analysis of behavior. "Profitability" cannot be directly placed in the context of an A→B→C contingency. On the other hand, the specific behavior leading to profitability, when reduced to behavioral events, plays a vital role in functional analysis. O. B. Mod. requires that organizational activity be reduced to behavioral events.

A major task for the contingency manager is to identify performance-related behavior in employees' behavior repertoires. Also, it is important to identify behavior which threatens to restrict performance and behavior which has no impact on performance. Finally, it is vital to successful human resource management to have the employees learn the behavior not currently part of their repertoire that leads to effective performance.

Behavioral events, performance, and organizational consequences

Campbell et al. (1970 and 1973) have made a distinction among three outcomes of organizational roles: (1) *behavior,* specific things people do in the course of working; (2) *performance,* behavior measured in terms of its contribution to organizational goal achievement; and (3) *effectiveness,* summary indices of organizational success. Although initially used in reference to managerial activity, this categorization seems directly applicable to all organizational behavior. Translated into the language of O. B. Mod., the three levels of organizational activity become: (1) *behavioral events;* (2) *performance;* and (3) *organizational consequences.*

This breakdown provides a conceptual framework for relating behavior and performance in an organizational context. Figure 4–1 illustrates how these three levels of organizational activity relate to an individual employee's behavior repertoire and the behavioral demands of the job.

O. B. Mod., by definition, starts at the first level of organizational activity, behavioral events. Conventional performance appraisals, on the other hand, deal almost exclusively with performance and organizational consequences. Management by Objectives (MBO), for example, attempts to tie individual performance to quantifiable organizational consequences.

However, in its normal application, MBO does not tie behavioral events to subsequent organizational consequences. The practicing manager using an O. B. Mod. approach must consider all three levels of organizational activity but concentrate on the behavioral level. He/she must identify those behaviors which contribute to successful performance and ultimately to desired organizational consequences.

Identification of performance-related behavior can begin at either end of the behavioral event–performance–organizational consequence chain. Consider the example of the secretary who rapidly types an error-free memo. This behavior enables the secretary to accomplish productive, quality work which in turn helps the organization reduce its costs and increase its profits. The actual contribution that the rapid typing of an error-free memo makes to the secretary's performance and the exact amount of labor costs that subsequently will be saved can be calculated by tracing the behavioral event through to its organizational consequence(s). Working in the opposite direction, from general to specific, it may be discovered that labor costs are cut if the secretary's performance improves. Thus, from either direction, this particular behavioral event should lead to improved organizational consequences.

Figure 4–2 lists some common examples of behavioral event–performance–organizational consequence relationships and notes the varying levels of specificity. The examples show that only the behavioral event level is specific enough for a meaningful functional analysis. For instance, telling a shopworker to be safety conscious is much less specific than telling him to immediately clean up any oil spills. Both safety consciousness and cleaning up oil spills are intended to have the organizational consequence of fewer accidents, but only the cleaning up of oil spills is a specific behavioral event that can be measured in terms of response frequency.

At this point, it will be instructive for the reader to identify and record some personally observed examples of the three levels of organizational activity, using Figure 4–2 as a guide. Special effort should be made to ensure that each behavioral event identified does in fact lead to the specified organizational consequence. This exercise will help the reader make the important distinction between behavioral events, performance, and organizational consequences and demonstrate the relationship between them.

Naturally, as one proceeds up the organizational hierarchy, from relatively simple and repetitive tasks to more complex executive-level problem solving and decision making, the identification of performance-related behavioral events becomes more difficult. However, this is not to say that the identification becomes impossible. Behavior can be observed throughout the organizational hierarchy. Problem-solving executives emit behavioral events just as drill-press operators do. The latter are simply more readily observed than the former. In cases where employees work by themselves, self-observation and self-control may also be learned. An O. B. Mod. approach can be used with any organizational behavior to the extent that performance-related behavioral events can be identified and measured.

FIGURE 4–2.   Examples of Behavioral Event, Performance, and Organizational Consequence.

Very specific	Intermediate	Very general
Behavioral Event	*Performance*	*Organizational Consequence*
Recording the solution to a complex management problem	Personal effectiveness	Increased productivity Greater return on investment Increased rate of growth
Praising a hard-working subordinate	Rapport with subordinates	Greater job satisfaction Lower absenteeism Lower grievance rate
Replacing a worn-out drill bit	Attention to detail	Cost effectiveness Decreased scrap and rework
Recalculating a capital budget figure after finding an error	Professional knowledge	Lower cost of capital
Working in an extra sales call at quitting time	Personal commitment	Greater share of the market
Immediately cleaning up an oil spill on the shop floor	Safety	Prevention of accidents

Managers using an O. B. Mod. approach should deal only with performance-related behavior—behavior which directly or indirectly enhances or inhibits performance. Valuable time and resources should not be wasted on shaping, strengthening, or weakening behavior with no impact on performance. A careful analysis of behavioral event–performance–organizational consequence relationships serves as the point of departure for the application of specific O. B. Mod. techniques such as behavioral contingency management. After a brief look at what happened at Emery Air Freight, attention is given to the specific steps of this technique.

THE EMERY AIR FREIGHT
EXPERIENCE

The case of Emery Air Freight demonstrates the practical and economic benefits of dealing in terms of specific job behavior and its consequences. At first glance, the widely publicized Emery success story appears too simple, too pat an answer to be believable. Yet, detailed analysis reveals some very interesting implications for human resource management. The techniques used at Emery, like the behavior modification principles upon which they are based, possess one overriding characteristic—they work.

Under the general guidance of Edward J. Feeney, who was then vice president of the company and is currently a private consultant, Emery was able to save a reported $2 million over a three-year period by identifying performance-related behaviors and strengthening them with positive reinforcement (Performance Audit, 1972). In Feeny's words, "Our end is improved performance, and we've been damned effective in getting it" (At Emery Air Freight, 1973). Feeney put a few basic behavior modification techniques to the practical test of modifying on-the-job behavior and succeeded. Certainly, the emphasis placed on providing feedback to employees about their performance contributed more than any other single factor to the program's success.

A careful performance audit was first conducted to identify the relatively few job behaviors with the greatest impact on profit. The approach taken by Feeney was then to simply tell those responsible for the high-payoff behaviors how they were doing. Despite all the information generated by industrial engineering, many employees learned for the first time how they were really doing at their job. This feedback was very important to them.

The air-freight container utilization at Emery provides the best example of the value of a performance audit. As a major air-freight forwarder, Emery requires the extensive use of freight containers. Economic, space, and time constraints collectively operate to necessitate maximum utilization of these containers. Emery loses money if a container is not full when the truck leaves for the airport. Because of the importance of maximizing container utilization, the warehousemen who loaded the containers had been thoroughly trained and frequently encouraged to increase their use of empty container space. Because of this extensive effort, both managers and dock workers believed that containers were being used 90 percent of the time (Where Skinner's Theories Work, 1972). However, Feeney and his five-man performance audit team found the container utilization to be around 45 percent, not 90 percent.

The need for more training was discounted in favor of Feeney's program of feedback and positive reinforcement. Self-feedback was provided by the dockworker as he kept a checklist when his container utilization rate fell between 45 percent and 95 percent a day. As a consequence, container utilization jumped tremendously almost immediately and Emery benefited from the program in the form of a savings of $520,000 in the first year.

Effective simplicity characterizes the Emery program. First, the performance audit identifies key performance-related behaviors. Second, management establishes a realistic output goal and gives the relevant employees feedback, mostly provided by the employees themselves, of how they are performing. Finally, increases in performance are systematically strengthened through the use of contingent positive reinforcement (P.R.):

> "In those areas in which Emery uses P.R. as a motivational tool, nothing is left to chance. Each manager receives two elaborate programmed instruction workbooks prepared in-house and geared to the specific work situation at Emery. One deals with recognition and rewards, the other with feedback. Under recognition and rewards, the workbook enumerates no less than 150 kinds, ranging from a smile and a nod of encouragement, to 'Let me buy you a coffee,' to detailed praise for a job well done" (At Emery Air Freight, 1973).

Under this program, Emery employees get accurate and reliable feedback on their performance and positive reinforcement contingent upon improvement. This deceptively simple human resource management approach has paid off handsomely for Emery Air Freight. Provided that a program makes effective use of the performance audit, Feeney is confident that his approach can work elsewhere. He states, "I have yet to see any performance area that can function effectively without an effective feedback system and a program of consequences—positive consequences—for the right behaviors." (Performance Audit, 1972). It is important to remember that Feeney is not talking in empty platitudes. His program saved Emery Air Freight $2 million in three years. These "bottom-line" results cannot be overlooked.

THE BEHAVIORAL CONTINGENCY MANAGEMENT MODEL

The Emery Air Freight experience marks an important beginning for the direct application of behavioral concepts and techniques to human resource management. Yet the approach taken by Feeney, although successful and certainly worthy of future attention, is not the final answer. Because people and organizational situations are so different, it would be virtually impossible to formulate one specific O. B. Mod. strategy with universal applicability. Consistent with a general contingency theory of management (Luthans, 1973b), specific human resource management concepts and techniques should only be applied contingent upon the situational conditions.

For example, Feeney's program of feedback and positive reinforcement may work well at Emery Air Freight, but not in a different type of situation. Feeney himself may have been a big factor in Emery's success. On the other hand, other managers could conceivably fail with the Feeney approach but succeed with significantly different behavioral approaches. What is needed is a problem-solving model which is specific enough to demonstrate how behavior modification can be used in practical work settings but, at the same time, general enough to allow for situational variations.

The authors (Luthans and Kreitner, 1974) have formulated a general O. B. Mod. problem-solving model, called *behavioral contingency management* or BCM. The model provides a general methodology for identifying and contingently managing the critical performance-related behaviors of employees in all types of organizations. Figure 4–3 shows the BCM model arranged in its logical flow. Very simply, BCM can be summarized by five one-word steps: (1) identify; (2) measure; (3) analyze; (4) intervene; and (5) evaluate. Each of the five basic steps and related substeps is described and analyzed in the balance of the chapter.

While reviewing the steps, the reader is urged to remember that the authors are only suggesting that BCM is "an" approach to managing human resources; it is not necessarily "the" approach. Successful application of any management concept or technique can come only through the efforts of problem-solving managers who possess the appropriate skills and a thorough knowledge of the situation. In other words, BCM, like any other management concept or technique (process, quantitative, behavioral, or systems), must be applied contingent on the situation (Luthans, 1973b).

Step 1: Identify performance-related behavioral events

As discussed earlier, organizational activity may be broken down into three different levels: behavioral events, performance, and organizational consequences. Any O. B. Mod. technique tries to deal with the most specific level of organizational activity, behavioral events.

FIGURE 4–3.   Behavioral Contingency Management.

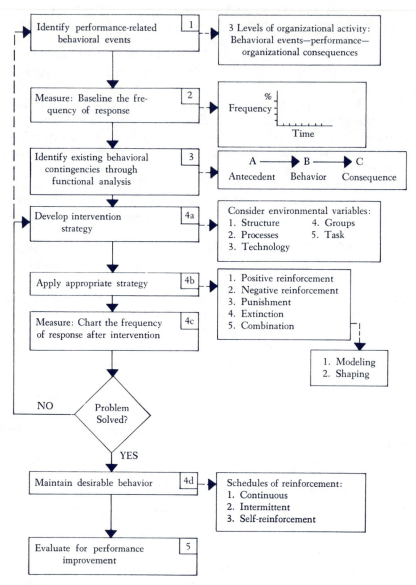

Source: Luthans and Kreitner, 1974, p. 13. Reprinted by permission of
the publisher from Personnel, July-August 1974 © 1974 by AMACOM,
a division of American Management Associations.

From the standpoint of performance, behavioral events may be classified as desirable, undesirable, or irrelevant. Intervention is required when desirable behavioral events occur too infrequently or undesirable behavioral events occur too frequently. Once identified, desirable behaviors must be strengthened and maintained and undesirable behaviors must be weakened and extinguished.

Although value loaded, the term "desirable" is simply used to identify those behaviors which eventually lead to the accomplishment of predetermined organizational objectives. "Undesirable" behaviors, on the other hand, refer to those which directly or indirectly inhibit or detract from the accomplishment of predetermined organizational objectives. The process whereby desirable and undesirable performance-related behavioral events are identified is the focus of Step 1 in BCM.

As a guide for the practitioner using BCM, the following four basic questions should be answered:

1) Can the behavior in question be reduced to *observable* behavioral events?
2) Can I *count* how often each behavioral event occurs?
3) *Exactly* what must the person do before I record a response?
4) Is this a key *performance-related* behavioral event?

The answers to these questions will lead to the identification of an appropriate behavior for BCM.

Observable and countable behavior • The importance of dealing only with observable, countable behavioral events has been repeatedly mentioned. A matter that has not received as much attention so far has been the exact meaning of behavioral events. Consistent with a precise technology of learned behavior, the dependent variable (behavior) must be precisely defined. First of all, each behavioral event must have a distinct beginning and a distinct end. Behavioral events are units which change the direction of complex behavior chains. As Brandt (1972) has observed: "No clear-cut standards have been established for determining the size of behavioral units to be measured. These seem to vary primarily with the purposes of the investigation and the specification of variables to be studied" (p. 130).

While manual tasks in an organization consist of a series of readily observed behavioral events, other on-the-job activity is not so obviously delineated. For example, consider the case of the applicant taking a personnel test. A typical observation of this activity would be that the applicant is sitting there "thinking." The behaviorist, however, cannot deal in terms of thinking because it is not observable; only the overt behavioral manifestations of thinking can be observed. Looking away from the test, attending to the test, completing responses, and correctly completing responses satisfy two fundamental behaviorist requirements. They are (1) observable and

(2) countable, and thus are acceptable measures of performance. For convenience, an extended behavior, such as attending to a work task, can be readily broken up into minutes or any other time span. One-minute periods of uninterrupted attention to a task can be easily recorded, especially on a random time-sampling basis.

Only performance-related behavior • Ensuring that the behavior is performance related is as important as identifying observable, countable, and definable behavioral events. Numerous behaviors are emitted in any work situation. Some of these behaviors are related to performance and some of them are not. For example, a supervisor may focus on a subordinate's complaining behavior. However, even though it is irritating to the supervisor, this complaining behavior may have nothing to do with the subordinate's performance. He/she may complain all the time but perform outstandingly on assigned tasks. If so, the complaining behavior has no place in BCM.

On the other hand, if the supervisor determines that the complaining behavior is disruptive and counterproductive with the subordinate's and/or others' performance, then this would be an appropriate target for BCM. If the behavior is not performance related, then the subsequent steps of the model become meaningless. The purpose of BCM is to improve performance, not merely to change behavior.

The manager should search for organizational consequences of behavior as an aid to identifying performance-related behavior. For example, the manager might ask the question: What would happen to production records or quality standards if employees did not emit response X ? Workers on an assembly line who do not show up for work generally cause lost time production that may not be recoverable. On the other hand, a clerical worker who is absent may have the work sitting on her desk when she returns, with no lost time production. In the former case, *attendance* is a critical performance-related behavior, while in the latter case it may not be.

The issue of identifying critical performance-related behavior becomes more complex when collective performance is considered. The goal is to identify those behavioral events, individual or collective, with the greatest impact on performance. An example of where collective behavior comes into play would be in the fast-food industry. Heavy emphasis is placed on how long it takes to complete a customer's order. Getting hot, tasty food to customers as quickly as possible is the very essence of their business. Presenting a customer with a properly filled order within a specified period of time would be a critical behavioral event. But this is directly or indirectly the result of the behaviors of several people. In this case, the behaviors must be broken down further and the priority of performance-related behavioral events must be established.

Nonbehavioral performance problems • To identify performance-related behavior and assign priorities, the manager using BCM may find the framework shown in Figure 4–4 useful. The framework makes a clear distinction between behavioral and nonbehavioral performance problems. Just as not all behavior is related to performance, not all performance problems are related to behavior. Sometimes an employee simply can not "cut the mustard" because of a lack of the necessary ability to perform adequately; this constitutes a selection problem, not a behavior problem. Someone with the appropriate ability should be found for the job. On other occasions some training may be necessary to erase a skill deficiency. The employee simply does not know the proper procedures necessary to do the job adequately. In other cases, a malfunctioning, outdated, or inefficient machine may be the source of the performance problem. This problem could be labeled technological inefficiencies. The machine portion of the worker/machine interaction must be remedied. BCM can not directly remedy performance problems caused by mechanical or technical shortcomings.

Another source of potential performance problems is unfair output standards. A worker producing at 75 percent of standard may be doing a tremendous job but be working with a standard which was mistakenly set too high. BCM will not help this "performance" problem. Unsatisfactory subordinate performance may also be due to improper supervision or undesirable behavior on the part of the supervisor. BCM can be applied in this case, but with the supervisor, not the subordinate.

As with all management techniques, BCM must be carefully implemented. Ability/selection, training, technology, standards, and supervision problems could rule out the application of BCM. On the other hand, these are not the major problems facing human resource managers. As the introductory comments of the book pointed out, there are numerous behavioral problems facing today's management. BCM is one systematic approach to help solve performance-related behavior problems. The ability to identify this behavior will largely determine the subsequent success of BCM.

Step 2: Measure the frequency of response

The second basic step in BCM involves measuring the strength of the performance-related behavioral event(s) identified in the first step. A baseline measure of response frequency indicates how often the behavior is occurring prior to attempts to change it. This baseline measure in and of itself is often very revealing. Sometimes the behavior turns out to be very low frequency and the manager realizes that it is not a problem at all.

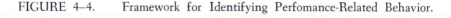

FIGURE 4–4.   Framework for Identifying Perfomance-Related Behavior.

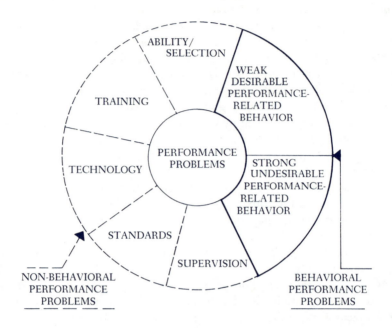

For example, a supervisor may feel that one of his subordinates has a tardiness behavior problem because "that guy is never on time." Upon objective measurement of tardiness behavior, he finds that the subordinate, on the average, is late once a week. With this objective data in hand, the supervisor decides that the tardiness behavior does not affect the performance of his department. In other instances, the reverse is true. In the case of the Emery Air Freight container utilization problem cited earlier, upon measuring the frequency, management discovered that the behavior problem was much greater than was thought. In any case, the measure serves as a baseline for comparative purposes when a manager intervenes in an attempt to change behavior (Step 4 of BCM).

There are many ways of measuring frequency of response; the best method depends on many factors. Some methods are more comfortable or natural to managers than others. The key is not in choosing a method of measurement but rather in accurately recording frequencies. In some cases the data for baseline purposes may already be on hand (for example, from production or absenteeism records). Most often, however, the two general approaches to recording are to observe and count every response, or to observe and count samples of on-the-job responses. The former technique can be used where the observer can devote considerable time to the measuring task. However, because time is limited for most practicing managers, time-sampling techniques (similar to the common work-sampling techniques of industrial engineering) are more realistic and, if used properly, equally accurate.

Tally sheet • A tailor-made tally sheet must be devised to gather the frequency data. The observer should have definite predetermined criteria for the data. For example, what is the criterion for tardiness— punching in one second late on a time clock or five minutes and over? What constitutes being away from the machine—is it any time the operator isn't there or are allowances made for getting material? The criteria can be determined by the relevant manager but, for measuring purposes, must be consistently applied. Another important facet of gathering the data is to attempt to reduce the observation into only two alternatives, yes or no. Yes, the employee is tardy or, no, he/she isn't. Yes, the operator is away from the machine or, no, he/she isn't. This greatly simplifies the observer's data gathering and eliminates the possibility of subjectiveness entering the measurement.

Figure 4–5 gives an example of a typical tally sheet. Remember, the tallies must be tailor-made because each situation will be different.

FIGURE 4–5.   Sample Tally Sheet for Frequency Data.

John Jones
employee

Bookkeeper
position

Tardiness (starting time,
breaks, mid-lunch)
Behavior Description

Ruth Smith, Office Manager
observer/recorder

6/1/74 — 6/6/74
observation period

Times	Monday		Tuesday		Wednesday		Thursday		Friday	
	Yes	No	Yes	No	Yes	No	Yes	No	Yes	No
8:05										
10:20										
1:05										
2:35										

Awareness of measurement • An important issue in measuring is whether or not the person being measured should be aware of it. BCM is and should be completely aboveboard. However, there is the possibility, in gathering certain types of behavioral data, that the data will be distorted because the person is aware of being measured. Therefore, if the manager feels this is the case, then he/she should devise the tally to minimize this effect. This could be accomplished by keeping a mental record and then recording the data on the tally a short time after, or using a wrist counter (Lindsley, 1968) similar to those used by golfers or supermarket shoppers and then transfering the data to the tally at a later time. Under some circumstances, self-observation may be used. Usable data may be obtained by positively reinforcing accurate self-observation response frequency tallies (this was done successfully at Emery). Also, self-observation may be an effective behavior change strategy. An exact knowledge of how often a person is emitting an undesirable response will often induce him/her to exercise self-control.

Even with the techniques mentioned above, data distortion due to awareness can still occur. The old approaches to time and motion analysis are an example. Time-study specialists were often frustrated in their efforts to collect valid data because those being observed could change the normal work environment and thus affect the rate of response. Yet, the awareness problem is not as predominant in a modern work environment as it was earlier. The reason is that industrial engineers and supervisors are constantly gathering every kind of imaginable data from today's employees. As a result, employees are relatively immune to being observed and receiving special attention. Thus, distortion stemming from awareness of being measured may not be as big a problem as it appears to be on the surface.

Time sampling • Another practical problem is that busy managers cannot tally every response of a high-frequency behavior. This, of course, is why the time-sampling technique is so useful. When the behavior occurs regularly throughout the working day, the observer may randomly pick one or more short time periods during which to observe and tally the frequency. For example, suppose a foreman in a fabricating shop determines that a particular operator's frequent absences from the work area have the effect of reducing output. Being too busy to stand around and inconspicuously record numerous responses per day, the foreman may choose to randomly pick five minutes during every hour to sample the response frequency. While the resulting baseline data does not include all instances of the response, if the observations are truly random, there is an accurate indication of the response strength. If the behavior is as important to performance as it should be, the time invested should pay off handsomely for the manager using BCM.

Transferring tally data to graphs • The same reasoning applies when the tally data is transferred to the actual graph. Normally, the vertical axis of the graph is *percentage* frequency and the horizontal axis is the time dimension. Percentage frequency is stressed because if the manager misses observing the employee for some reason, he/she can still get a representative frequency from the percentage data.

Figure 4–6 shows a typical graph derived from tally sheets. Through visual inspection, the manager can quickly obtain an accurate picture of the baseline measure of the performance-related behavior. When an intervention strategy is implemented in Step 4, the manager can visually see the results in terms of response frequency. Seeing this frequency movement in visual, graphic terms in and of itself can be very reinforcing for the manager using BCM. The manager is receiving direct feedback on the success or failure of his/her intervention.

Step 3: Identify existing contingencies through functional analysis

Before the manager using BCM can intervene and actually begin to manage contingencies, one more preliminary step must be taken. This step involves a functional analysis of the behavior that has been identified and measured. A functional analysis answers two key questions: (1) where does the responding take place (the antecedent A); and (2) what are its consequences (the C)? Functional analysis can be accomplished during the baseline period. The basis of this analysis is that the identified behavior (desirable or undesirable) is being maintained by the environment. In the case of undesirable behavior, in order to decrease it, the functional analysis must determine what the consequences reinforcing it are so they can be removed or replaced. In terms of the A→B→C contingency, it is not enough to simply identify the B's; the A's and C's must also be identified and analyzed.

An example of functional analysis • As an example of functional analysis, imagine a supervisor who determined that his people took an excessive number of rest-room breaks. He calculated that if the operators were attending to the task the time they spent at the rest room, his production record would show a significant increase.

In functionally analyzing this behavior, he found that the "A" was the clock. The workers were taking the breaks almost precisely at 9 A.M., midway between starting time and their first regularly scheduled break, and 11 A.M., midway between their scheduled break and lunch. The clock served as the antecedent condition (A) for emitting the rest-room break behavior (B). Significantly, the clock did not cause the behavior; it only set the occasion for the behavior to be emitted.

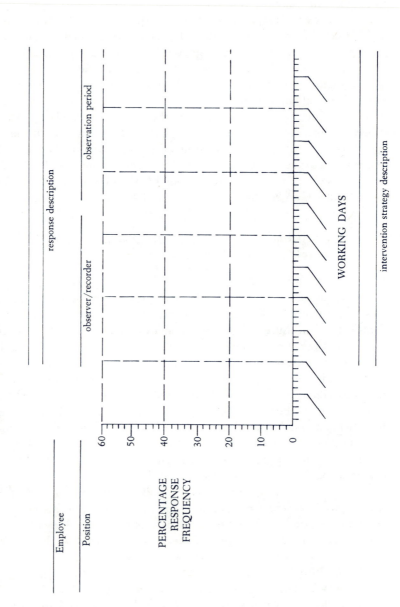

FIGURE 4-6.   Response Frequency Chart.

The consequence of the employees' rest-room behavior was not necessarily to relieve themselves but instead to socialize with their friends and get away from their boring job for a while. These were the consequences maintaining the behavior at such a high frequency. The antecedent (A) could not be changed. The supervisor could not alter time. If he wanted to change the behavior he had to change or replace the consequences. In this particular example, changing or replacing the consequences would be no easy task either, but it was not impossible.

The discussion of intervention in the next section and of reinforcement and punishment in the next two chapters will suggest ways that this supervisor could change the behavior. The point of this example, which is representative of most cases, is that antecedents can be difficult for managers to change. Most often, the functional analysis will reveal that the consequences are more adaptable to BCM.

Problems in functional analysis • Dealing with consequences can also present problems, however. For example, the same consequence may control the frequency of two or more behaviors or a single response may have more than one contingent consequence (Skinner, 1953, pp. 205–13). The following is a good example of how a single consequence may play a role in more than one contingency. A section boss praises a hard-working machine-shop employee as they leave the plant together. Unknown to the boss, the machine-shop worker has fifty dollars worth of company tools in his lunch bucket. While the section boss intended to reinforce the hard-working behavior, he may have accidentally reinforced the theft of company property.

In cases where cooperative effort is involved, a single consequence may simultaneously affect the contingencies of two or more people. When a supervisor compliments one of a pair of equally performing subordinates and the performance of the ignored subordinate drops, the supervisor's action has affected more than one individual's behavior. So we see that a single consequence may at the same time control: (1) two or more behaviors of the same person or (2) the behavior of two or more people.

Another technical problem encountered when functionally analyzing organizational behavior centers around the manner in which a single response may have two or more contingent consequences. This situation frequently occurs when organizational behavior comes under the control of both the formal and informal organizations. Joke telling on the job may be punished formally and at the same time reinforced informally. The organizational participant is caught in a dilemma between two mutually attractive sources of reinforcement. To resolve the conflict, the manager must make the formal consequences more attractive or potent than the informal consequences.

Step 4: Intervention strategies

The first three steps of BCM provide the necessary background and data for the fourth step. Passive identification, measurement, and analysis turn into active intervention and control in Step 4. As Figure 4–3 indicated, Step 4 is the most extensive and actually consists of four substeps: (4a) developing and (4b) applying intervention strategies; (4c) measuring the impact of the intervention strategy on response frequency; and (4d) maintaining desirable behavioral outcomes.

Variables affecting intervention strategies • When attention shifts to the development of appropriate intervention strategies, certain variables within the work environment should be considered. The structure of the organization is one such variable. For example, different interventions may be needed for organizations that are mechanistic or centralized than for those that are organic or decentralized (Burns and Stalker, 1961). Self-controlled contingencies would probably be more appropriate in the organic, decentralized organizations. On the other hand, carefully delineated and closely controlled contingencies may be more appropriate in the mechanistic, centralized organizations.

Internal organizational processes such as decision making, communication, and control are also variables (Luthans, 1973a). These processes may individually or collectively contribute to the eventual success or failure of a particular contingency management strategy. Technology, which includes knowledge, procedures, and techniques as well as machinery, may also limit or promote the applicability of certain intervention strategies. As stressed earlier, BCM cannot be applied to performance problems caused by lack of knowledge, inefficient procedures, outdated techniques, or malfunctioning machinery. It must also be remembered that organizational environments are largely social environments, and as such they possess all the complexities associated with group dynamics. Before an intervention strategy is implemented, its impact on other members of the work group as well as the impact of other work group members on the intervention strategy should be considered. The complicating nature of groups, with all of their force and influence on organizational behavior, can not and should not be underestimated in BCM. Yet, the problems associated with groups are certainly not insurmountable.

A final major environmental variable is the nature of the task. Some tasks lend themselves to behavioral interventions and some do not. The goal of BCM is to implement intervention strategies on tasks that have a great deal of behavioral input and, in turn, have a great impact on performance. In total, these environmental givens must be related in a contingent manner to the appropriate intervention strategies. Like the overall theory and practice of contingency management (Luthans, 1973b), the goal of BCM is to determine that *if* the organization has a certain structure, processes, and technology, and there are certain group and task elements, *then* what is the most appropriate intervention strategy to use that will lead to the greatest performance improvement.

Selecting and implementing a strategy • After identifying relevant variables in the organizational environment, the manager must select and implement an appropriate intervention strategy. The basic strategies are positive and negative reinforcement, punishment, extinction, or a combination of these. The goal of the intervention is to change the frequency of response of the identified behavior. Once applied, the results of the intervention strategy are monitored and charted on the response frequency chart similar to the one shown in Figure 4–7.

This chart is, of course, a continuation of the one started in Step 2. The wavy vertical line marks the beginning of the intervention period. During the intervention period (the area to the right of the intervention line), the response frequency is continually monitored. The response frequency chart, such as the one in Figure 4–7, tells the manager three things: (1) the baseline strength of the response; (2) the type and date of intervention; and (3) the effect of the intervention strategy on response frequency.

In a sense, the practicing manager using BCM has conducted a behavioral science experiment. The chart reveals at a glance whether the intervention strategy has worked or not. When the chart reveals that the intervention strategy did not bring about the desired change in response frequency, then the manager must attempt to use another intervention strategy. This points out the value of measuring. The manager thought a particular intervention would work one way but objective measurement proves that it actually had the opposite effect. For example, a supervisor may think that a verbal reprimand is punishing to a subordinate. However, upon contingent application of the reprimand to an undesirable behavior, the data shows that the behavior increased instead of decreased in frequency. In other words, the reprimand was actually a reinforcer, not a punisher, for this subordinate. It may be that this is the only time the supervisor pays any attention to the subordinate and, regardless of being "chewed out," this attention reinforces the undersirable behavior. Obviously, in this case another type of intervention strategy must be applied. In some cases, the manager may even have to go all the way back to Step 1 and redefine the behavior.

Maintaining desirable behavioral outcomes • In most cases, however, the result is that the undesirable response is emitted less often or the desirable response is emitted more often. When measurement reveals this intervention is working, appropriate schedules of reinforcement can

FIGURE 4-7.   Response Frequency Chart.

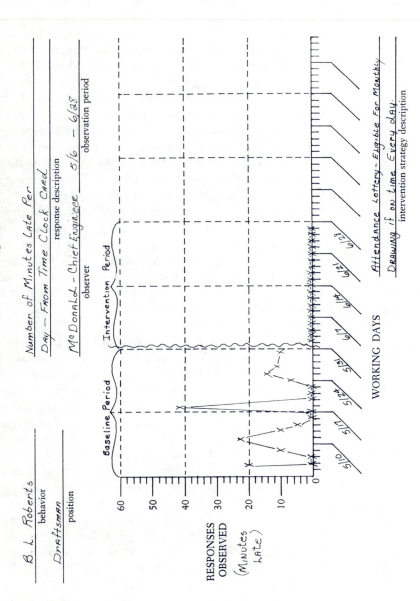

be employed to maintain the desired behavioral rate. Initially, at least, a weak response may need the steady support of continuous reinforcement. As the behavior gains strength, as indicated by its increase in frequency, intermittent reinforcement should be used. The ultimate goal is to develop a self-reinforcing participant in the pursuit of organizational objectives.

Step 5: Evaluate

The fifth and final step is the real test of the effectiveness of BCM. Almost without exception, human resource management techniques in the past have, at best, only conducted sketchy or surface evaluations of effectiveness. The typical approach was to get some affective reactions—"I think it's great" or "The employees seem to be responding"—but make no objective evaluation of the impact on performance and organizational consequences (the "bottom line"). BCM is geared directly to performance improvement (PI) and bottom-line results. If the evaluation determines that BCM is not positively affecting the performance of the individual or group whose behavior has been identified, measured, analyzed, and intervened, then corrective action must be taken. As emphasized earlier, BCM is not attempting to change behavior for the sake of behavioral change. BCM must be able to improve performance in order to be effective.

Positive Control 5

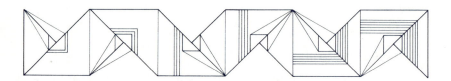

Reinforcement has been presented thus far as the key to operant learning theory and the most important principle of behavior modification. The simple fact is that positive reinforcement, contingently applied, can effectively control human behavior. In contrast to punishment and negative reinforcement, it is a positive type of control. With the possible exception of the contingency concept itself, the understanding and appropriate use of positive reinforcement is most important to success in O. B. Mod.

The major goal of human resource management is the attainment of organizational goals through people. This goal is commonly accomplished through either negative (punishment or negative reinforcement) or positive (positive reinforcement) control of organizational participants. Both approaches are generally not used very effectively in today's human resource management.

The premise of O. B. Mod. is that positive control of organizational behavior is much more effective than negative control for goal attainment in modern organizations. After reading this chapter, the practitioner and student of management will hopefully have a better understanding of and be able to effectively apply positive control. Since negative control is so widely used, the next chapter is devoted to it. The point to remember is that positive reinforcement is the most socially desirable and effective method of controlling behavior in organizations.

TECHNICAL REFINEMENTS OF REINFORCEMENT

Because positive reinforcement is so important to O. B. Mod., a clear distinction must be made between positive and negative reinforcement, positive reinforcement and rewards, and primary and generalized

conditioned reinforcers. An understanding of such distinctions is a necessary prerequisite for identifying and successfully applying positive reinforcement on the job.

Positive and negative reinforcement

As Chapter 3 pointed out, there are two general types of reinforcement, positive and negative. Both positive and negative reinforcement
strengthen behavior, but while positive reinforcement strengthens behavior
by the *presentation* of a desirable consequence, negative reinforcement
strengthens behavior by the *withdrawal* of an aversive stimulus.

An organizational example can clarify the distinction. If a key
performance-related response of an assistant shipping room manager is
strengthened through the use of performance-contingent time off, positive
reinforcement is being used. The *presentation* of time off is made contingent on improved performance. On the other hand, if the boss consistently
relies on threats of docked pay, demotion, transfer, dismissal, or just on
"chewing out" to stimulate the assistant's performance, a negative reinforcement strategy is in operation. In short, the assistant works harder so
that the threat will not be carried out. In this latter case, the hard work
responses are said to be negatively reinforced because they lead to the *withdrawal* of threatened undesirable consequences.

Both positive and negative reinforcers are widely used in contemporary human resource management. Yet, most often they are used in-
tuitively and randomly rather than knowledgeably and systematically. As
the next chapter points out, negative reinforcement, like punishment, has
some undesirable side effects. With positive reinforcement, on the other
hand, about the worst that can happen is its failure to work or the inad-
vertent strengthening of undesirable or otherwise unwanted responses.
Technically, in the case of failure, the approach cannot really be called
positive reinforcement. Remember that the behavior must be strengthened
and subsequent frequency must increase if positive reinforcement has actually been applied.

Reward and positive reinforcement

Contrary to common belief, reward and positive reinforcement
are not one and the same. Although closely related, there is a technical
and very important difference. All positive reinforcers can be called rewards, but not all rewards turn out to be positive reinforcers. To clarify
this point, we must first distinguish between positive reinforcer and posi-

tive reinforcement. A positive *reinforcer* is a consequence which, when presented, strengthens a behavior. Positive *reinforcement* is the name used to identify the entire process whereby behavior is strengthened by the contingent presentation of a consequence. In other words, a positive reinforcer is a *consequence* and positive reinforcement is the overall *process*.

The technical distinction between a reward and a positive reinforcer, of course, relates to how the terms are defined. Rewards are commonly subjectively defined while positive reinforcers are functionally defined. Reward, as the term is commonly used, simply refers to the presentation of something desirable. The word "desirable" accounts for the subjective nature of the definition. Frequently, employee performance is "rewarded" with consequences that the manager *feels* are desirable.

A recent true story demonstrates that employees do not always share management's opinion of what is rewarding. A Christmas tradition at a manufacturing plant in a small Midwestern town had been to invite all personnel to a big dinner at the local country club. Prior to last year's party, much to the surprise of the managers, who were practically all club members, a petition was received which asked if the party could be replaced by equivalent cash. Upon investigation, the managers discovered that many of the hourly personnel felt extremely out of place at the country club. They did not go to the country club during the year and felt awkward going there only at Christmas time. Management saw the Christmas party as a reward while many of the operating personnel found it very aversive. The subjective definition of rewards has led to many such problems.

In contrast to subjectively defined rewards, positive reinforcers are functionally defined. Based on Skinner's interpretation of Thorndike's law of effect, the term positive reinforcement has come to mean something very specific in behavior modification and, in turn, in O. B. Mod. A contingent consequence is called a positive reinforcer because it *functions* as a positive reinforcer. Positive reinforcers strengthen the behavior upon which they are contingent and make the reoccurrence of the behavior more probable. In other words, a consequence is not a positive reinforcer simply because someone has arbitrarily judged it to be such; it must pass the test of being able to increase response frequency. If the response frequency increases, then, and only then, is it a positive reinforcer. Importantly, this functional definition precludes the subjective or a priori definition of positive reinforcers. The key lies in the basic datum of behavior modification—response frequency.

The process of defining a positive reinforcer is further illustrated in Figure 5–1, in A→B→C terms. This figure helps clarify the earlier statement that positive reinforcers may be called rewards, but not all rewards may turn out to be positive reinforcers. Such a distinction is crucial

FIGURE 5–1.   The Process of Functionally Defining Positive Reinforcers.

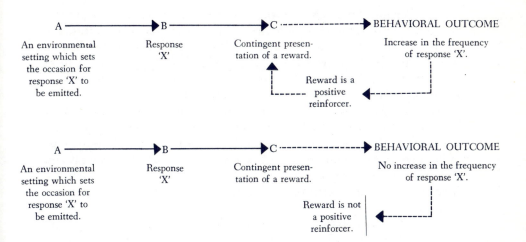

to the successful positive control of organizational behavior. Traditional "rewards" may not be positive reinforcers. The difference between rewards and positive reinforcers is analogous to the difference between the traditional human relations approaches to human resource management and O. B. Mod.

Another important distinction between rewards and positive reinforcers relates to the contingency concept. Rewards can and often are presented in a noncontingent manner by managers. Tardiness, dependence, dishonesty, immaturity, output restriction and other such undesirable behaviors are frequently maintained through the inappropriate use of rewards. In O. B. Mod., positive reinforcers are only presented contingent on the successful performance of objectively defined responses. When the store manager says, "I have rewarded Joe with an extra day of summer vacation," two important bits of information are missing: the "if" and the "then" or, the contingency and the effect on response frequency. When the office manager says, "Mary's Monday-through-Thursday performance rating has improved 20 percent since she was given the opportunity to work at her favorite job on Friday if she improved her Monday-through-Thursday performance," precise information on both the contingency and the effect on response frequency are given. The store manager's statement is too general and nontechnical for O. B. Mod. purposes, but the office manager's statement presents useful data and is representative of an O. B. Mod. approach.

Primary and generalized conditioned reinforcers

Another important refinement is the difference between primary and generalized conditioned reinforcers. In an organizational context, employees are not paid with beef steaks, tickets to movies, suburban houses, or shoes for the kids. Although it is true that everyone may need these types of things, it is just not feasible to use them as pay. A person can not possibly eat enough steaks at one sitting to last a year until payment is made in steaks again, or the kids might not need shoes at the time of the payment in shoes. On the other hand, money allows us to have steaks when we are hungry, to go to the movies when we like, to buy the type of house we need, to buy shoes for the kids when their old ones wear out, and most importantly, through saving, to defer any of our purchases. Money gives us the opportunity to efficiently manage our own personal economy.

The above examples lead to the distinction between primary and generalized conditioned reinforcers. Each is a reinforcer and each plays a unique role in the human–environment interaction. Representing food in general, steaks are examples of primary reinforcers. In more technical terms, steaks are related to a state of relative deprivation–satiation, namely common hunger. Primary reinforcers include food, water, sex, and sleep. They can satiate (satisfy) a deprived organism. All of us depend on the primary reinforcers for physiological well-being. However, most of our learned behavior depends on the conditioned reinforcers.

Through operant conditioning, people learn to associate primary reinforcers with other environmental stimuli. These latter stimuli take on reinforcing properties and are known as conditioned reinforcers. For example, as a child grows up, parental affection becomes associated with food. As conditioned reinforcers (parental affection) come to be associated with a number of primary reinforcers (food), *generalized* conditioned reinforcers emerge (Skinner, 1953, p. 77).

The most widely used generalized conditioned reinforcer today is money (McGinnies, 1970, p. 45; Millenson, 1967, p. 245; Skinner, 1953, p. 79). Money may be used to purchase food, drink, and a place to sleep. Hence, money obviously has value. But since money does not possess any inherent reinforcing properties such as nutritional value, it is not a primary reinforcer. We have *learned* to associate money with a wide variety of primary reinforcers. Money is a generalized conditioned reinforcer and is a very potent positive reinforcer available to management. In addition, other important generalized conditioned reinforcers include attention, affection, approval, and recognition, the so-called social reinforcers. Even status symbols are generalized conditioned reinforcers. All of these generalized conditioned reinforcers are extremely vital to the positive control of organizational behavior. More will be said about money as a reinforcer at the end of the chapter.

POSITIVE REINFORCEMENT
AND HUMAN RESOURCE MANAGEMENT

In behavioral science laboratory and field experiments, positive reinforcement has been repeatedly demonstrated to be a powerful tool for the positive control of human behavior. Although the exact theoretical explanations of how it works are still subject to debate, few behavioral scientists dispute the validity of the principle of reinforcement (Bandura, 1969, p. 217), i.e., positive reinforcement works. It is particularly popular with behavioral scientists because it does not lead to the undesirable side effects associated with negative control. With positive reinforcement, people emit certain behavior in order to receive a desirable consequence rather than to escape or avoid something bad.

Positive reinforcement has been widely used in the positive control of behavior over the last fifteen years. At first it was used exclusively with abnormal children and institutionalized adults. Then it was successfully applied to normal school children and, finally and most importantly for O. B. Mod., to normal adults in complex social settings. The Emery Air Freight program reviewed in the last Chapter is based on performance-contingent positive reinforcement and has been very successful. Recent rigidly controlled experimental studies on the efficacy of positive reinforcers for controlling "everyday" types of behaviors are also encouraging. For example, one group of researchers (Burgess, Clark, and Hendee, 1971) increased the freqency with which litter was properly disposed of in a public theater and strengthened anti-litter behavior in a public campground (Clark, Burgess, and Hendee, 1972). Another group (Everett, Hayward, and Meyers, 1974) increased bus ridership through positive reinforcement.

Aside from the fact that each is a successful demonstration of positive reinforcement, all three of these experiments have one thing in common. In each case, a behavior with important current social ramifications (i.e., properly disposing of litter and using mass transit) has been strengthened by systematic application of positive consequences. These target behaviors had not been systematically reinforced in the past. Yet, once positively reinforced, they showed dramatic improvement. Consistent with the law of effect, each positively reinforced behavior became stronger. With this background, the application of positive reinforcement to human resource management seems limited only by practicing managers' singular and collective ingenuity and problem-solving ability.

Willingness to serve

In his classic work, *The Functions of the Executive,* Chester I. Barnard (1938, p. 82) listed the three basic elements of any formal organization as communication, willingness to serve, and common purpose. The principle of teamwork or cooperation is largely derived from Barnard's second element, willingness to serve. In the broadest sense, willingness to serve in today's organizations represents a mutually beneficial employment contract. The slaves who built the great Egyptian and Roman edifices in ancient times certainly did not have the same type of willingness to serve. Slaves served to avoid a cruel death. In the formative years of this country, workers generally served in order to receive one thing and to avoid something else. They served the organization in order to earn enough money to enable them and their families to avoid starvation and the cold.

In today's "future-shock" society where the burden of the welfare of people has been assumed by the government instead of the family, starvation is not a threat for the bulk of the population. People now generally serve the organization in order to receive the benefits associated with gainful employment. In other words, people no longer serve organizations to avoid dire consequences. Like a pendulum, the willingness to serve has swung a full arc, first from a willingness to serve in order to avoid something, to a willingness to serve in order to receive one thing and avoid something else, to the present willingness to serve in order to receive many things. The many things that people *expect* to receive from serving today's organizations can and should be used in the positive control of human resources for goal attainment.

Perhaps one of the biggest challenges facing modern human resource management relates to the fact that the willingness of employees to serve is not great enough for the successful attainment of organizational objectives. In short, a willingness-to-serve gap exists. Studies as far back as those at Hawthorne during the late 1920s and early 1930s suggest that this gap has been around for a long time—it seems to still be with us. Recent Gallup Poll results indicate that half of the wage earners surveyed said they could accomplish more each day if they tried and, of that group, three out of five said they could improve their output by 20 percent or more (Job Satisfaction, 1973, p. 1).

Inducing willingness to serve

Willingness to serve is obviously a relative dimension. The relevant question for human resource managment becomes: willingness to serve to what extent? The gap between the level of willingness to serve which is brought to the job and that which is ultimately needed by the organization, if it is to achieve its stated goals, must be filled by *induced* willingness to serve. The question now becomes: exactly how can management go about inducing additional willingness to serve?

The most common inducement, of course, is pay or monetary reward. Lawler (1971, p. 1) has suggested that pay can increase job satisfaction, improve performance, and keep employees in the organization. However, O. B. Mod. recognizes that although money is a commonly used reward, it may not prove to be a positive reinforcer. In addition, money is recognized as but one of a practically limitless supply of positive reinforcers controlled by practicing managers. Money should not be equated with inducement as traditional approaches sometimes assume or, at least, imply. A manager using an O. B. Mod. approach must constantly survey the work environment for positive reinforcers with which to strengthen the behavior associated with willingness to serve. Money alone is not the answer. The next section suggests some specific ways of identifying positive reinforcers in the work environment.

IDENTIFYING POSITIVE REINFORCERS

The first thing to remember when attempting to identify reinforcers for the positive control of organizational behavior is that they are idiosyncratic. A recent episode illustrates this. After hearing several lectures on the value of positive reinforcement, a student presented one of the authors with a cartoon. It showed a manager picking a sugar cube out of a box and throwing it into the gaping mouth of an employee. The caption read, "He always rewards good work." The cartoon is now prominently posted on the author's door but with an added notation that reads, "Regarding idiosyncratic reinforcers, not everyone likes sugar."

This comeback was attempting to make the point that rewards are not necessarily positive reinforcers, and that there is no universal reinforcer. Because all reinforcers must be defined in terms of their effect on response frequency, there is no single, surefire reinforcer that will effectively control all behavior in a single person or control a single behavior in all people. Technically, the identification of reinforcers becomes a case-by-case proposition. For example, while one employee may work very hard for occasional praise from a relevant supervisor, another will scoff at praise and ask for money. Still another, unimpressed with praise or money, will only be reinforced by the self-satisfaction of a job well done. Because of this idiosyncratic nature of reinforcers, a concerted effort is often needed to identify the positive reinforcers that work for a particular employee.

The problem of identifying reinforcers is alleviated somewhat by the fact that not every response of every person requires a unique reinforcer. During the socialization process in childhood, a person learns to play various socially acceptable roles and consequently comes to behave like many other members of his/her culture (McGinnies, 1970). Consider, for example, the commonality of waking up in a suburban home, having a glass of orange juice, reading the morning newspaper, and joining the morning rush hour. It follows that these common behaviors may come under the control of common consequences. Because of this, many specific reinforcers may be able to strengthen a similar response in a great number of people. Thus, the idiosyncrasy of reinforcers is relative rather than absolute. The collection of reinforcers which positively controls the behavior repertoires of people can be thought of as a kaliedoscope; each person is reinforced by a unique pattern of common parts.

The following discussion summarizes three general approaches that can aid the manager in identifying positive reinforcers on the job. These are: analyzing histories of reinforcement, using self-report instruments, and using systematic trial-and-error techniques. The use of any one of these approaches or the use of a combination of two or more can help the practicing manager be more effective in the positive control of organizational behavior.

Analyzing histories of reinforcement

From a technical standpoint, there is only one correct way to identify positive reinforcers. As illustrated in Figure 5–1, the correct way involves an A→B→C analysis of contingencies. In Skinner's words (1969), "An experimental analysis permits us to relate behavior to a history of reinforcement" (p. 126). Each behavior in an individual's behavior repertoire has a history of reinforcement. Empirical investigation involves measuring the effect of the managed contingencies of behavior.

A sample functional analysis worksheet is shown in Figure 5–2. It may be used in conjunction with the response frequency chart illustrated and discussed in the last chapter (Steps 2 and 3 of BCM). This approach gives the practicing manager a workable set of tools for systematically analyzing histories of reinforcement. Initially, a particular consequence is made contingent on a performance-related response. Next, a functional analysis worksheet is used to identify all three elements (the A, B, C's) in the contingency. The frequency of the target response can then be charted on the response frequency graph. If the response frequency moves upward, then the consequence in question is a reinforcer. More specifically, the consequence is a positive reinforcer if it consists of the *presentation* of some environmental condition and the frequency of response increases.

FIGURE 5–2.   Functional Analysis Worksheet.

_____
   behavior

_____   _____ _____
   position   observer   observation period

Note: Describe each antecedent condition, behavior, and consequence carefully.

Date/time   ANTECEDENT ⟶ BEHAVIORAL EVENT ⟶ CONSEQUENCE
_____

In addition to measuring the effect of consequences in experimentally monitored contingencies, the procedure may also be used to identify positive reinforcers in naturally occurring contingencies. Ongoing work environments are not always amenable to experimental manipulation of contingencies for the purpose of identifying positive reinforcers. If such is the case, an alternative method of identifying positive reinforcers is available to the practicing manager. It involves only observation as opposed to the management of consequences and observation. Naturally occurring contingencies can be functionally analyzed by use of a worksheet, observed, and recorded on a response frequency chart. The frequencies can then be analyzed and interpreted. Positive reinforcers which support both desirable and undesirable performance-related behaviors may be identified in this manner. Conceivably, an appropriate intervention strategy as discussed in Step 4 of BCM could shift the positive reinforcers of undesirable behavior to desirable behavior. This approach represents effective use of data uncovered through the analysis of histories of reinforcement.

It should be remembered that the further away one gets from functionally analyzing histories of reinforcement, the less accurate will be the specific identification of true positive reinforcers. An analysis of history of reinforcement reveals the idiosyncratic nature of positive reinforcers. Also, this approach has the advantage of forcing the manager to view organizational behavior in A→B→C terms and thus use an O. B. Mod. approach to human resource management.

Self-reporting of reinforcers

Due to time, behavioral, or economic constraints, it may not be possible to analyze histories of reinforcement in order to identify on-the-job positive reinforcers. Like any technique which involves the systematic collection of empirical data, the analysis of histories of reinforcement can be very time consuming and tedious for a busy manager. An alternative is to use self-report approaches.

Ask what is reinforcing • The most basic self-report approach would be to simply ask an employee what is reinforcing for him/her. Although this approach can work and is the most straightforward, caution should be used. A verbal self-report that a certain consequence is reinforcing is not the same as the results of a history of reinforcement analysis. In other words, verbal opinion is one thing, actual behavior is another. With reference to this point, Skinner (1969) has cautioned that the information derived by asking a person what his/her intentions, plans, or expectations are ". . . may be worth investigating, but it is not a substitute for the behavior observed in an operant analysis" (p. 116). Stated another way, the most reliable indicator of consequences that are positive reinforcers will always remain the history of reinforcement, in which frequency of response is the basic datum. Because of the realistic limitations of such an approach, though, self-report techniques are relied upon in O. B. Mod. (This, of course, is the type of thing that separates O. B. Mod. from the more technical B. Mod.)

An ipsative test • Some relatively sophisticated self-report instruments are emerging that the manager can use to assist him/her in identifying positive reinforcers on the job. One particularly effective technique is reported by Blood (1973). He developed and experimentally tested a self-report instrument which yields an ipsative score for rewards an individual might expect to receive on the job. In direct contrast to normative scales, ipsative scores show the relative importance of various dimensions *within* a single individual. A normative test might tell us that money means more to Joe than it does to Mary or Curt but an ipsatively scored test tells us that Joe prefers job security to achievement or sense of accomplishment. Normative instruments measure similar dimensions across a number of people while ipsative instruments measure the relative importance of several dimensions in one person.

Blood's ipsative test is designed to identify job-related rewards. However, it should be remembered that each reward is only a potential positive reinforcer. Referring to the relevance of his ipsative measure to human resource management, Blood (1973) noted: "If we are to translate the concepts of behavior modification into the work situation, we must begin to get an understanding of the rewards which are available to the worker."

In finished form, the ipsative instrument, labeled the Job Orientation Inventory (JOI) Scales, contains forty-five pairs of statements. The respondent selects his/her preference in each pair. Each of ten different reward categories is represented in corresponding pairs of statements. The number of times the respondent agrees with a statement from a particular reward category determines its relative position in a hierarchy of preference. The ten reward categories are the following:

1) Achievement or sense of accomplishment.
2) Responsibility or control.
3) Opportunity for personal growth.
4) Recognition from the community and from friends.
5) Job or company status.
6) Interpersonal relationships or friendships.
7) Pay or monetary reward.
8) Job security.
9) Provision for family.
10) Support for hobbies or avocational activities.

Blood carefully points out that this list is not exhaustive and may overlook some idiosyncratic reinforcers. However, the experimentally derived results of the application of the JOI seems to indicate, so far at least, the validity and practical potential of such an approach.

Contingency questionnaires • A second questionnaire self-report method of identifying reinforcers is suggested in a study reported by Reitz (1971). He employed a contingency questionnaire to measure perceived performance-outcome probabilities. Respondents select one of six responses (100 percent certain, very probable, fairly probable, uncertain, fairly improbable, and very improbable) for each of twenty items. The net result is a self-report selection of contingencies.

In terms of the practical implications of such an approach, contingency questionnaires can give the practicing manager a reasonably good idea of what types of consequences are important to individual subordinates. Fourteen of the items used by Reitz (1971) identify positive reinforcement contingencies. They include the following:

1) Your supervisor would personally pay you a compliment if you did outstanding work.

2) Your supervisor would lend a sympathetic ear if you had a complaint.

3) You will eventually go as far as you would like to go in this company if your work is consistently above average.

4) You would be promoted if your work was better than others who were otherwise equally qualified.

5) Your supervisor would help you get a transfer if you asked for one.

6) Your supervisor's boss or others in higher management would know about it if your work was outstanding.

7) Your supervisor's recommendation for a pay increase for you would be consistent with his evaluation of your performance.

8) Your supervisor would show a great deal of interest if you suggested a new and better way of doing things.

9) You would receive special recognition if your work performance was especially good.

10) Your supervisor would do all he could to help you if you were having problems in your work.

11) Your supervisor's evaluation of your performance would be in agreement with your own evaluation of your performance.

12) Your next pay increase will be consistent with the amount recommended by your supervisor.

13) Your supervisor would encourage you to do better if your performance was unacceptable but well below what you are capable of doing.

14) You would be promoted within the next two years if your work was consistently better than the work of others in your department.

While the data generated from this type of self-report instrument is not as precise as that obtained from analyses of histories of reinforcement, the approach can still potentially identify behavior that requires reinforcement and identify already effective positive reinforcers. Being contingencies, all fourteen of the above statements are if-then statements. The "ifs" refer to peformance or results of performance and the "thens" refer to rewards or potential positive reinforcers. The low probability responses to the statements represent an area that probably needs attention by the manager. In other words, the "then" side of the contingency relationship is deficient. Appropriate contingent consequences would have to be identified and applied.

A close look at the contingency questionnaire reported by Reitz reveals that the rewards include a compliment, sympathy, promotion, transfer, recognition from top management, a pay increase, attention, special recognition, help with problems, recognition from the supervisor, and support. Some or all of these rewards may, in fact, turn out to be positive reinforcers that are currently maintaining goal-directed performance. For example, a high-performing employee might indicate low pay and promotion probabilities but a high special-recognition probability. On the basis of such information, the manager could then turn directly to the task of analyzing the histories of reinforcement where special recognition is involved to determine objectively if special recognition is, in fact, a positive reinforcer. Conceivably, a self-report instrument of this nature could be used to identify a general class of potential reinforcers. Subsequent refinements could be carried out with an analysis of reinforcement histories.

Another contingency questionnaire is proposed in Figure 5–3. The test is designed to simply have the respondent fill in the missing if-then contingency elements. The purpose of this test format is to assist in the identification of idiosyncratic reinforcers. It is important to note that this performance/consequence questionnaire is only a suggested prototype. The validity and reliability have not been tested. Obviously, such an instrument would not have universal applicability. Figure 5–3 is intended to show how a manager using O. B. Mod. could tailor an instrument so that the ifs would be key performance-related responses and the thens would be rewards (potential positive reinforcers) actually controlled by management. Such a tailor-made instrument could help the manager using O. B. Mod. to measure the degree of contingency in the work environment and help identify positive reinforcers.

Self-selection technique • Another self-report method for identifying positive reinforcers is the self-selection technique. Rather than responding to a carefully developed questionnaire, the individual employee chooses his/her own rewards from a broad selection. This approach is really a hybrid evolving from two separate, but not altogether unrelated, trends. The first trend occurred in education. Originally formulated by Premack (1959) and later developed by Addison and Homme (1966), a so-called reinforcement menu technique has been designed to involve reluctant school children in their school work by allowing them to "pick their own reinforcers." Under this system, the children start working for rewards they desire, not rewards the teacher arbitrarily thinks they desire or should desire. A reinforcement menu typically involves items such as playtime, time away from the task, recess, and favorite curricular and extracurricular activities. Importantly, all reinforcers are given contingent upon the achievement of desirable performance criteria. *If* a student properly completes an assigned activity, *then* he/she gets to pick a desired reward from the menu. This technique has proven successful for many teachers (Blackham and Silberman, 1971, pp. 128–29).

A trend parallel to that in education has developed in business, in executive compensation programs. These are the so-called smorgasbord (Cathey, 1970) or cafeteria (Oates, 1973) compensation plans. The approach is to tailor the compensation package to fit the individual executive. He/she is allowed to select a total compensation package from a vast assortment of options. For example, an executive may choose more time off instead of cash, or select a deferred income plan instead of immediate cash, or take the cash right now. The total dollar cost is the same in each

FIGURE 5–3.   Sample Performance/Consequence Questionnaire.

Directions: After carefully considering your present job, fill in the following
                 blanks as specifically as possible.

| *Performance* | *Consequence* |

If _____, then I will get a raise.

If I ask for a transfer, then _____.

If _____, then I will be complimented by my supervisor.

If I am having problems with my work, then _____.

If _____, then my supervisor will show interest in my
work.

If I do my job better than usual, then _____.

If _____, then I will get more sense of accomplishment
from my job.

If I make a suggestion, then _____.

If _____, then I will be promoted.

If I take proper care of my equipment, then _____.

If _____, then I will like my job more.

If my work is outstanding, then _____ _____.

If _____, then I will be formally recognized by top management.

If I get to work on time, then _____.

If _____, then I will get some help from my supervisor.

If I save the company some money, then _____.

Other relationships not mentioned above

If _____, then _____.

If _____, then _____.

If _____, then _____.

If _____, then _____.

case but the way it is split up can widely differ. From an O. B. Mod. standpoint, the probability that the selected rewards from such a plan will turn out to be positive reinforcers is greatly increased.

Any personnel manager or compensation specialist will readily admit that the task of employee compensation is getting progressively more difficult. Like everything else, employee likes and dislikes are undergoing drastic change. Much time and effort is being devoted to ensure that there is equal pay for equal work. In addition, there has been a steady growth in nonwage benefits and services, and continual changes in tax legislation and Internal Revenue Service interpretations of various types of compensation. The base wage or salary has become secondary in many instances. With this type of situation, smorgasbord and cafeteria compensation plans are becoming more and more popular. If a contingency relationship between performance and reward is assured, these new approaches to compensation can increase the number of positive reinforcers available on the job.

Admittedly, contingency management in a classroom setting with youngsters and contingency management in a complex organization are two different matters. Contingencies in organizations cannot be as clear-cut and time-efficient as the classroom contingencies. For example, allowing a student who has completed a math assignment to immediately select a privilege from a reinforcement menu is much more efficient than having an executive work for a paid-up life insurance policy that he/she selected from a cafeteria compensation plan six months earlier and will not benefit from for many years to come. Nevertheless, significant parallels do exist. The self-selection approach has exciting possibilities as a method of identifying positive reinforcers on the job. Successful application depends on establishing contingencies between key performance-related behavior and the chosen forms of compensation.

Identifying positive reinforcers through trial and error

Besides analyzing reinforcement histories and using self-report techniques, the manager can turn to systematic trial and error to identify on-the-job positive reinforcers. This last approach, of course, is much less precise and efficient than the other two approaches discussed thus far. It is, however, much more convenient and readily applicable and, if done systematically, is certainly better than no approach at all. The approach is very straightforward: make a reward contingent on a particular per-formance-related response and objectively observe what happens. Increased frequency of response identifies a positive reinforcer and decreased fre-quency eliminates the consequence as a reinforcer. Once systematically identified this way, positive reinforcers can be made contingent on similar performance-related behavior to see if their ability to positively control generalizes to other behavior.

On the surface, the trial-and-error method appears to be the same as the history of reinforcement technique described earlier. They are similar in intent, but that is where the similarity ends. One of the major differences between the two is that in the trial-and-error method the manager relies on rewards to induce performance, without distinguishing between rewards and positive reinforcers. Unlike the analysis of the his-tory of reinforcement, no special attempt is made to ensure a contingency relationship between response and consequence and no accurate response frequency records are kept. With trial and error, the manager often guesses at the reinforcing ability of various consequences. Once again, what re-inforces one person may not reinforce another: the idiosyncrasy of rein-forcement. A more systematic approach toward trial-and-error identification would be the development of a classification scheme of on-the-job rewards.

Classification of on-the-job rewards • Although practically all managers unwittingly use trial and error, an O. B. Mod. approach re-quires that it be done much more systematically than is usually the case. The starting point is categorization of all positive consequences available to a given manager. Although most of today's human resource managers cannot directly give more money or time off or a promotion on the spot, they still have many potential reinforcers available to them. To ensure that all possible forms of rewards are considered, a classification framework would be helpful. Such a scheme was proposed by Meacham and Wiesen (1969, p. 46) for identifying reinforcers available to school teachers, as follows: (1) consumables; (2) manipulatables; (3) visual and auditory stimuli; (4) social stimuli; (5) tokens; and (6) Premack. This breakdown seems directly adaptable to the trial-and-error identification of rewards in O. B. Mod. The word *reward* is used here deliberately to emphasize that this approach does not necessarily identify positive reinforcers. Only follow-up measures will reveal if in fact the rewards are positive rein-forcers.

Examples of all the categories are listed in Figure 5–4. The con-sumables, manipulatables, visual and auditory stimuli, and tokens are placed under the general heading of contrived rewards. The natural re-wards, which are much more important to O. B. Mod., are shown to be social stimuli and Premack.

FIGURE 5–4.   Classifications of On-The-Job Rewards.

| Contrived On-The-Job Rewards | | | Natural Rewards | | |
Consumables	Manipulatables	Visual and Auditory	Tokens	Social	Premack
Coffee-break treats	Desk accessories	Office with a window	Money	Friendly greetings	Job with more responsibility
Free lunches	Wall plaques	Piped-in music	Stocks	Informal recognition	Job rotation
Food baskets	Company car	Redecoration of work environment	Stock options	Formal acknowledgment of achievement	Early time off with pay
Easter hams	Watches	Company literature	Movie passes	Invitations to coffee/lunch	Extended breaks
Christmas turkeys	Trophies	Private office	Trading stamps (green stamps)	Solicitations of suggestions	Extended lunch period
Dinners for the family on the company	Commendations	Popular speakers or lectures	Paid-up insurance policies	Solicitations of advice	Personal time off with pay
Company picnics	Rings/tie pins	Book club discussions	Dinner theater tickets	Compliment on work progress	Work on personal project on company time
After-work wine and cheese parties	Appliances and furniture for the home	Feedback about performance	Vacation trips	Recognition in house organ	Use of company machinery or facilities for personal projects
Beer parties	Home shop tools		Coupons redeemable at local stores	Pat on the back	Use of company recreation facilities
	Garden tools		Profit sharing	Smile	
	Clothing			Verbal or non-verbal recognition or praise	
	Club privileges				
	Special assignments				

Contrived rewards • The contrived rewards are largely brought in from outside the natural work environment and generally involve costs for the organization over and above the existing situation. It is the contrived rewards which usually come quickly to mind when practitioners are asked about possible rewards for employees. These are the "jellybeans" that Frederick Herzberg critically refers to in his movie "Jumping for Jellybeans." Although they can be used to positively reinforce organizational behavior, besides being costly, they also tend to lead to satiation rather quickly. An employee can be reinforced by movie passes or wall plaques only so long before he/she becomes satiated. In other words, people get tired of most contrived rewards.

An even greater problem with contrived rewards is that they are seldom administered on a contingent basis. The watch given after twenty-five years of "loyal" service to the organization is noncontingent on the individual's performance. About the only thing the watch does is reinforce walking up to the boss and shaking his hand as it is presented. A Christmas turkey, an annual bonus, or two tickets to the local dinner theater for perfect attendance are all administered on a noncontingent basis. Even the weekly, biweekly, or monthly paycheck is noncontingent on day-to-day job behavior. Most often the paycheck simply reinforces walking up to a pay window or opening an envelope. In some cases, where employees have their checks automatically deposited in their checking account, they never see any money from the organization, let alone establish a contingency with their job performance.

A good example of the use of contrived rewards is the fairly common practice of awarding green stamps or some other reward, such as free dinners or movie tickets, to increase the attendance behavior of employees (reduce absenteeism). Although these programs almost always initially work, they soon begin to fizzle because the employees become satiated. However, an interesting variation is worthy of mention. One company wrote to each employee's wife announcing the green stamp attendance program, rather than announcing the program to the employees in the normal way by memo or bulletin board. The men did not seem to be particularly reinforced by green stamps, but the company found out that the wives were. It soon became evident that the wives were getting their spouses to work in the morning in order to receive the green stamps. The behavior used by the wives to induce their husbands to go to work increased in frequency when the contingent consequence was green stamps. As mentioned in the last chapter, the administration of the reinforcement may be more important than its content. This company was able to increase attendance by the way they administered a contrived reinforcement program.

Natural rewards • The natural rewards are of much more value than the contrived rewards in O. B. Mod. These are the rewards that exist in the natural occurrence of events. The social category listed in Figure 5–4 almost always contains natural reinforcers, as do all the *existing* work procedures, schedules, task assignments, and personnel policies concerning incentive pay, transfers, time off, breaks, etc. Whereas the contrived reinforcers generally cost the organization additional money, the natural rewards do not. Social reinforcers and existing procedures and policies cost nothing extra. The natural social rewards are potentially the most powerful and universally applicable reinforcers. In contrast to the contrived rewards, they do not generally lead to satiation (people seldom get tired of compliments, attention, or recognition) and can be administered on a very contingent basis. The supervisor of any group of employees at any level in the organization is the major source of potential reinforcement. He/she can not normally dole out consumables, manipulatables, visual and auditory rewards, or tokens, but he/she can and does constantly give out social rewards. In the O. B. Mod. approach, however, these social rewards are contingent on desired performance-related behavior and the results are measured to see if they in fact turn out to be positive reinforcers.

The natural rewards stemming from existing procedures and policies can be made into positive reinforcers by the Premack Principle. Named for the work of David Premack (1965), this category of rewards involves the use of high probability behavior to reinforce low probability behavior. Undoubtedly, many of us vividly remember our parents saying to us when we were young, "You don't get your dessert until you have finished your dinner" or "You can go out and play with friends after you clean up your room." Whether they realized it or not, our parents were using the Premack Principle. This principle takes advantage of the reinforcing properties of an opportunity to engage in a preferred activity that is already natural to the job. Although frequently overlooked in human resource management, there are many preferred activities that can be made contingent on less preferred but organizationally important activities.

In other words, assume an employee has two tasks to do, A and B. If he likes to do B better than A, then the Premack Principle would say that A should be performed first and followed by B. In this manner B becomes a reinforcer for first performing the less desirable A. Performance-contingent time off and rotation to more desirable tasks are some practical examples. Getting off early from work may have strong reinforcing properties for personnel performing tedious, routine tasks such as sorting checks or mail. As an illustration of the reinforcing properties of leaving work one need only observe and contrast the speed with which employees punch in and start work and later punch out and leave. One manager recently remarked that he wouldn't want to be standing in the exit door when quitting time came around. The key to taking advantage of the reinforcing properties of leaving the work place lies in making it contingent on performance. More precisely, the work environment must be arranged so that early time off with pay can be earned through improved performance. This particular strategy does not normally involve any additional costs to the organization that uses it and is thus considered a natural reinforcer.

A number of rewards listed in Figure 5–4 actually qualify for two or more categories but have been arbitrarily listed under one. Too, the list is only representative and suggestive rather than absolute and exhaustive. At this point, as a beneficial exercise the reader may want to (1) consider his/her own past, present, or future work environment; (2) check off the applicable rewards listed in Figure 5–4, giving particular attention to any natural reinforcers; and (3) fill in the balance of each category with a personal list of additional job-related rewards. Once the job-related rewards have been identified, the trial-and-error approach to identifying positive reinforcers may begin. Even if analysis of reinforcement history or self-report approaches are used, a classification list of this type can still be very helpful.

MONEY AS A REWARD
FOR PERFORMANCE

There are two major reasons for giving special attention to money as a reward in the positive control of organizational behavior. First, the extensive use of money makes it the closest thing there is to a universal reward in the practice of management. Second, the use of money as a reward for performance is as controversial as it is widespread. Discussing money from an O. B. Mod. perspective will certainly not end the controversy, but it will give emphasis to the dual role of money as a reward *and* a positive reinforcer.

The complexity of money

During the last fifteen years, human resource management experts have generally agreed that monetary reward should be tied to performance in order to get at least some "motivational" impact. The solution was various types of individual or group incentive pay for hourly workers and some type of merit or bonus plan for salaried personnel. For example, some operations management experts, citing the successful use of piece-rate pay plans since the time of Frederick W. Taylor's scientific management movement at the turn of the century, still recommend the use of incentive wage plans today (McManis and Dick, 1973). On the other hand, organizational behavior theorists generally stress the administrative, technical, and psychological problems associated with piece-rate compensation. Some of the important "human" problems mentioned are output restriction (Vroom, 1964, p. 258), diminished intrinsic motivation (Deci, 1973), and reduced satisfaction (Schwab, 1974). There is also strong evidence to suggest that incentive pay plans are not being used as widely as is supposed (Evans, 1970; Lawler, 1971, p. 158). The net result is general confusion and few useful guidelines for the practitioner in tying pay to performance and using money as a motivator.

Money was described earlier as a generalized conditioned reinforcer. It has also been noted that money, in spite of being the most common *reward* for organizational performance, is not necessarily a *positive reinforcer*. Once again, money is not a positive reinforcer until its performance-contingent presentation demonstrably increases response frequency. This fundamental point is often overlooked by those advocating wage-incentive plans or by the expectancy motivational theorists who are concerned with valence, expectancy, and instrumentality. While these latter terms may help us understand the psychological process of motivation and, more specifically, the role of money as a motivator, they have done little in the way of demonstrating how to control organizational behavior with money. Only situation-specific experimentation on a case-by-case basis will tell the practicing manager whether money is a reward *and* a positive reinforcer or just a reward with no known impact on performance. The key from an O. B. Mod. perspective lies in analyzing the histories of reinforcement for money.

The changing environment (both social and economic) suggests that the reinforcing potential of money may be diminishing. First, unemployment insurance and other forms of social welfare have diminished the significance of money earned through work (Conversation with B. F. Skinner, 1973). Second, and perhaps more important, as was pointed out earlier, the contingency connection between performance and pay is slowly but steadily being eroded mainly through the increasing use of time-based pay plans (Aldis, 1961; Luthans and White, 1971; Nord, 1969). For example, a weekly, biweekly, or monthly paycheck is administered on a fixed interval schedule of reinforcement (described in Chapter 3 as being one of the least efficient reinforcement schedules). Thus, the reward of money is weakened as a positive reinforcer because of a diminution of its reinforcing properties (for example, because of less materialistic social values and a relative abundance of money for everyone) and the inefficient manner in which it is typically administered in the modern organization. Economic factors like inflation also do little to enhance the reinforcing properties of money as its purchasing value is eroded.

Making money contingent

As far as conventional pay plans are concerned, there is no question that the piece-rate method is the most contingent. An increment of pay is given for a defined increment of work. During the scientific management era dramatic improvements in performance were attained through the use of such piece-rate incentive plans. They appeared to be one of the keys to greater human productivity. Workers were generally very poor economically, the tasks were relatively simple to perform, and the strategic variable was the speed at which the individual worked. However, as twentieth-century technology pervaded and began to dominate industrial organizations, the resulting man/machine interface began to complicate the conventional piece-rate plans. Technology gradually began to replace humans as the strategic variable. More often than not, machines rather than people determined the quality and speed of production. As a result of this new technological variable and administrative problems with establishing and maintaining meaningful standards, piece-rate plans fell into a state of limbo and confusion, where they seem to remain today.

The best means of getting piece-rate incentive plans out of their current state is to start making money truly contingent on key performance-related responses. The same holds true for merit pay plans for managerial personnel, although the process would be more difficult. At the minimum, a portion of the paycheck should always be made contingent on performance (Cummings and Schwab, 1973, p. 53.) Appropriate consideration must also be given to task, technology, personal, group, and other relevant work-environment variables. The key for the practitioner using O. B. Mod. is to identify key performance-related behavior and then make monetary rewards contingent upon improvement. By following this guideline, at least part of the paycheck becomes more than a reward for simply showing up at work. Performance is also rewarded.

A study reported by Hermann et al. (1973) illustrates the practical utility of making money contingent on a specific on-the-job response. In this study money was more than a reward; it became a positive reinforcer. The general problem studied was chronic tardiness. The subjects were workers at a Mexican division of a large U.S. corporation. Several workers with chronic tardiness records were experimentally exposed to some systematic positive consequences. The target response was punctuality —defined as punching a time-clock card on or before the designated starting time. Punching in later was the incompatible, undesirable response of tardiness. Each worker in the experiment was instructed that every day he arrived on time the plant guard would give him a slip of paper saying he was entitled to a small cash bonus (approximately 3 percent of an average day's pay). At the end of each work week the workers could exchange their punctuality bonus slips for cash. This arrangement had the effect of making the slips of paper conditioned reinforcers; they had value because of their association with cash.

Baseline punctuality figures covering the previous year were obtained from punch-card records. All together, there were three experimental treatment periods and three baseline periods. The baseline/treatment/baseline research design allows the individual or group exposed to the experimental contingencies to serve as its own control across time. To ensure that any changes in tardiness were due to the presence or absence of the punctuality bonus plan, an equivalent control group was also selected and observed. Tardiness increased during the baseline periods (the control periods) when the bonus plan was not in effect and clearly decreased during the treatment periods when the workers were able to earn a bonus for punctual arrival at work. The last treatment period covering thirty-two weeks demonstrated the durability of the bonus effect. More tardy arrivals at work were recorded for the control group which was not under the punctuality bonus plan than for the experimental group which was. Clearly, the punctuality bonus plan helped this company overcome its tardiness problem with the workers studied.

The primary value of the above reported study is the manner in which it demonstrates how problem-solving managers using an O. B. Mod. approach can turn rewards like money into positive reinforcers. Consistent with the whole behavior modification approach, the techniques and application of performance-contingent pay must necessarily be objective and precise which, of course, takes time, but the benefits accruing to the organization in the form of greater organizational effectiveness can make the effort worthwhile. This or any other O. B. Mod. approach must continually monitor the results to make sure the desired change is being maintained and is always pointed toward performance improvement.

Negative Control 6

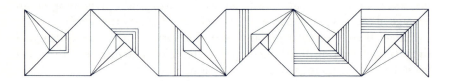

In the first half of the book, the idea that future behavior is largely determined by present consequences has been emphasized repeatedly. The overriding theme of the book is that behavior is a function of its consequences. Although there are numerous types of consequences, we have categorized them into two general types—positive and negative. The last chapter strongly recommended positive control in an O. B. Mod. approach to human resource management. However, an O. B. Mod. approach is also realistic enough to recognize that negative control is and will be used to manage people in modern organizations. Thus, this chapter is devoted to developing an understanding of and effectiveness in using negative control.

FUNCTIONAL DEFINITIONS OF TERMS

Punishment and negative reinforcement are two key concepts in understanding the negative control of behavior. After a detailed look at these two aspects of negative control, we will examine the closely related but yet quite different concepts of extinction, and escape and avoidance behavior. The meanings of these terms must be fully understood before they can be critically analyzed from an O. B. Mod. perspective.

The functional definition of punishment

Realistically, punishment probably plays as much a role in the control of human behavior as does reinforcement. As with reinforcement,

punishment should be functionally defined. In other words, the consequences involved in the process called punishment must be labeled in
terms of their *effect* on frequency of response. In a punishment contingency, the effect is a *reduction* of response frequency; punishment weakens
behavior. As in the other O. B. Mod. concepts discussed thus far, this
definition centers around the action of the individual, the reaction of the
environment, and the subsequent effect on response frequency. Figure
6–1 illustrates how each of these elements relate to one another.

FIGURE 6–1.   The Process of Functionally Defining Punishment.

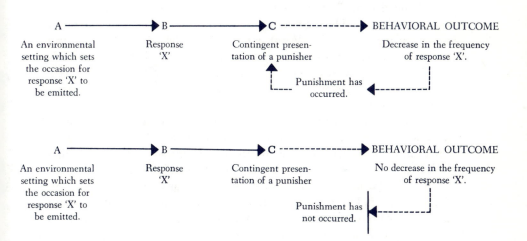

An important distinction to make is that between the subjective
use of the term punisher and what is meant here by functional punishment. Like a reward, a punisher is often a subjectively defined consequence.
Like positive reinforcement, punishment is a functionally defined process.
The term punishment is used to identify a consequence that has demonstrably weakened a particular response (the frequency has decreased).
A subjectively defined aversive consequence could be called a punisher
while a functionally defined consequence is called punishment.

The example of a manager publicly berating a subordinate helps
clarify this distinction. From the manager's viewpoint, the public berating
was felt to be punishing for the subordinate, supposedly possessing the

power to weaken the undersirable response. However, precisely the opposite may occur. The subordinate in this case may go out of his way to misbehave to "get the manager's goat" or, perhaps, he may see misbehaving as the only way to receive any attention from his boss. In this example, the assumed punisher actually turns out to be a positive reinforcer. The use of negative control commonly backfires this way when managers fail to make the important distinction between subjective punishers and functional punishment. An O. B. Mod. approach depends on response frequency when defining punishment. Again, punishment weakens behavior and decreases response frequency. If the consequence does not have this effect, punishment has not occurred.

Skinner and punishment • To give added depth to the meaning of punishment a Skinnerian interpretation is useful. Skinner (1953) outlined the nature of punishing consequences in terms of positive and negative reinforcers. He suggested: "In solving the problem of [defining] punishment we simply ask: What is the effect of *withdrawing* a *positive* reinforcer or *presenting* a *negative* reinforcer?" (p. 185). If punishment has taken place, the general effect is a weakened behavior as evidenced by a lower response frequency. The key to understanding Skinner's interpretation is to recall how positive and negative reinforcers have been defined. To reiterate, positive reinforcers strengthen behavior by their presentation and negative reinforcers strengthen behavior by their withdrawal. According to Skinner, every behavior modification intervention strategy, including punishment, can be explained in terms of positive and negative reinforcers.

Reinforcement versus punishment • Relative to the manner in which positive and negative reinforcers are employed, reinforcement and punishment can be thought of as opposites. Reinforcement strengthens behavior through the presentation of a positive reinforcer or the withdrawal of a negative reinforcer, while punishment weakens behavior through the withdrawal of a positive reinforcer or the presentation of a negative reinforcer. Of course, the consequences must always be contingent for this to occur. Wenrich (1970, p. 53) has summarized the four operations identified in this comparison between reinforcement and punishment as follows:

1) If a *positive reinforcer* is *presented* to an organism following a response, the result is *positive reinforcement*.

2) If a *positive reinforcer* is *withdrawn* following an organism's response, the result is *punishment*.

3) If a *negative reinforcer* is *presented* to an organism following a response, the result is *punishment*.

4) If a *negative reinforcer* is *withdrawn* following an organism's response, the result is *negative reinforcement*.

This chapter is concerned with the last three operations in the above list because each falls under the general heading of negative control. In spite of the strengthening effect of negative reinforcement, it is considered a form of negative control because punishing consequences are at least indirectly involved.

The idiosyncrasy of punishment • A final parallel in functionally defining punishment is to recognize that, like reinforcement, punishment is idiosyncratic. Using the example cited earlier, a manager's public berating of an employee because of performance deficiencies may be punishing for some but not for others. Only the decreased frequency of a particular response stands as an accurate and reliable indicator of the effects of various so-called punishers. Because punishment is idiosyncratic, thus producing different effects in different people, a hard and fast list of universally effective punishers is just as difficult to formulate as a list of universally effective positive reinforcers. Consequences are not punishing simply because the manager feels they are or should be punishing. However, punishers can be identified in much the same manner as is used for reinforcers.

The role of negative reinforcement

Some may argue that negative reinforcement contributes to positive rather than negative control of behavior. However, as we pointed out earlier, negative reinforcement, although having the opposite effect of punishment on behavior, controls behavior in a negative manner. Because punishing consequences are present in negative reinforcement, it is considered a form of negative control in O. B. Mod.

Like punishment, negative reinforcement is widely used and abused. Most discussions of human behavior either ignore it or lump it together with positive reinforcement or punishment. One major reason for the confusion surrounding negative reinforcement is that it is a concept that is much more difficult to explain verbally or in writing than it is to apply in the actual control of behavior. Although much of everyone's behavior is a function of negative reinforcement, most people, including managers who greatly depend on it, do not understand it. Negative reinforcement and punishment are not the same. Behavior is strengthened rather than weakened through negative reinforcement. When a response leads to the termination of a punishing consequence and is thereby strengthened, negative reinforcement has occurred. Put into everyday terms, when certain behavior gets us out of trouble, we tend to repeat that behavior when we are again faced with the same trouble.

Negative reinforcement starts to control behavior at a very early age. Once a child learns that the mother will finally give in to various demands after a period of progressively louder crying, the process of negative reinforcement begins to control behavior. The tantrum-throwing child who is pacified with a cookie is being positively reinforced for throwing tantrums. More importantly, however, is that the behavior of the mother (the response of giving her misbehaving child a cookie) is negatively reinforced by the termination of the bothersome crying. Thus, the child gets a cookie from the mother's negative reinforcement. It is interesting to note who the *real* behavior modifier is in this example. Learning from experience, the child makes greater and greater demands. Later, as an adult, the individual possesses a whole repertoire of disruptive behavior with which to exact compliance to personal demands.

In a technical sense, there are normally two key roles in the use of negative reinforcement: (1) the person who controls the aversive situation and stands to gain if the other person responds in a certain manner; and (2) the person who is negatively reinforced for emitting the appropriate response which terminates the aversive situation. In the following discussion, these two roles are simply referred to as Role 1 and Role 2. In effect, from the standpoint of the Role 1 person, a negative reinforcement strategy constitutes a form of social blackmail. The Role 2 person must do something or continue to be punished. The logic of labeling negative reinforcement as a form of negative control is now clear.

Examples of negative reinforcement in human resource management are plentiful. A nagging head nurse (Role 1) is positively reinforced by a staff nurse's return to a necessary but distasteful task. The staff nurse (Role 2), meanwhile, is negatively reinforced for returning to the task because the head nurse stops nagging. Similarly, a busy executive (Role 2) is negatively reinforced for answering the phone. When a manufacturing company's collective bargaining team (Role 2) yields to the demands of a striking union (Role 1), their action is negatively reinforced by the termination of the strike. In each case, the Role 2 person(s) had to behave in a prescribed manner in order to escape an unpleasant situation.

Negative reinforcement has many of the same undesirable side effects as punishment. These will be mentioned later. For now, it is hoped that the reader has a clear understanding of the difficult area of negative reinforcement. This understanding is important when using the O. B. Mod. approach to human resource management.

The role of extinction

Whereas negative reinforcement has the opposite effect of punishment on behavior, extinction has the same effect. Both punishment and extinction reduce response frequency and weaken behavior. Notably, each reduces the response frequency in a distinctively different manner

—punishment through the withdrawal of positive reinforcers or the presentation of negative reinforcers, and extinction through the failure to provide *any* type of contingent consequence. Angrily telling someone that their opinion has offended you would constitute punishment while ignoring or not paying any attention to their opinion would constitute extinction. Both strategies are attempting to prevent further expression of the opinion. However, undesirable side effects are much less probable with an extinction strategy. On the other hand, an extinction strategy generally takes much longer to decrease frequencies than does punishment.

There is a very fine line between punishment by withdrawal of a positive reinforcer and extinction. According to Bandura (1969): "In extinction, consequences that ordinarily follow the behavior are simply discontinued; in punishment, behavior results in the application of aversive consequences through forfeiture of positive reinforcers" (p. 338). Thus, the failure to formally or informally recognize an employee's superior performance could be construed as extinction. The withdrawal of recognition, pay, or privileges because of substandard performance would be punishment. In the former case a desirable behavior may be unintentionally weakened. In the latter case an undesirable behavior is intentionally weakened. Regardless of the intent, both extinction and punishment weaken behavior. As will be discussed later, extinction may be effectively employed as an alternative to punishment for weakening undesirable behavior.

Escape and avoidance behavior

Much of the day-to-day behavior that occurs in today's organizations involves escaping from or avoiding punishing situations. The physical and social organizational environment is literally filled with potential and actual punishing consequences. Criticism, undesirable tasks, nagging, unsatisfactory performance evaluations, layoffs, pay docks, and terminations are common punishing consequences of organizational behavior. Each of these real or imagined consequences may lead to escape behavior. When a harried executive leaves work a few hours early to play golf, he is emitting escape behavior. He is escaping the stress and pressure of his job by playing golf. In this case, the aversive situation is both physiologically and psychologically based. In a more social context, the securities broker who snaps at a complaining client after the stock market goes down again may also be emitting escape behavior.

A careful functional analysis generally reveals that a person who punishes others is exhibiting escape behavior. In other words, punishment begets more punishment. Recalling the earlier discussion of negative reinforcement, it is easy to see why escape behavior is so common. People in punishing situations are negatively reinforced for behaving in a way that will terminate the punishment.

The unfortunate aspect of escape behavior is that it usually detracts from rather than facilitates effective job performance. For a government welfare agency employee, the short-run personal objective of expeditiously passing along a troublesome case may take precedence over the organizational objective of efficient, thorough service. Immediate negative reinforcement resulting from escape behavior is very appealing, particularly when the pressure is on as it is in most organizations. Unfortunately, high-pressure situations often demand problem solvers who can persevere and resist the negative reinforcement associated with expedient escape behavior. To the extent that performance-related behavior is at the same time escape behavior (employees performing to escape punishing situations), many aggressive, emotional, and otherwise dysfunctional behaviors will emerge. Performance in the name of placating a punitive boss will tend to be reluctant, marginal, and of relatively short duration. Furthermore, the desirable goal of self-control is highly improbable when organizational participants must perform in order to escape negative consequences.

Avoidance is conceptually different from escape behavior. As a result of experience with punishing consequences, people learn to associate environmental cues (the antecedent of the behavioral contingency) with punishment. These cues, through their association with past punishing consequences, take on aversive properties and serve as warnings of impending punishment. Threats of various undesirable consequences such as layoff, unsatisfactory performance ratings, and termination signal impending punishment. These threatening cues serve as antecedent events which set the occasion for avoidance behavior. Employees living under expressed or implied threats work to *avoid* having the manager carry out the threats.

As will be discussed in greater detail later, punitive managers themselves often become so closely associated with the punishment they inflict that their mere presence in the work environment cues or sets the occasion for all sorts of avoidance behavior. For example, subordinates will *look* busy to avoid being reprimanded. A manager with this stigma has little hope of being viewed as a source of positive reinforcement for desirable performance. Like escape behavior, avoidance behavior is not typically associated with efficient and highly productive organizational behavior. With escape and avoidance behavior, employees are literally looking over their shoulders for trouble or signs of trouble rather than straight ahead at what must be done in order to get the reinforcing consequences associated with satisfactory performance. This type of inefficient behavior is symptomatic of the use of negative control.

THE POPULARITY OF NEGATIVE CONTROL

As we mentioned earlier, the importance of studying negative control derives from its extensive use in society at large and in organizations in particular. Why negative control and, specifically, punishment are so popular is a question which deserves special attention.

Most behavioral scientists generally agree that punishment is used widely in our society (Skinner, 1953, p. 182; Nord, 1969) and deplore its indiscriminate use. A paper written by the authors pointed out the widespread use and abuse of punishment in human resource management (Luthans and Kreitner, 1973).

The subject of punishment is clouded by misunderstanding and doubt, and by conflicting terminology, empirical evidence, and interpretations. However, detailed study of punishment reveals some traces of consistency. In brief, the status of punishment as a controller of behavior is as follows: (1) we know little about the long-range effects and systematic consequences of controlling human behavior with punishment (Campbell and Masterson, 1969, p. 3); (2) what we have learned from systematic research indicates that punishment has a number of undesirable side effects (Azrin and Holz, 1966, pp. 436–38; Estes and Skinner, 1941; Johnston, 1972); and (3) punishment remains a widely used tool for social control today.

Importantly, it is the functional definition of punishment which is at issue here, not the traditional subjective definition. A frown, a verbal put-down, a layoff, an embarrassing remark, or the failure to grant a pay raise or promotion may be just as much a part of punishment as incarceration, physical violence or discomfort, or fines. A whole spectrum of types, degrees, and durations of punishment is available in contemporary society and its organizations.

Punishing consequences in the environment

From a childhood experience of falling off a bike to the experience of being snubbed by a friend at work, we learn that the physical and social environment is filled with a complex assortment of punishing consequences. These punishing consequences relentlessly shape and direct our lives both away from and toward various modes of behavior. Sometimes punishment is carefully planned, programmed, and carried out. More often, however, punishment is arbitrarily and hastily inflicted, or altogether random and accidental. Regardless of method or intent, punishment does modify behavior. Our daily behavior is continually being modified by aversive consequences in our environment. Consider, for example, the poor guy who is awakened by a blaring alarm clock, cuts himself shaving, drinks some sour milk, trips over the dog on the way to his car, gets a speeding ticket in a radar trap on the way to work, finds his parking spot taken, and gets the silent treatment from his boss for missing an early morning briefing. Tell him it's not a punishing world! From a more academic perspective it is important to note that each of these negative consequences affects a particular response.

The principal concern of O. B. Mod. is with the punitive social consequences rather than the negative aspects of the physical environment. The complex framework of bureaucratic rules and regulations which is so much a part of modern large organizations, upon close scrutiny, turns out to be nothing more than a system of negative contingencies.

Whether expressed or implied, the threatened consequences of breaking rules and not following regulations are negative. They are "do it or else" types of propositions. The work environment is full of examples: "If you fail to fill out your monthly sales report sheet properly, headquarters will really raise hell"; "You lose one more tool and your pay will be docked"; "I'm warning you, one more Friday absence and you're through"; "The boss really gets mad when he sees people standing around"; "The president wants everyone to attend the banquet." Statements of this type are the rule rather than the exception in today's organizational environments.

Of both interest and importance is the fact that each of the foregoing statements has an exact counterpart in the form of positive consequences for incompatible, desirable behavior. For example, contrast the following with its counterpart above: "Say, I notice how you've qualified for the tool return bonus for three straight weeks now. I appreciate how you've helped us cut down on tool loss expense and I'm happy you can share in the savings." Unfortunately, negative consequences seem to persist in spite of their easy reversibility to a positive orientation.

Why punishment is popular

There are numerous philosophical, sociological, and anthropological explanations for the popularity of punishment as a form of social control. Justice, equity, and the "eye for an eye" doctrine all enter into the subject. All of these explanations notwithstanding, a less frequently heard behaviorist explanation is offered here. From an O. B. Mod. standpoint, punishment appears to be a popular strategy because it is very reinforcing to its user. More precisely, administrators of punishment are generally negatively reinforced. In most social situations one person's behavior is frequently another's consequence. People commonly fall back on the use of punishment to terminate the annoying behavior of others. If the punishing behavior has the immediate consequence of terminating the annoyance, it has been negatively reinforced.

For example, an executive may yell at his secretary for tying up the office phone with private calls. The secretary's response of getting off the phone negatively reinforces the executive's punitive behavior. Consistent with the law of effect, the executive's punitive behavior is strengthened and will increase in subsequent frequency. The executive yells because yelling pays off. By examining the contingencies under which administrators of punishment operate, we can get a good idea of why punishment is so widely used.

The seemingly overwhelming use of punishment is not completely hopeless. As human resource managers come to recognize the questionable side effects and long-range implications of punitive control, they can begin to put themselves under the control of different contingencies. Specifically, the short-run negative reinforcement associated with the use of punishment may be passed up in favor of long-run positive reinforcement derived from working in a nonpunitive and self-controlling, supportive environment. Although tempting, punishment's immediate payoffs should most often be resisted. The next section explains why.

THE CASE AGAINST NEGATIVE CONTROL

An entirely unique combination of variables goes into action every time an individual is faced with a negatively based if–then behavioral contingency. The behavior modifiers, in turn, operate under their own if–then contingencies. In general, many unpredictable things may happen if punishment is used.

To build a case against the use of negative control, it is first of all important to note that punishment does not weaken behavior as efficiently as positive reinforcement strengthens behavior. This disparity is due to the possibility, with punishment, of undesirable and unpredictable side effects. This is not saying that punishment does not work, but rather that it does *more* than work.

In the following discussion, specific attention is focused on the four long-run side effects of punishment as identified in Figure 6–2: temporary suppression of behavior rather than permanent change; the generation of emotional behavior; the possibility of behavioral inflexibility; and the generalization of aversiveness to the controller of the punishing consequences. These side effects are so dysfunctional that they present an effective case against punishment. Conceivably, if more managers were aware of the undesirable side effects of punishment, they would not rely so heavily on it for changing the behavior of organizational participants.

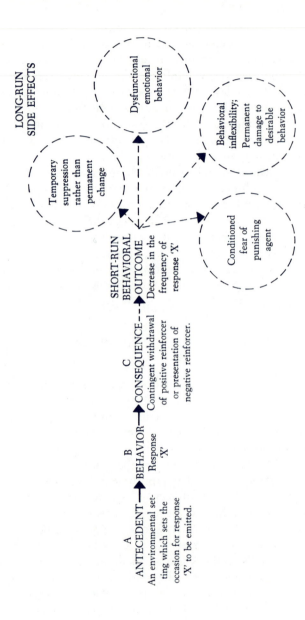

FIGURE 6–2.   The Effects of Punishment in Contingency Terms.

Temporary suppression of behavior

As many parents, teachers, and managers have discovered, the old adage that "when the cat's away, the mice will play" is true. Punishment will eventually operate against the person using it. Once a practicing manager depends on punitive control, he/she will have to continue to rely on it to exact compliance. Punishment only temporarily suppresses rather than permanently changes behavior. (Skinner, 1953, pp. 183–84). Empirical research shows that punishment initially reduces response frequency, but once the aversive consequence is withdrawn or not salient (in the forefront of awareness), the punished response reemerges. Continued negative control becomes necessary for sustained suppression and, hence, punishment leads to more punishment.

Consider, for example, the undesirable response of wasting time by telling stories on the job. After warning her subordinate a number of times about idly standing around telling stories, a food service manager catches a glimpse of the subordinate distracting three co-workers with a story. Knowing the subordinate is sensitive to criticism, the food service manager decides to really "chew out" the subordinate right in front of her co-workers. Besides, the manager feels her action will serve as a warning to the other members of the work group. So the manager proceeds to berate her subordinate for stealing valuable time and keeping others from their work. As soon as the manager finishes talking, everyone goes back to their own job and the food service manager returns to her desk with the feeling that she has put things back on the straight and narrow.

Now let us take a look at what has happened from an O. B. Mod perspective. The manager's action, as intended, put an immediate stop to the unproductive storytelling. What the manager does not realize, however, is that the action has just begun rather than just ended. From an O. B. Mod. standpoint, the storytelling response has been punished and the incompatible response of returning to work has been negatively reinforced, the former through the contingent presentation of a negative reinforcer and the latter through the contingent withdrawal of the same negative reinforcer. In other words, the food service manager's aversive berating started because of the storytelling and did not stop until the subordinate returned to work. Both responses, storytelling and the immediate return to work, were followed by contingent consequences controlled by the manager. If the food service manager has some reliable way of accurately measuring the frequency of her subordinate's storytelling response, she will probably discover one or both of two things. First, after the "chewing out" the storytelling will initially diminish and then return to its former strength. Second, when she (the manager) is in the general vicinity, the subordinate will refrain from telling stories—but in the manager's absence, the subordinate's storytelling will go on as usual.

In this example, as a result of behavior/consequence interaction social learning has taken place. Unfortunately for the manager, the subordinate has learned more than initially meets the eye. In short, the subordinate has learned not to tell stories when the manager is around. In A→B→C terms, the food service manager has become an antecedent condition (A) in the subordinate's work environment signaling the high probability of punishment (C) for storytelling (B). Accordingly, the subordinate has learned that storytelling is safe and will go unpunished as long as the boss is not around. The food service manager, meanwhile, is tied to intermittently punishing her subordinate's deviant behavior to keep it suppressed. Unfortunately, an employee who actively pursues organizational goals because of the positive reinforcement associated with such pursuit is a far cry from an employee who passively works to achieve organizational goals in order to avoid the punishment associated with not pursuing those goals.

Generation of emotional behavior

Emotional behavior is very complex and, frankly, not fully understood at this time. Some behavioral scientists feel that emotion lies in a gray area somewhere between respondent and operant behavior. For example, McGinnis (1970, p. 30) suggests that emotion is more than a unique set of cognitive, physiological, and behavioral manifestations; he feels that emotion is most appropriately viewed as a reaction that disrupts or otherwise interferes with ongoing behavior. The commonly heard terms used by psychologists and laymen such as anger, aggression, frustration, regression, fear, and withdrawal are examples of what is meant in this discussion by the term emotional behavior. Angrily yelling back or perhaps striking at a superior, kicking a candy machine which will not work, loudly announcing the intention to quit, sabotaging an important piece of equipment or a production run or computer program, getting drunk after work, and storming out of the office after a conference with the boss all qualify as behavioral manifestations of what we commonly call emotion. This type of behavior is considered here to be mainly dysfunctional behavior which may inhibit the achievement of personal and organizational objectives.

What does emotion have to do with punishment? Simply stated, punishment appears to increase the incidence of emotional behavior. Skinner (1953, p. 188) has noted that behavior temporarily suppressed with contingent punishment is commonly replaced by an emotional reaction. Returning for the moment to the example of the storytelling subordinate cited earlier, the subordinate's immediate cessation of storytelling after the food service manager's punishment could easily have been accompanied by emotional behavior. Emotional reactions to the food service manager's public censure could have taken the form of angrily snapping back at the boss, ripping up some worksheets or damaging equipment back at the work station, or telling the other members of the work group what a so-and-so the boss is. Importantly, each of these emotional displays threatens to diminish rather than enhance personal performance effectiveness and organizational goal attainment.

Possibility of behavioral inflexibility

A third undesirable side effect of punishment contains especially important implications for today's human resource managers. Bandura (1969, pp. 310–12) has noted that punishment via the presentation of negative reinforcers may sometimes permanently stifle behavior. In light of the first side effect (punished behavior is only temporarily suppressed rather than permanently changed), this observation by Bandura may seem to be a favorable turn of events. The catch, however, is that behavior that is viewed as undesirable at one time but highly desirable at another may be permanently repressed by ill-timed punishment. For example, a child severely punished for sex-related behavior may suffer problems later in life when sexual behavior becomes both appropriate and desirable. In other words, punishment may permanently suppress the wrong responses.

Extended to an organizational context, important performance-related behaviors involving decision making, creativity, or problem solving may be severely weakened by early punishment. Suppose, for instance, that a new management trainee with the ink still wet on her M.B.A. degree is subjected to embarrassing derogatory comments from her superiors and peers for making a seemingly creative suggestion at a management meeting. Not stopping to realize how sensitive new employees are to reinforcement and punishment, her critics may permanently stifle her creative contributions in the future. Later on, when the management team actively solicits creative contributions, they should not be surprised to hear none from the now "experienced" trainee.

In a similar manner, the consequence climate of most subordinate positions does not tend to prepare one for eventually assuming a responsible leadership role. If management demands leadership and responsibility from superiors, then they should see to it that the relevant behavior of subordinates is nurtured and shaped with positive consequences instead of permanently damaged with indiscriminate punishment. With the fast-paced change facing today's organizations, inflexible behavior created by punitive control is highly undesirable.

Generalization of aversiveness to the administrator

A fourth undesirable side effect of punishment is very common in contemporary organizations. The aversiveness of a punisher may generalize to the supervisor through frequent and close association between the punisher and the supervisor who administers it. The manager who uses punitive control becomes a cue for punishment; i.e., when the punitive manager is present, the probability of punishment increases. In effect, the punitive manager becomes what is technically called a conditioned aversive stimulus (Skinner, 1953, p. 173). We have all had experience with this type of individual. All he/she has to do is appear on the scene and everyone is suddenly hard at their task. As long as the punitive manager is breathing down people's necks, he/she is effective at stimulating performance—or at least what outwardly appears to be performance.

In the long run, the punitive manager actually turns out to be quite ineffective. It is almost impossible to assume the dual roles of punisher and reinforcer. As a conditioned aversive stimulus, the punitive manager's ability to positively reinforce is eroded by fear and distrust. Also, once the punitive manager leaves the work area, the now unrestrained subordinates get the all-clear cue and control begins to break down. Self-discipline and self-control in the absence of authority are not usually associated with a punishing environment.

A steady exposure to punishment typically leads to aggressiveness, defensiveness, dependence, passivity, and immature, emotional behavior. Moreover, the productivity stimulated by the presence of a manager who relies a great deal on punishment may be just a masquerade. The behavior which the punitive manager's presence creates is defensive; its goal is to avoid rather than to seek. Organizational goals are not efficiently and effectively achieved through such defensive behavior.

A final word on negative control

The four undesirable side effects just discussed provide a strong case against the use of punishment. The discussion attempted to show that punishment is not nearly as effective as positive reinforcement in controlling human behavior. In some cases, punishment may create permanent inflexibility where it can least be afforded. On the other hand, when permanent change is desired, punishment may effect only temporary suppression. Punitive control may not only fail to weaken undesirable behavior, it may actually facilitate the emergence of emotional behavior which generally erodes organizational effectiveness.

Negative reinforcement is subject to many of the same problems and limitations attributed to punishment. Although the person who controls the aversive situation may exact the compliance demanded, such pressure tactics may eventually breed ill feelings and threaten superior–subordinate openness and rapport. Also, since a punishing situation is first created and later terminated, punishing contingencies may accidentally be established with other prior behavior. As an example of this last problem, take the case of a foreman who started criticizing a machine operator, without first checking on his performance, for standing around and talking to a friend. Suppose the operator has exceeded the production standard all day. While the criticism for standing around has the immediate effect of getting the operator back to his machine, a long-run effect may be lower performance as the operator resolves to get back at his boss by doing less work. High performance has been accidentally punished through the inappropriate use of a negative reinforcement strategy.

In summary, whether punishment or negative reinforcement is used, the result can be very ineffective in modifying behavior in general and organizational behavior in particular. Consequently, practicing human resource managers should actively seek alternative behavior change strategies which rely more on positive and less on negative control. When negative control is used, special effort must be made to avoid or diminish as much as possible its undesirable side effects. The next section suggests some way that this can be accomplished.

ALTERNATIVES FOR MORE EFFECTIVE APPLICATION

As stated at the beginning of the chapter, O. B. Mod. recognizes that even though positive control is much more effective in human resource management, negative control will still be used. The goal of O. B. Mod., then, is to make negative control as effective as possible. The practitioner is faced with a difficult dilemma in regard to negative control. Punishment is reinforcing to use because it leads to rapid termination of undesirable behavior, but it creates dysfunctional side effects.

Fortunately, experience with applied behavior analysis has uncovered some alternative intervention strategies which appear to avoid or at least ameliorate the undesirable side effects of punishment. Two of the most promising alternatives are a combination extinction/positive reinforcement strategy and a combination punishment/positive reinforcement strategy.

Extinction/positive reinforcement

Realistically, much job behavior needs to be weakened. The manager whose primary objective is to weaken an undesirable performance-related response but still avoid the undesirable side effects of a punishment strategy may effectively use a combination extinction/positive reinforcement strategy. Meacham and Wiesen (1969) contend that in such a strategy, "What is really involved is a systematic redistribution of reinforcers, be they tangible or social, so that undesirable behavior is deprived of reinforcement but competing desirable behavior is heavily reinforced" (p. 75). Ideally, extinction weakens the undesirable response while positive reinforcement concurrently strengthens an incompatible, desirable response.

Two stages are involved. The first stage is extinction, the carefully programmed absence of any contingent consequences. Undesirable behavior will eventually weaken under this strategy. As Skinner (1953) points out, ". . . when we engage in behavior which no longer 'pays off,' we find ourselves less inclined to behave that way again" (p. 69). The second stage is positive reinforcement, which is made contingent upon desirable responses that will eventually replace the undesirable target response. Placed into the behavioral contingency management (BCM) model of Chapter 4, the following steps would take place:

1) Identify the undesirable performance-related response and an incompatible, desirable response.

2) Obtain a baseline measure.

3) Identify antecedents and supporting consequences through an A→B→C functional analysis.

4) Terminate supporting consequences of undesirable response and positively reinforce incompatible, desirable response(s). Assess the effectiveness of the intervention strategy in terms of response frequency and maintain with appropriate schedules of reinforcement.

5) Evaluate to assure performance improvement.

As we discussed in Chapter 3, the combination extinction/positive reinforcement strategy is recommended for use with either-or behavior (in other words, incompatible behavior.) As examples, being at the work station is incompatible with being somewhere else; promptness is incompatible with tardiness; following an order is incompatible with failing to follow an order; and making relevant comments at committee meetings is incompatible with making irrelevant comments. The following example shows how a combination extinction/positive reinforcement strategy might work:

Phil James is a bright young marketing specialist with an M.B.A. from a prestigious Midwestern university. He is married and has one small child. Alpha Company had hired Phil on the basis of his appealing combination of high grade-point average and active participation in extracurricular activities. From the beginning, Phil had been tabbed for big things at Alpha. In fact, after only two years with the company, Phil is being considered for his second promotion. The promotion would be to assistant brand manager. The position demands problem-solving, communication, and human-relations skills and abilities. Phil's boss, the vice president of marketing, feels that Phil has the requisite skills but is reluctant to recommend Phil for the promotion because of a single weakness. This one small problem is beginning to erode Phil's credibility and is a potential threat to his rapport with several key executives. Specifically, at the weekly departmental meetings, Phil acts more like a comedian than an aspiring young executive. He interjects one-liners and wisecracks, and generally disrupts the constructive flow of the meetings. To date, repeated informal requests from the boss to cease the disruptive behavior have produced no results. Phil seems to think his remarks are very funny and his problem has actually become worse during the last month. The boss definitely feels that this problem must improve if Phil is to get ahead at Alpha.

Being familiar with the undesirable side effects of punishment and knowing from past experience that Phil is quite sensitive to public criticism, Phil's boss rejects the possibility of punishing Phil's disruptive behavior by "putting him down" in front of everyone at the next meeting. Instead, Phil's boss decides to measure and functionally analyze Phil's comical behavior at the departmental meetings. After two meetings, the boss finds an interesting consistency in his data. It seems that out of the ten committee members, two consistently acknowledge Phil's disruptive behavior by attending to him, laughing, nodding approval, and smiling. In fact, Phil has developed the habit of looking at one or both of his social supporters immediately after each of his disruptive comments. He appears to actually solicit their support.

On the basis of this data, Phil's boss decides to implement a combination extinction/positive reinforcement BCM strategy. The incompatible responses are defined as Phil's *disruptive* and *constructive* comments. This operational definition is both specific enough to discriminate and broad enough for easy identification. An extinction strategy for the undesirable disruptive comments is put into action by the boss, who asks the two supporters to refrain from laughing at or otherwise acknowledging Phil's disruptive behavior. He explains how they are inadvertently getting Phil into trouble. The two are contingently reinforced for complying with praise from the boss. For positive reinforcement, the boss, with the help of three other ranking members of the committee who like Phil, plans to shape Phil's constructive contributions with recognition, compliments, and other social positive reinforcers deemed appropriate at the time.

At the next meeting the measured effects of the intervention strategy begin to show up almost immediately. Phil slips in a couple of one-liners, looks to his supporters who continue to attend to the meeting and not him, and falls silent for approximately fifteen minutes. Again Phil tries a pun but there is no acknowledgment and he is silent for ten minutes. To ensure that Phil is positively reinforced for an incompatible construc-tive comment, Phil's boss asks him a question concerning a proposed policy change. Phil comes up with a very appropriate response and is im-mediately reinforced by the boss and the three ranking committee mem-bers. He sits back, looks around, and breaks into a smile. During the course of the next four meetings Phil makes only two disruptive com-ments, each early in the meeting. Gradually his incompatible constructive contributions have increased in frequency, even without prompting ques-tions or continuous reinforcement.

Although this rather lengthy example may seem insignificant to some, it does show that by systematically and consistently managing the relevant antecedent events and consequences of this young executive's behavior at the departmental meetings, his boss has helped him learn how to become a more effective committee member and improved the man's chances of getting a promotion. Examples like this are relevant to effective human resource management. In particular, the negative side effects of punitive control were avoided.

Punishment/positive reinforcement

As has been stated, O. B. Mod. is realistic enough to recognize that punishment is and will continue to be used. Obviously, extremely undesirable organizational behavior must be terminated as quickly as pos-sible. The practitioner often does not have the luxury of waiting for an extinction strategy to decrease the behavior. But this does not mean that managers can not learn to use punishment more appropriately and avoid some of the pitfalls. Some help toward this end can be gained from the experience of behavior modification researchers and applied behavior anal-ysis experts (Herman and Azrin, 1964; Azrin and Holz, 1966). They point out that whenever punishment is used, there must be a correspond-ing presentation of an opportunity to emit one or more incompatible re-sponses which are then positively reinforced. A combination punishment/ positive reinforcement strategy limits as much as possible punishment's un-desirable side effects. Success or failure of this strategy hinges on shaping and strengthening the incompatible response(s) with positive reinforcement so that desirable responses will eventually replace the undesirable response.

The major advantage of the punishment/positive reinforcement strategy is that it avoids putting pressure on the punished person and backing him/her into a corner. The opportunity to behave in positively reinforced alternative ways acts as a safety valve. As a result, the undesirable side effect of emotional responding is minimized. The major strength of punishment, an ability to immediately terminate a response, is retained while the major liabilities are, to some extent, neutralized. For example, this intervention strategy can be applied to the respective pairings of tardiness, absence, sloppiness, disobedience, and unsafe behavior on the one hand, and positively reinforced promptness, attendance, neatness, obedience, and safe behavior on the other. Instructions, directions, requests, or more sophisticated modeling or restructuring of the physical or social environment may be used to increase the probability that the incompatible, desirable responses will in fact be emitted. Contingent positive reinforcement then takes over.

When a punishment/positive reinforcement strategy is used, the steps are as follows:

1) Identify the undesirable performance-related response and an incompatible, desirable response.

2) Obtain a baseline measure.

3) Identify antecedents and supporting consequences through an A→B→C functional analysis.

4) Contingently apply a punisher to the undesirable response and a contingent positive reinforcer to the incompatible, desirable response(s). Assess the effectiveness of the intervention strategy in terms of response frequencies and maintain with appropriate schedules of reinforcement.

5) Evaluate to assure performance improvement.

If punishment *must* be used, the available research indicates that combining it with positive reinforcement makes it as effective as possible. The following case illustrates how a punishment/positive reinforcement strategy might be applied in practice:

Pete Jones has been working for a large warehousing firm for seven years. He is presently employed as a lift-truck operator, the highest paid nonsupervisory job in the warehouse. It took Pete five and a half years to work his way from a stock handler to his present high-status position. Being a bit of a show-off, Pete occasionally lapses into unsafe driving habits such as speeding, taking corners too close, and backing up without sounding his horn. Except for this habit of unsafe driving, Pete's supervisor is generally pleased with his performance. Because of the increased pressures from the front office on complying with OSHA (Occupational Safety and Health Act), Pete's supervisor has increasingly had to "chew him out" for his unsafe driving. This approach has proven fruitless because Pete's dangerous behavior on the lift truck has actually increased in frequency. Also, the informal warnings Pete has received from the union steward seemed to have had no effect.

After being introduced to O. B. Mod., Pete's supervisor identifies the problem behavior and some possible incompatible desirable behaviors. During the first week, a baseline measure is taken. The supervisor realizes that the frequency is as serious as he suspected. Pete is a very unsafe driver and corrective action is needed quickly. Next, the supervisor performs a functional analysis by examining the antecedent events and supporting consequences. Several significant facts emerge from the functional analysis and development of an intervention strategy:

1) The work group's laughter and attention seems to be positively reinforcing Pete's unsafe driving.

2) The unsafe driving is very dangerous and must be stopped immediately.

3) Getting fifteen co-workers to put Pete's unsafe driving behavior on extinction is unrealistic.

4) Punishment seems to be the only viable intervention strategy.

5) Firing Pete is an undesirable punisher.

6) In Pete's particular case, an immediate reassignment to a warehouse floor job for the balance of the working day after one of his reckless behaviors *might* be an effective punisher.

7) Whether the temporary reassignment is in fact punishment or not will depend on the frequency of Pete's unsafe driving behavior after the intervention.

8) The incompatible, desirable behavior which must be positively reinforced is safe lift-truck operation.

9) Positive reinforcers, based on the supervisor's knowledge of Pete's history of reinforcement, *might* be supervisory attention, solicitation of advice by the supervisor, or compliments on safe and effective performance.

10) Whether attention, asking advice, or praise are positive reinforcers or not will depend on the frequency of Pete's safe driving behavior after the intervention.

After only one intervention (reassignment to a floor job), Pete's unsafe driving stops. The safe driving behavior which is positively reinforced strengthens and increases in frequency. In this case, which is typical of many contemporary work settings, the supervisor has had to pit the positive and negative consequences at his command against competing consequences in the work environment. The individual's reinforcement hierarchy determines the outcome of a tug-of-war of this kind. Because of the supervisor's systematic punishment/positive reinforcement intervention, the warehouse is a safer place and an otherwise good employee has not been fired. Such outcomes are the goal of O. B. Mod. As a rule of thumb, if punishment is used, a desirable alternative behavior should be made available and positively reinforced. In this manner, punishment is used as effectively as possible.

Shaping, Modeling, and Self-Control

7

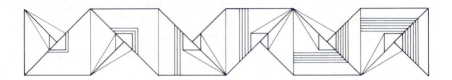

This chapter discusses the overall process of shaping and modeling, with particular attention given to organizational socialization through shaping and three basic effects of modeling. For both processes, a seven-step strategy for effective human resource management is presented. The last section of the chapter is devoted to self-control. This section attempts to dispel the mistaken notion that O. B. Mod. deals only with a manager exercising behavioral control over human resources. In fact, self-control is a goal of O. B. Mod.

THE SHAPING PROCESS

At the time of joining an organization, an individual possesses a behavior repertoire which can be classified into four general categories: (1) desirable performance-related behavior; (2) potentially disruptive performance-related behavior; (3) behavior unrelated to performance; and (4) performance behavior deficiencies.

Positive control can be used to maintain and increase the strength of desirable performance-related behavior. Appropriate negative control may weaken undesirable performance-related behavior. Behavior unrelated to performance can simply be ignored. However, if an individual is deficient in some performance-related behavior, the behavior must, in a sense, be developed. The obvious question is, how can the practicing manager "develop" new desirable behavior? The manager does not somehow mystically develop behavior. Rather, using an O. B. Mod. approach, he/she may *shape* appropriate organizational behavior. This section explains how such a shaping process works and how it can be implemented in human resource management.

The meaning of shaping

The old adage, "A thousand-mile journey begins with a single step," can be applied to the shaping process. Most complex organizational behavior must begin with a single step and then build. In other words, if the first step is positively reinforced, then another step will be taken. Hill (1963) described how relatively simple behavior may be eventually shaped into more complex organizational behavior, as follows: "The behavior is shaped through a series of successive approximations, each made possible by selectively reinforcing certain responses and not others. Thus behavior is gradually brought closer and closer to the desired pattern" (p. 71).

The shaping of organizational behavior involves the careful use of a combination extinction/positive reinforcement intervention strategy. Successively closer approximations to a target organizational behavior are first positively reinforced and then put on extinction as closer approximations are reinforced. The earlier illustration of how on-the-job behavior of hard-core unemployables was systematically shaped to a level consistent with gainful employment demonstrates the practical utility that the shaping process has for human resource management. Most training programs, whether deliberate or not, depend largely on the shaping process. Of even more importance is the role shaping can and does play in organizational behavior in general.

Organizational socialization through shaping

The process whereby organizational participants learn to play performance roles leading to organizational goal attainment, can be called, for lack of a better term, organizational socialization. McGinnies (1970) has noted the following about such a process: "It seems likely that much of what we call socialization is achieved by various methods of *behavior shaping,* that is, selective reinforcement of performances that approach some socially acceptable standard" (p. 97).

Socialization begins early in life. A person growing up is influenced by family, church, school, and peers. More important from an O. B. Mod. perspective, however, socialization also occurs in a person's adult life. Since adults spend about half of their waking life in the organization that employs them, the organization is an important component of the socialization process. Although the consequence sources of an adult operat ing in a complex, modern organization differ from those in childhood, the shaping process is omnipresent.

Even Chester Barnard (1938), the pioneering management theorist, noted the presence of the shaping process as an aspect of organizational socialization when he observed: ". . . the process of decision is one of successive approximations—constant refinement of purpose, closer and closer discrimination of fact—in which the march of time is essential" (p. 206). In other words, Barnard depicted decision making as a shaping process. Just as a quarterback is shaped into passing accuracy by the reinforcement of completions, the busy executive is shaped into making effective decisions by desirable outcomes. Greater profit, a lower cost of capital, an adequate supply of scarce raw material, a greater return on investment, or a greater share of the market are all desirable organizational outcomes that serve to differentially reinforce or shape effective managerial decision making. Organizational socialization consists of things like following rules, working on tasks, solving problems and making decisions. In general, the successful achievement of organizational objectives can be thought of as a shaping process in which closer and closer approximations of established objectives are positively reinforced.

The shaping process will take place regardless of managerial action or intent. Since shaping plays such an important role in organizational socialization, it is crucial to O. B. Mod. that it be properly controlled. The choice is between the haphazard shaping of random behavior, some productive and some counterproductive, or the careful systematic shaping of key performance-related behavior. Consequently, the challenge for O. B. Mod. is to create a work environment in which positive reinforcement is made systematically contingent on steadily improving performance. Systematic shaping should play an important role in vestibule training, on-the-job training, management development, and, most importantly for organizational socialization, the management of everyday performance.

Odiorne (1970, p. 316), in discussing the manager as a teacher, identified three types: (1) the manager who does his subordinates' work for them; (2) the manager who does his own job competently by intuition; and (3) the manager who does his own work well and teaches others. It is the last type who is capable of incorporating the shaping process into everyday human resource management, resulting in effective organizational socialization.

A shaping strategy for human resource management

To implement an effective shaping strategy, several specific steps should be followed. For example, an O. B. Mod. approach to shaping would involve the following:

1) Precisely define the goal or target behavior. This target behavior should always be related to performance.

2) If the target behavior is a complex chain of behavior, reduce it to a discrete, observable, and thus measurable sequence of behavioral events or steps.

3) Make sure the individual is capable of meeting the technical skill or ability requirements for each step.

4) Select potentially effective positive reinforcers on the basis of the individual's history of reinforcement.

5) Structure the contingent environment so that appropriate antecedent conditions will increase the probability of the desired behavior.

6) Make all positive reinforcement contingent upon successively closer approximations to the target behavior. The behavioral chain must be built link by link.

7) Once achieved, maintain and strengthen the target behavior, first with continuous reinforcement and later with an intermittent schedule of reinforcement.

To obtain a better understanding of the shaping process, it would be helpful to expand the steps listed above.

Define the target behavior • What must the employee do to effectively accomplish organizational objectives? This is a fundamental question in O. B. Mod. Answers such as "greater initiative," "more independence," "better performance," "improved attitude," and "increased responsibility" are too general to be appropriate target behavior for a shaping strategy. Specific behavior is the key. According to Mathis et al. (1970): "Unless terminal objectives can be specified as behaviors, it is impossible to determine the reinforcement contingencies needed to accomplish those terminal objectives" (p. 127). Examples of more appropriate target behavior would include: "Punch in at 8:00 A.M. every workday"; "Eliminate temper tantrums as soon as possible when dealing with subordinates"; "Take action on customers' complaints within two days"; and "Reduce work-order errors to 3 percent by the end of the month."

Notice how each of these examples directly expresses or at least implies a definite time dimension. The net result is a clear definition of the desired state of the target behavior (or of the effect of that behavior in terms of performance) by a specified time. Even the example of the elimination of temper tantrums has a time dimension (i.e., as soon as the systematic shaping of incompatible responses with positive consequences will permit).

This first step in the shaping process is closely related to Management By Objectives (MBO). MBO was developed by Peter Drucker (1954) and is currently a widely used and accepted method of management. It can be simply defined as setting objectives and appraising performance results. It can be both a total philosophy of management and a specific technique of planning and control. In addition, MBO can be thought of as an effective blend of both the plan, organize, and control requirements and the necessary behavioral requirements for effective modern management.

One thing that all MBO experts tend to agree upon is the need for specific, quantifiable objectives. This, of course, is directly comparable to the shaping process in O. B. Mod. For example, one MBO expert (Murray, 1973) listed three important elements of effective management objectives. They include: (1) a statement of specific results in behavioral terms; (2) a statement of a specific time frame; and (3) a statement of specific criteria. The close parallel between such objectives and target behavior descriptions in the shaping process is obvious. However, there are differences.

For example, the O. B. Mod. shaping process gives closer attention to specific performance-related behavioral events. MBO relies heavily on self-control with the commitment to and accomplishment of mutually determined objectives. Shaping entails a more precise and systematic program of positive consequences for improvement than the typical MBO approach. However, the self-control concept found in MBO can be incorporated into O. B. Mod.

As indicated a few years ago (Luthans and White, 1971), there is a very close relationship between O. B. Mod. and MBO. (Interestingly, the initials for O. B. Mod. put in reverse order are MBO.) One of the eventual goals of O. B. Mod., as will be discussed in the last chapter, is to bring MBO and O. B. Mod. even closer together in actual practice. Both approaches can learn from each other and improve each other's effectiveness.

Once the target behavior has been precisely defined in the shaping process, the subsequent steps fall into place. But overgeneralization or imprecision during this first step will negate the subsequent steps and permanently cripple any attempts to successfully shape organizational behavior. Precise definitions of target behavior not only help the controller of the consequences in a shaping strategy, but also help the behaver know what is expected of him/her. As emphasized before, knowledge of self-improvement can be a very potent positive reinforcer.

Break behavior down into sequential steps • A natural followup to the first step of the shaping process is to break down complex behavior chains into sequences of observable behavioral events. As you will recall from the discussion of behavior chaining in Chapter 3, the consequence in one contingency is often the antecedent in another contingency. If positive reinforcement is to be made contingent on successive approximations to the precisely defined target behavior, then those successive approximations also must be precisely defined.

Consider, for example, the common case of the overly dependent subordinate—the one who asks for answers to daily problems rather than attempting to solve the problems himself/herself. Generally, the appropriate strategy should involve removing the supporting consequences of the dependent behavior and implementing a program of positive consequences for the weaker, incompatible problem-solving behavior. The former could be achieved with an extinction strategy while the latter could be systematically shaped. Shaping is simply a systematic way of administering positive reinforcement.

More specifically, some approximations of the target behavior that would be reinforced in this example include: (1) paying any attention at all to a problem; (2) giving more extensive attention to a problem—five minutes, ten minutes, fifteen minutes, and so on; (3) carefully studying and analyzing all facets of a problem; (4) making early attempts at actually solving a problem; (5) making successively closer approximations to a workable solution to a problem; and (6) developing final workable solution(s) to problems. By reducing a rather complex behavior such as problem solving down to a sequence of observable and thus reinforceable steps, the practitioner using O. B. Mod. can effectively shape a desirable organizational behavior.

Meet skill requirements • This third step emphasizes that the manager using a shaping strategy must consider all technical skill requirements which, if not mastered by the individual, could block the attainment of the target behavior. As examples, a touch-typing skill and the ability to insert the drum card in a keypunch machine are key determinants of success in rapidly and efficiently typing letters and punching data cards. In describing a two-step clerical training program for the hard-core unemployed using a token economy, Brief and Filley (1974) explain how the problem of technical skills may be overcome: "Each trainee works independently on various learning tasks such as typing or record keeping. The learning tasks are broken down into modules allowing each trainee to learn at her own pace and to allow [the manager] to frequently evaluate each trainee's performance." This suggests that each requisite technical skill can be shaped to a level of desired proficiency before it can become a reinforceable step in a larger shaping strategy for organizational socialization.

Select positive reinforcers • Just as the target behavior and its component parts must be identified, the appropriate positive reinforcers must be identified as well. Any one of the methods for identifying potential positive reinforcers (analyzing histories of reinforcement, self-report instruments, or trial and error) may be used. The important point is to make sure that the most potentially powerful positive consequences are made part of the shaping process. Rewarding successive approximations with consequences which turn out not to be positive reinforcers will postpone the ultimate successful achievement of the target behavior in the shaping process.

Favorably structure the antecedent environment • An O. B. Mod. approach involves not only the systematic programming of contingent consequences, but attention to antecedent conditions. In terms of the A→B→C contingency, the antecedent conditions (A) set the occasion for behavior (B) to be emitted by the individual. Once emitted, a program of positive consequences (C) ensures the reoccurrence of the behavior. When organizational behavior is being shaped, the practicing manager cannot rely on consequences alone. Coaching techniques, directions, instructions or rules, or simulated exercises (role playing or experiential games) may provide the appropriate antecedent conditions for cueing or prompting the successive approximations of desired behavior.

Returning to the example of the overly dependent subordinate, the manager using a shaping strategy may increase the probability of an early approximation of the target behavior (such as simply studying a problem) by presenting a relatively simple but highly interesting (for the individual) problem. In the O. B. Mod. terms, the presentation of a simple but highly interesting problem is the antecedent condition (A) which sets the occasion for the response of studying the problem (B) which, in turn, is positively reinforced (C) by the manager. As closer and closer approximations are required for contingent reinforcement, other antecedent conditions may be used.

Apply contingent reinforcers to approximations • Complex chains of responses leading to target behavior must be built link by link. This is accomplished through a carefully managed program of positive consequences. As mentioned earlier, shaping most effectively results from a combination extinction/positive reinforcement strategy. Each link in the behavioral chain is first positively reinforced and later put on extinction as the reinforcement criterion is stretched to require the successful performance of an additional link. Because self-reinforcement is a part of goal achievement, this reinforcement stretching effect should always be completely aboveboard in terms of the employee's knowledge of what is happening and what the manager expects.

Maintain and strengthen target behavior • Once the desired target response is emitted, it must be continually monitored and managed. Continuous or at least high-frequency fixed or variable ratio schedules of reinforcement must be employed initially to ensure the steady emission of the shaped behavior. Once established in the individual's behavior repertoire, the desirable behavior can be maintained and strengthened through an appropriate program of antecedent conditions, intermittent positive reinforcement, and eventually self-reinforcement.

The foregoing seven-step shaping strategy, closely related to the BCM problem-solving model discussed in Chapter 4, permits the practicing manager to systematically reduce behavioral performance deficits in an employee's behavior repertoire. In a sense, shaping permits the development of desirable (from the viewpoint of goal attainment) organizational behavior. Practicing human resource managers can benefit from a working knowledge and systematic strategy of shaping organizational behavior.

THE MODELING PROCESS

Shaping accounts for a great deal of organizational behavior acquisition. Whether systematically managed or not, organizational behavior is constantly being shaped into new or varied forms. However, the shaping process does not account for the learning of all organizational behavior. In contrast to shaping, whereby simple responses eventually evolve into complex behaviors, some complex behaviors appear relatively suddenly. Behavioral scientists working in the area called psychological modeling (e.g., Bandura, 1971) have formulated some explanations of how complex behavior can suddenly emerge without benefit of a long shaping process.

A significant portion of what we call organizational behavior is learned through modeling or, more simply stated, through imitation. One person behaves in a certain manner, another person observes the behavior of the first and then behaves in the same manner. In any social environment, much of our behavior is a function of behaving like those around us. We commonly pattern our behavior after live or symbolic models which serve as examples or behavioral standards.

According to Albert Bandura (1969), generally recognized as the foremost expert on modeling: "One of the fundamental means by which new modes of behavior are acquired and existing patterns are modified entails modeling and vicarious processes" (p. 118). A vicarious process is an imagined participation in the model's experience. Besides modeling and vicarious processes, other terms associated with this form of learning include: "identification," "copying," "imitation," "social facilitation," and "contagion."

The threefold purpose of this section is to examine how organizational participants learn by modeling, discuss the implications of modeling for human resource management, and present a specific modeling strategy for the practicing human resource manager.

Three basic modeling effects

Bandura (1969, p. 120) identified three effects of exposure to modeling influences. They are: (1) an observational learning or modeling effect; (2) an inhibitory or disinhibitory effect; and (3) a response facilitation effect.

In O. B. Mod. terms, the first effect is concerned with the learning of new responses by imitation; the second effect relates to the manner in which the consequences of one individual's behavior may vicariously affect the behavior of another individual; and the third effect identifies the process whereby one individual's behavior cues a similar behavior in another individual. Each of these modeling effects, although having only subtle differences, plays a unique and important role in day-to-day organizational behavior. Understanding the three basic modeling effects can contribute to successful application of O. B. Mod.

Learning through imitation • This first effect occurs when an individual learns a new response by identically reproducing a response observed in another individual. This new or novel response is behavior that has a very low or zero probability of occurrence in the presence of appropriate stimuli (Bandura, 1969, p. 120).

An example of such a response (actually a number of closely related responses) in an organization might be the efficient operation of a keypunch machine by an individual who has never touched a keypunch machine before. With no prior "hands on" experience, the responses associated with successful and efficient keypunching are not part of the individual's behavior repertoire. Suppose that this person is observed sitting down and successfully loading, programming, and operating a keypunch machine. While this behavior may have been the result of a shaping strategy as outlined earlier, assume that it has not been shaped in this instance. Instead, a novel response has suddenly appeared. No successive approximations have been emitted and systematically reinforced. Obviously, the learning process of modeling has occurred.

In the case of the keypuncher, assume that the employee has just finished watching a training film supplied by the manufacturer of the keypunch machine. The modeling effect that has occurred in this example is *imitation*. In a sense, a long and otherwise time-consuming shaping process has been replaced by a fast-acting modeling (specifically, imitation) approach.

New responses may be learned from both live and symbolic models. A supermarket manager who takes time to show a stock clerk how to operate a labeling machine is acting as a live model. The keypunch operator mentioned above made use of a symbolic model (a film). Symbolic models may be presented pictorially (Bandura and Walters, 1963, p. 49) in the form of movies, television, still pictures, slides, or videotape, or can be presented in the form of textbooks, records, cassette tapes, manuals, graphic presentations, charts, and common verbal or written directions. This book you are reading can be thought of as a symbolic model.

Regardless of whether the model is live or symbolic, however, imitation helps explain how a significant amount of complex organizational behavior, both desirable and undesirable, is learned. The challenge for O. B. Mod. is to understand and manage the imitative effect of modeling rather than passively watch models facilitate the learning of dysfunctional as well as functional organizational behavior.

Learning from others' consequences • Consequences play an important role in modeling. With regard to the learning of novel responses through imitation, successful imitation, by itself, seems to have very strong reinforcing properties. In addition, consequences experienced by others, especially relevant behavior models, play an important role in determining what behavior is imitated and what behavior is ignored. The inhibitory or disinhibitory effect comes into play when we witness a model experiencing positive or negative consequences. Tempered by the extent to which we identify with the model, the status of the model, and the nature of the consequence(s), we tend to imitate behavior which pays off for the model and avoid imitating behavior which does not pay off or has negative consequences for the model. Television advertising of personal care products such as toothpaste, deodorant, perfume, and shave creams rely heavily on this effect. An advertisement implies, for example, that if we buy and use "Toothy Grin" toothpaste we will enjoy the same consequences (affection, friendship, love, or esteem) received by the model in the advertisement.

Equal opportunity and treatment are desirable goals for most members of contemporary American society. It follows that those socialized with such cultural values are highly sensitive to the consequences of others. Many people feel that what one person gets, everyone should get, and what one person avoids, everyone should avoid. Given this cultural environment, the inhibitory or disinhibitory effect of modeling takes on added meaning. If properly handled, the reinforcing quality of equitable treatment can become a powerful management tool. Publicly giving generalized positive reinforcers to those who display desirable organizational behavior should not only improve the performance of those reinforced, but should improve the performance of others as well. Thus, members of the work group can become behavior models for their co-workers.

This aspect of modeling suggests how one potential problem of BCM can be overcome. If a manager using BCM singles out one of his employees for special treatment and attention, how will the rest of the work group react? In modeling, by reinforcing the desirable behavior of the targeted individual, the others in the group could also be reinforced. Of course, it may not always work out this way, but if the individual being reinforced is part of the group and a relevant model, the others in the group will generally also be reinforced. By the same token, the effective human resource manager must ensure that the negative consequences of one work group member do not erode the performance of the other members.

Using the behavior of others as a cue • Whereas new responses may be learned by imitating others, responses already in an individual's behavior repertoire may be cued by a model's behavior. Some typical examples would be: at an executive board meeting everyone sits down when the chairperson sits down; dinner guests begin eating when the hostess begins; and everyone in the machine shop loafs when the foreman loafs.

In each instance, the behavior in question did not have to be learned by imitating the model; each behavior was already part of the individual's present repertoire. Previously acquired responses may be cued by similar responses on the part of others. In O. B. Mod. terms, the model's response serves as an antecedent condition which sets the occasion for the emission of a matching response by an observer. In a sense, the organizational behavior of relevant models serves as a reminder for organizational participants to behave in a similar fashion.

It may be an interesting exercise for the reader to chart the frequency with which he/she follows the behavioral lead of others. An objective determination of who are relevant models may turn out to be a surprise.

A modeling strategy for human resource management

The seven-step modeling strategy presented below suggests one possible way of putting the three modeling effects into practice. Other factors, such as alternative model selection, media selection, target-behavior specification, presentation, and consequence programming are involved. However, an on-the-job modeling strategy generally should include the following steps:

1) Precisely identify the goal or target behavior that will lead to performance improvement.

2) Select the appropriate model and modeling medium, i.e., live demonstration, training film, video tape, etc.

3) Make sure the employee is capable of meeting the technical skill requirements of the target behavior.

4) Structure a favorable learning environment which increases the probability of attention, participation, and, ultimately, the target behavior.

5) Model the target behavior and carry out supporting activities such as role playing. Clearly demonstrate the positive consequences of the modeled target behavior.

6) Positively reinforce all progress of the modeled behavior.

7) Once achieved, maintain and strengthen the target behavior first with a continuous schedule of reinforcement and later with an intermittent schedule.

As with the discussion of the shaping strategy, a more detailed explanation of the above steps should help in developing more effective human resource management.

Identify the target behavior • Both shaping and modeling strategies must necessarily start at the same point—the precise definition of target or goal behavior. This target behavior must be observable, countable, and reinforceable. To be appropriate for O. B. Mod., the target behavior must also be related to performance. Complex chains of organizational behavior must be reduced to key behavioral events that can be efficiently modeled.

As an example of this first step, imagine a sales manager who runs a performance audit on his sales staff and determines that they are not closing as many sales as expected. He concludes that a personal selling course is necessary. Knowing the importance of breaking complex behavior down into key target behavior, the sales manager formulates a list of six key personal-selling behaviors: (1) the greeting, (2) rapport building, (3) preparation, (4) the pitch, (5) the close, and (6) the exit. In its own way, each step is critical to successful personal selling. This specific behavioral breakdown gives the sales manager a solid base for designing an effective modeling strategy. Each step, initially representing a separate target behavior, can be modeled and learned. Later, all six steps, in proper sequence, can become the target behavior.

Select the model and medium • Selecting the appropriate model(s) and the modeling medium (media) is a very important step in the modeling strategy. The first decision is between live or symbolic models. In certain cases a combination of both may be used. Generally, high-status relevant individuals are the best live models. For example, an informal group leader (not necessarily the appointed leader) makes an effective model. The more the observer identifies with the model, the greater the observational learning effect.

Sorcher and Goldstein (1972) note that, "Most training programs are not adequately structured to the principles that enhance learning, e.g., involvement rather than passive listening, imitation of appropriate behavior, reinforcement, and practice of new skills." They proposed a comprehensive behavior modeling approach to training in industry. Desirable behavior is first modeled on videotape by high-status members of the work group. After watching the videotaped presentation of the desirable target behavior and the associated positive consequences received by the model, the observers/trainees discuss and role-play the target behavior. Role playing which closely approximates the target behavior is positively reinforced by the trainer. The success of this modeling/role playing/reinforcement sequence largely depends upon the appropriate selection of models and modeling media.

Videotape media for modeling are relatively inexpensive, flexible, and readily adaptable to specific work settings. Other methods include coaching. Day-to-day coaching in the form of live modeling by the manager and positive reinforcement for successful replication is relatively easy to conduct. The model used and media selected will depend on the nature of the target behavior, budget constraints, personal and group variables, organizational tradition, and other situational factors.

Meet skill requirements • This step is identical to the one discussed in the shaping strategy. The necessary skills, if not mastered, can stand in the way of successful performance of target behavior. Frequently, it may become necessary to model or shape skills such as the use of machines, complex administrative procedures, and special forms and documents before an attempt is made to teach key performance-related behavior through modeling.

Structure a favorable learning environment • This step is important in order to avoid the relatively common occurrence of training sessions being rendered ineffective by poor learning environments. Special efforts should be made to reduce the potentially disruptive influence of noise, work-group peers, and various other environmental stimuli which compete for the attention of the learner. This holds true regardless of whether the modeling strategy is carried out as part of an apprenticeship program, on-the-job training, coaching, vestibule training, or off-the-job training.

Many modern organizations have special training facilities containing classrooms, blackboards, overhead and movie projectors, and videotape equipment. Such modern facilities offer an excellent environment for improving performance through modeling. Besides the facilities, however, there must be carefully programmed positive consequences to increase the probability that the observer(s) will positively attend to and emulate the model(s).

Model the behavior • Whereas the previous steps are preparatory, this is an action step in which the learner is finally exposed to the model and given the opportunity to imitate the model. Structured imitative experience may take the form of role playing. A previously prepared sketch or scenario may be used to prompt or otherwise cue the matching response (e.g., Margulies and Wallace, 1973, pp. 88–91). The manager should take advantage of the inhibitory or disinhibitory effect of modeling discussed earlier.

Reinforce progress • Positive reinforcement should follow as soon as the observer successfully imitates the modeled behavior. Where immediate imitation of a complex modeled behavior is impossible, successful performance of successive approximations must be positively reinforced as in shaping. The shaping strategy may be used to pick up where a modeling strategy leaves off. In this manner, the two procedures can be used in combination.

Maintain and strengthen the target behavior • As in the shaping strategy, new behavior learned from models must be maintained and strengthened, at first with continuous or high-frequency fixed or variable ratio positive reinforcement, and then with less frequent intermittent schedules of reinforcement.

In summary, a modeling strategy permits the practicing human resource manager to take advantage of the manner in which organizational participants learn, by observing those around them, *how* to behave, *what* behavior pays off, and *when* to behave. Like other O. B. Mod. techniques, modeling occurs regardless of intent or desire. Therefore, the challenge is to actively manage rather than passively observe this important aspect of organizational behavior. Also, the very common "do as I say, not as I do" approach to managing human resources becomes absolutely indefensible in view of the knowledge about modeling. Teaching effective performance-related organizational behavior through a modeling strategy can become a part of everyday human resource management.

SELF-CONTROL IN O. B. MOD.

The inclusion of self-control in a book on O. B. Mod. may come as a surprise or appear contradictory. However, it should be remembered that O. B. Mod. does not always depend upon one person or group of people "doing something" to or controlling another person or group of people. O. B. Mod. is much more. The fact is, self-control on the part of both the "modifier" and the "modifiee" is an important part of O. B. Mod.

Self-control is a legitimate objective in any human resource management approach. If for no other reason than the cost involved, self-controlled pursuit of organizational objectives seems preferable to formally programmed control by someone else. It is much less expensive to have someone control himself/herself than it is to have someone manage him/her.

In addition, by incorporating self-control, O. B. Mod. can meet head-on some of the criticisms coming from proponents of the more traditional internal approaches to human resource management. Self-control is the cornerstone of the internal (motivational) approach to human resource management. The conflict model of a person fighting an internal battle between good and evil, and concepts such as "will power" have been popular internal explanations of self-control. Skinner (1953), stressing the alternative external view, proposed an organism/environment interaction explanation of self-control:

> "When a man controls himself, chooses a course of action, thinks out the solution to a problem, or strives toward an increase in self-knowledge, he is *behaving*. He controls himself precisely as he would control the behavior of anyone else—through the manipulation of variables of which behavior is a function" (p. 228).

In other words, like any other type of learned behavior, self-control behavior is a function of its consequences.

An individual exercising self-control is actually managing the consequences of his/her own behavior. For example, when a department store clerk patiently explains the store's return policy to an angry, shouting customer without getting angry in return, the clerk is exercising self-control. The store clerk, by being patient, is choosing the consequences of being patient over the consequences of getting angry. Whether carried out in the name of self-discipline, being nice, staying cool, or resisting temptation, the action still centers around self-control.

Self-control typically involves selecting one set of consequences from two or more alternatives. It involves careful consideration of the consequences of one's own alternative behavior. Most often the person using self-control will choose behavior which leads to desirable consequences rather than behavior of a rash, impulsive, and indecisive nature that leads to undesirable consequences. If the attainment of objectives requires self-control on the part of organizational participants, then they must learn to consider the consequences of various on-the-job behavior before acting. Shaping, modeling, and the positive reinforcement of desirable performance-related behavior are all involved with increasing the probability of self-control.

Learning self-control

Although more cognitive than behaviorist in approach, Argyris' (1957, p. 50) presentation of the immaturity-maturity continuum of personality can be used as a point of departure for a behaviorist explanation of self-control. Figure 7–1 illustrates the seven dimensions along a continuum. An individual's maturity profile may be plotted at any given time. For seventeen years Argyris (1973) has contended that the natural psychological maturation (not necessarily synonymous with chronological maturation) of individuals is blocked by organizations. Participants in formal organizations are forced to behave in relatively immature ways. In other words, there is a basic incongruency between the needs of the mature individual and the requirements of the formal organization.

FIGURE 7–1.   Argyris' Dimensions of Immaturity and Maturity.

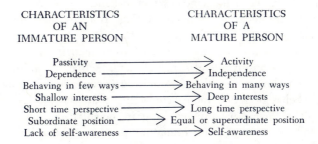

CHARACTERISTICS
OF AN
IMMATURE PERSON

CHARACTERISTICS
OF A
MATURE PERSON

Passivity ⟶ Activity
Dependence ⟶ Independence
Behaving in few ways ⟶ Behaving in many ways
Shallow interests ⟶ Deep interests
Short time perspective ⟶ Long time perspective
Subordinate position ⟶ Equal or superordinate position
Lack of self-awareness ⟶ Self-awareness

Working from the dimensions found in Figure 7–1, the assumption is that mature employees will exercise more self-control than will immature employees. Accordingly, to learn self-control the employee must move along each of the seven immaturity-maturity dimensions from left to right. In an O. B. Mod. approach, the specific behavioral definitions for each of the seven dimensions should be formulated. There will, of course, always be situational differences in the definitions. For example, independent activity on the part of a bricklayer would represent different behavior than that of an insurance company executive.

In any case, the complex organizational behavior must be reduced to specific behavioral events. For each individual, in each job, there would be specific behavioral events associated with mature characteristics, which in turn would lead to self-control. To shape mature self-controlled organizational behavior, the practicing manager using an O. B. Mod. approach would first determine the employee's relative position on the immaturity-maturity dimensions and then manage the contingent environment in which progressively mature, self-controlled behavior is positively reinforced.

As the individual matures and uses self-control, the manager may place less reliance on contrived reinforcers and give more emphasis to natural reinforcers. Contingencies of self-reinforcement should eventually replace formally programmed contingencies of reinforcement. A person who finds work on an interesting and challenging job positively reinforcing is more valuable to the organization than the person who puts up with a dull, tedious job in order to receive contrived (money or physical trappings) positive reinforcers. Self-control is much more probable in the first instance because the job is conducive to mature behavior. A job enrichment program is one method of making the work itself more positively reinforcing (see: Luthans and Knod, 1974; Luthans and Reif, 1973).

The purpose of learning self-control, of course, is not to do away with the manager. As long as there is a need for a formal organization, there will always be management functions such as planning, organizing, directing, communicating, and controlling. But the goal for human resource management should be to strive for self-control wherever possible. Unfortunately, many organizations and their management provide little in the way of a positive reinforcing climate. Active, committed, and self-controlled employees capable of exercising independent judgment should find such behavior much more reinforcing than the passive, dependent, and simple behavior usually resulting in negative consequences. Using O. B. Mod., movement from immature to mature behavior may be systematically shaped with appropriate positive reinforcement.

Manager self-control

Self-control by the modifier/manager is fundamental to O. B. Mod. Systematically managing the environmental contingencies of others' organizational behavior demands a great deal of self-control on the part of the practicing manager; maturity must prevail over immaturity. This is especially true when one recognizes how important the manager is to the contingent environment of a subordinate. Blowing up at a subordinate on a particularly hectic day when the air conditioning system is broken down may erase weeks of careful shaping with positive consequences. Failing to note response frequencies or forgetting to positively reinforce a newly shaped performance-related behavior may negate the effectiveness of an O. B. Mod. approach. For example, missing an opportunity to positively reinforce an independent action by a usually dependent work group member may strengthen rather than solve the problem behavior.

Each of these examples relates at least indirectly to the need for self-control on the part of the manager using O. B. Mod. It is clear that the practicing manager cannot hope to effectively modify the organizational behavior of others without first being able to exercise control over his/her own behavior. Modifier/manager self-control is a function of its consequences, primary among which is the attainment of organizational objectives through human resources.

Subordinate self-control

The top management of an organization is subject to a great deal of external control (board of directors, government, public opinion, organized labor, and economic and market conditions). They are controlled by overall organizational consequences such as survival, profitability, growth, market share, return on investment, and social responsibility.

Such noncontingent consequences require top management to have a great deal of self-control. Lower-level operating personnel in an organization, especially in a subordinate role, do not depend on such lofty consequences but nevertheless also need a great deal of self-control. To make the organization more effective, the manager should increase the opportunities of subordinates at all levels to develop more self-control. Two suggested approaches to improve self-control include participation in goal setting and contingency contracting.

Self-control through participation in goal setting • Starting with the classic Coch and French (1948) study on overcoming resistance to change, behaviorally oriented management experts have generally agreed that participation has a favorable impact on productivity, turnover, and attitudes. MBO, discussed earlier, is firmly based on the premise that subordinate participation in goal setting facilitates commitment to those goals. Such personal commitment, combined with the knowledge that subsequent performance will be judged in terms of actual results, ensures that each subordinate has a personal stake in organizational goal attainment. Subordinate self-control becomes a natural by-product of this participation in goal setting. The subordinate behaves in such a way that he/she knows what the consequences will be.

Recent empirical research (Latham and Kinne, 1974) indicates that training in goal setting improves subsequent job performance. In the Latham and Kinne study, logging crews which ordinarily did not set daily, weekly, or monthly production goals were given such goals. These output goals were tied to the performance of the sawhands because of the strategic importance of the cutting operation in pulpwood harvesting. The experimental group's output goals were calculated at the beginning of the work week by the trainer and the crew supervisors from carefully constructed production tables derived from company time-study data.

It is important to note that the crew members themselves did not participate in setting the goals but they did view the goals as realistic and attainable. During the study, the normal piece-rate plan remained in force; only verbal praise was made contingent on goal attainment. Experimental group sawhands were given tally meters so they could constantly monitor, evaluate, and provide themselves with reinforcing feedback on performance. The results were that production significantly increased and absenteeism decreased in the experimental group.

This study demonstrates the ability of realistic output goals to control productivity. Even without active participation in the goal-setting process by those ultimately affected, the mere existence of realistic, attainable goals seems to facilitate improved self-controlled performance.

The literature in general supports the fact that subordinate self-control is improved through participation in goal setting. The Latham and Kinne study discussed above suggests that the subordinates do not even have to participate as long as they know the goals are realistic and attainable. Goals give the subordinate something for which to strive. The attainment of realistic goals seems to possess strong reinforcing properties which increases the likelihood of subsequent self-controlled pursuit of organizational objectives.

Self-control through contingency contracting • Subordinate participation in goal setting is well established in management. Not given attention in the past is a behavior modification technique called contingency or behavioral contracting (Homme et al., 1970). Although the application of contingency contracting thus far has been largely restricted to classroom behavior of children, there appears to be no reason why it cannot be successfully extended to the adult work environment.

Basically, a contingency contract is an agreement (formalized in writing if necessary) between the superior and the subordinate specifying an if-then situation. The possible range may run from a complete specification of both the "if" and "then" components of the contingency by the boss (e.g., if you complete Project A by the end of the week, then you will receive a one-hundred-dollar bonus) to a complete specification of both components by the subordinate (e.g., if I come up with an improved method of inventory control, then I will receive a new desk calculator). Subordinate self-control should be directly related to the amount of participation in the contingency specification. Significantly, contingency contracting includes not only the process of mutual goal setting as in MBO, but also provides for specific programmed consequences—something that is noticeably absent from most MBO programs.

Under contingency contracting, superiors can conceivably maintain very loose, results-centered controls with mature subordinates. Self-controlled subordinates formulate their own work contingencies and behave accordingly. The major job of management would simply be to see to it that the agreed-upon consequences were forthcoming as soon as the behavioral criteria were satisfied. The day-to-day responsibility for living up to the contingency contract(s) falls squarely on the shoulders of the self-controlled subordinate. Mature, active, and independent employees, who dominate today's organizations, are capable of assuming such self-control resulting from contingency contracting.

Organizational Behavior Modification: Some Actual Cases

8

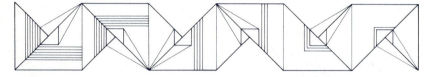

Thus far, the material in this book has been largely conceptual, using realistic examples as much as possible to illustrate the theory and principles of O. B. Mod. As the ultimate test of any theoretical/conceptual approach is actual practice, this chapter now turns to cases which demonstrate the direct application of O. B. Mod. and closely related approaches. Four applications have been selected to demonstrate how O. B. Mod. can be and is being applied in the actual management of human resources. The applications to a production operation of a light manufacturing firm, provision of customer service in an airline, the overall management system of a food processing firm, and the running of a military unit are presented. These particular cases were selected to represent production, service, and total organizational development applications in business organizations; the military case represents a nonbusiness application.

THE PRODUCTION CASE

Because of the newness of O. B. Mod., only a few empirically based research studies have been conducted to date. This case [1] reports one of them. It represents a viable approach to building a meaningful body

1. The authors are indebted to Dr. Robert Ottemann, Assistant Professor of Management, University of Nebraska, Omaha, for gathering the data for this case. The information is used with his permission. Dr. Ottemann and David Lyman were the trainers in this study under the general direction of Dr. Fred Luthans.

of knowledge about O. B. Mod. The firm in this study is a medium-sized industrial plant engaged in light manufacturing. Two groups of nine first-line supervisors from the production division participated in the study. One of the groups went through a training program and served as the experimental group. The other group, which was matched with the experimental group on the basis of age, education, experience as foremen, and mental test score, did not undergo any training and served as the control group. Spans of control for the supervisors ranged from ten to thirty. All had worked their way up from operative positions in the plant. For the most part, each had gained his managerial knowledge from the "school of hard knocks" rather than formal education or supervisory training.

Behavioral contingency management training

O. B. Mod. was applied by training the first-line supervisors how to use BCM. The training sessions were held in the plant's training room for ten ninety-minute sessions spread over ten consecutive weeks. A process rather than content training approach was used. This approach replaced the traditional lecture format, where the trainer has a dominant role, with a relatively free give-and-take discussion format, where the trainees themselves dominate.

In general, the content of the sessions was preplanned and sequenced but not rigidly structured during the session itself. Some of the assumptions made by the trainers included: it is easier to change the trainees' behavior first and overall style later than the reverse; appropriate trainee responses must be reinforced immediately and frequently; complex trainee behaviors must be gradually shaped; and allowances must be made for individual differences in learning speed.

The process approach resulted in an informal and relaxed learning environment. Importantly, the trainers served as models of what they were teaching by first cueing and then contingently reinforcing appropriate trainee behavior. Among the reinforced trainee behaviors were attendance, contributions to discussion, and data presentation and analysis. In effect, the BCM approach was taught to the trainees through the use of BCM.

The steps of BCM as taught to the trainees were as follows:

1) *Identifying target behavior*. The focus was on objective behavior rather than on internal states. Initial reliance upon internal explanations such as "Joe has a bad attitude" was eventually replaced in the training sessions and on the job by an attention to observable behavior. Identification of *performance-related* behavior was stressed. The trainees in the study identified behavior such as work-assignment completions, absences, rejects, quality-

control problems, complaints, excessive breaks, leaving the work area, and scrap rates.

2) *Measuring the frequency of behavior*. After learning the measuring techniques, the trainees charted real behavioral data on the job and discussed it during the training sessions. The resulting frequency charts provided both training session data and feedback for the trainees on their progress with implementing the BCM approach.

3) *Functionally analyzing behavior*. The trainees were taught to identify the three elements in the behavioral contingency (antecedent→behavior→consequence). By analyzing antecedents and especially contingent consequences, the supervisors began to see for themselves how target behavior could be predicted and controlled. Emphasis was placed on managing contingent consequences to change on-the-job behavior.

4) *Developing intervention strategies*. Strengthening desirable performance behavior and weakening undesirable behavior was the goal of the intervention. Shaping, modeling, and reinforcement were discussed in terms of strengthening behavior. Extinction, reinforcement of incompatible behavior, and, in exceptional cases, punishment were examined as strategies for reducing the frequency of unproductive or counterproductive behavior. Because of the difficulty of identifying reinforcers ahead of time, methods of selecting and establishing effective reinforcers were given a great deal of attention. Potential reinforcers that were proposed and used included attention, work scheduling, positive feedback on performance, approval, recognition, praise, responsibility, and contingent assignment to favorite tasks.

5) *Evaluating Results*. The supervisors continually monitored their interventions through measurement to see whether the intended effects were in fact taking place. The goal of the evaluations was to determine if performance improvement was occurring.

Importantly, emphasis throughout the entire ten-week training program was on getting the supervisors to identify and solve behavioral problems on their own. As much as possible, the trainers resisted offering any direct prescriptions. Occasionally in the sessions, a problem would be brought up by trainees and solutions suggested by the trainers, but mainly the trainees became problem-solving behavior contingency managers.

Results were measured on two levels to evaluate the overall effectiveness of the BCM training program. First, individual and group performance of the trainees' workers was analyzed to determine the trainees' ability to put the BCM approach into actual practice. Second, since performance improvement is the ultimate test, a comparison was made between the experimental and control groups in terms of the overall, "bottom-line" performance, to determine if the training had a significant impact on improving the performance of the experimental group's respective departments. These results are discussed below.

Changes in specific on-the-job behavior

Frequency of response was the dependent variable and the intervention strategy was the independent variable in measuring on-the-job behavioral changes. The supervisors/trainees measured the frequency of a target behavior of an individual subordinate or a group of subordinates during a baseline period and subsequently during the intervention period. Thus, the data for the behavioral change analysis was contained on response frequency charts. Four representative illustrations of these behavioral change problems are discussed in the following sections. They involve both individual and group problems and different types of intervention strategies.

The disruptive complainer • A particularly disruptive female machine operator was selected as a target for BCM by one supervisor/trainee in the program. She often complained bitterly about the production standards to the supervisor. In addition, she seemed to adversely affect the productivity of her co-workers by talking to them about their rates and production sheets. According to her, everyone else in the plant had an easier job. Close review of her case revealed that her complaints were unfounded.

After identifying the complaining behavior, the supervisor gathered baseline data on this behavior during a ten-day period. No new contingencies were introduced during this "before" baseline measure. In conducting a functional analysis of the target response during the baseline period, the supervisor determined that *he* was probably serving as a reinforcing consequence by paying attention to the complaints.

Armed with the baseline data and information gathered in the functional analysis, the supervisor decided to use a combination extinction/positive reinforcement intervention strategy. Extinction took the form of his withholding attention when she complained. Satisfactory production and constructive suggestions were socially reinforced by praise in an effort to strengthen the incompatible behavior. In addition, her constructive suggestions were implemented whenever possible.

The supervisor's chart, shown in Figure 8–1, illustrates that the combination intervention strategy did in fact have the desired effect. The complaining behavior decreased in frequency. The chart shows that a time-sampling technique was used. Rather than carrying out time-con-

FIGURE 8–1.   Frequency of Complaints.

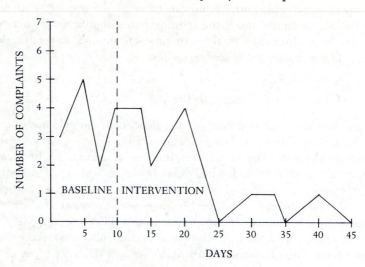

suming measures every day, the target response was charted on randomly selected days (the 1st, 5th, 7th, 10th, 13th, etc.). Implementing constructive suggestions turned out to be especially reinforcing in this case. The supervisor noted to the trainers that the rapid reduction in frequency of complaints was amazing because it had been such a long-standing problem.

Group scrap rate • Another supervisor/trainee identified group scrap rate as a growing performance problem in his department. Attempts at reducing the scrap by posting equipment maintenance rules and giving frequent reminders to his workers had not produced any noticeable improvement. The specific target response to be strengthened was identified as stopping the stamping mill when a defective piece was sighted and sharpening and realigning the dies.

During a two-week baseline period the supervisor kept a careful record of the group's scrap rate. Importantly, no new contingencies were introduced during this baseline period. The extent of the problem had to be determined before any intervention was attempted. After conducting a functional analysis, the supervisor decided to install a feedback system to inform the group of their scrap rate. This was accomplished by measuring, charting, and posting in the department work area the group scrap rate. The supervisor then actively solicited ideas from his workers on how to improve the scrap rate. Providing the feedback and implementing the suggestions turned out to be potent reinforcers.

FIGURE 8–2.   Group Scrap Rate.

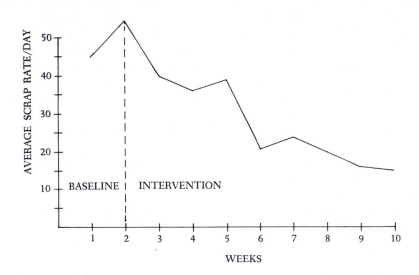

Figure 8–2 shows the results of the intervention. In this case, group, not individual, behavior was charted. In addition to the improved scrap rate, the supervisor noted an increase in interaction between himself and his workers and among the workers themselves. A number of social reinforcers were discovered in the process.

Group quality control • A third supervisor/trainee identified quality control in the paint line as a major performance problem in his department. The paint-line attendants' job consisted of hanging pieces on a paint-line conveyor, removing the painted pieces, and inspecting them for acceptance or rejection. "Getting on the men's backs" by the supervisor typically produced only temporary improvement in quality control. Soon after the supervisor reprimanded the men the defective pieces would again pass unnoticed. As defined by the supervisor, a desirable target response consisted of identifying and removing defective pieces from the paint line. An undesirable response involved overlooking a defective piece.

During the two-week baseline period the average daily number of overlooked defective pieces was recorded for the entire work group. Figures were charted weekly during both the baseline period, where contingencies remained unchanged, and the intervention period. The supervisor noted to the trainers that after conducting a functional analysis he had concluded that he had a group of "clock watchers" on his hands, particularly around break time, lunch time, and quitting time.

The supervisor developed his intervention strategy during a discussion session with his work group. It was decided that a group rate of eight or less overlooked defective pieces a day would qualify the group for an extra five minutes for each of two coffee breaks the next day. To increase the value of the potential reinforcer, the paint-line attendants were told each morning if they had qualified for the extended breaks.

Figure 8–3 shows that the extra time off in the form of extended coffee breaks did in fact prove to be reinforcing. Contingency contracting had been effectively used. With the average daily rate of defectives down around two or three, the supervisor confided to the trainers that he couldn't see much more room for improvement.

Individual performance problem • A fourth supervisor/trainee was having a problem with the quality of assembled components in his department. Upon detailed analysis of the problem, the supervisor discovered that most of the rejects were coming from a single assembler. The assembly work entailed the precise manipulation of intricate subcomponents and the individual in question had satisfactory scores on screening tests for dexterity and coordination. In addition, this assembler had received the standard training in assembly and checking. After initial consideration, the supervisor rejected the alternative of running the assembler through more training. In his previous experience with similar cases, more

FIGURE 8–3.   Frequency of Overlooked Defective Pieces.

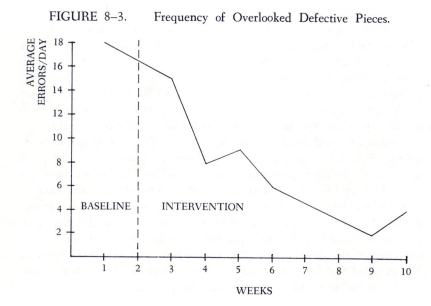

training had failed to improve poor performance. Thus, he decided to use the BCM approach on this particular employee.

The supervisor specifically identified undesirable behavior as more than two rejects per one hundred assembled components and desirable behavior as two or less. Without changing the existing contingencies, the supervisor obtained a two-week baseline measure. To facilitate measuring, boxes of assembled components were randomly sampled and the per box average recorded on a weekly basis. After a functional analysis, the supervisor decided that feedback on performance and compliments and praise for desirable behavior would be an appropriate positive reinforcement intervention strategy.

Beginning a shaping process at five or less errors, the supervisor contingently praised the assembler for any improved quality. As the reject level began to drop, the reinforcement schedule was gradually stretched. In other words, the worker had to have four, then three, and eventually only two rejects before praise was given by the supervisor. Summarized reject statistics were charted and presented to the assembler as a form of feedback on performance. Discussions of this feedback data between the assembler and the supervisor provided the opportunity for the supervisor to reinforce desirable behavior and ignore undesirable behavior.

Figure 8–4 illustrates the rapid improvement resulting from the feedback and positive reinforcement intervention strategy.

FIGURE 8–4.   Assembly Reject Rate.

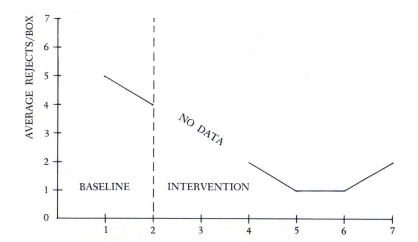

Overall performance improvement

The supervisors' ability to modify specific on-the-job individual and group behavior represents only one level of evaluation in BCM. Of more importance is overall performance improvement. The supervisors worked on the specific problems discussed above during the training program but the trainers' ultimate objective was to have BCM generalize to the supervisors' total method of managing their human resources. To evaluate the effectiveness of BCM as an overall method of managing, direct labor effectiveness (a ratio of actual to standard hours stated as a percent) was measured for each of the supervisors' departments both in the experimental group (those who received BCM training) and in the control group (those who received no training).

Figure 8–5 shows the results of the overall performance evaluation. The figure shows the experimental group's and the control group's mean direct labor effectiveness curves over a six-month period subsequent to the start of the training program at the end of September. The training program itself lasted ten weeks (until the middle of December). The figure clearly shows that the overall performance of the control group

FIGURE 8–5.   Intergroup Comparison of Overall Performance Using BCM.

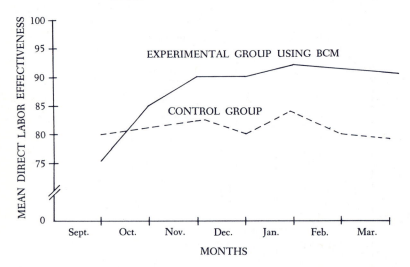

Source: Robert Ottemann and Fred Luthans, "Behavioral Contingency Management: An Empirical Analysis." Unpublished paper, Lincoln, Nebraska, 1974. Used with permission. Not to be reprinted without permission of the authors.

remained relatively stable over the six-month period, but the performance of the experimental group significantly improved and seemed to be maintained even after the training period was over. This evaluation demonstrated that the BCM training had generalized and paid off in terms of overall performance improvement.

Although not all the supervisors were able to obtain as clear-cut results of behavioral change as the four reported above, the overall performance was impressive. The other cases presented in this chapter do not provide as systematic and precise an evaluation. Some of the significant features of this production case are:

1) Specific performance-related problems were identified by the supervisors and reduced to desirable/undesirable behavioral events.

2) Baseline measures were obtained on target behavior. The frequency measures were accomplished with little difficulty.

3) A functional analysis was performed by the supervisors that determined actual and potential contingent consequences for positive control.

4) Making use of the functional analysis, the supervisors were able to design and generally successfully implement intervention strategies. Natural positive reinforcers were readily identified and contingently applied by the supervisors.

5) Both behavioral change and significant overall, "bottom-line" results were achieved by first-line supervisors using a BCM approach.

THE SERVICE CASE

This case [2] demonstrates the application of O. B. Mod. principles to improving customer service. It involves the customer service group of a major airline. The airline is proud of its reputation for friendly, efficient service and much of its marketing effort is built around this reputation. However, maintaining such a reputation has become increasingly difficult and new ways to improve the service to customers are constantly being sought.

Concerned with the overall morale and customer service record of his ticket agents, the manager of one of the airline's stations requested

2. The authors are indebted to Robert A. Esposito for providing the factual data for this case. The information is used with permission.

training assistance from the home office. Although the station was technically sound, there were definite human problems associated with the lack
of clearly defined performance goals, specific action plans, and effective
means of measuring and controlling performance.

After carefully assessing these problems, the training department
suggested an experimental training program based on the principles of
behavior modification. As the training director noted, "It was felt that the
use of behavior modification techniques would prompt the management
to more clearly define 'good work,' provide more specific performance feedback to employees, help reduce counterproductive behavior, and improve
performance and climate through recognition of good work." The station
manager agreed to this approach because of the stress it put on both greater
productivity and an improved behavioral climate.

The Reinforcement Management training program

A behavior-modification based training program called "Reinforcement Management" was jointly developed and administered by an outside
consulting firm and members of the airline's training department. The
trainees in the program consisted of managers, assistant managers, and
lead agents from the station's reservations and passenger ticketing operations. Although both the reservations and ticketing personnel work with
the same technical information (fares, rules, routine procedures, etc.),
their work situations differ with regard to direct customer contact. Reservations personnel deal with the public primarily over the telephone; ticketing
personnel interact with customers mainly on a face-to-face basis.

Two groups went through four training sessions, spaced at two
to three-week intervals. In the first group were the reservation and ticketing managers and their respective assistant managers. Lead agents formed
the second group. The management group preceded the lead agent group
through each of the four sessions. Skills learned during each session were
practiced between sessions and the results were discussed at the next meeting. Briefly, the content and duration of the four sessions were as follows:

1) Principles of behavior (8 hours).
2) Diagnosing reinforcers (4 hours).
3) Techniques for giving constructive criticism or feedback
(4 hours).
4) Formal performance review techniques (4 hours).

The first session focused on both classical and operant principles of behavior. The classical principles included pairing principles, the effect of reinforcing verbal equivalents of behavior, and the effect of mildly punishing versus strongly punishing verbal equivalents of behavior. The operant principles included: (1) reinforcement, (2) extinction, (3) the presentation of mild aversives and punishments, and (4) the withdrawal of aversives. Care was taken to show how each principle occurs in everyday life and how each can affect both desirable and undesirable behavior. Application to actual supervisory situations in the station followed.

The behavior principles discussed during the first session were intended to provide the supervisor with a repertoire of skills for diminishing inappropriate behavior and strengthening desired behavior as a means of attaining improved customer service. The second session covered identification and application of individualized reinforcers. In the third session the trainees learned how to give positive rather than negative feedback on performance. The fourth session explained traditional performance review techniques. Emphasis was placed on merging the Reinforcement Management approach with performance evaluations.

After completing the four training sessions, the trainees were instructed to identify work situations where Reinforcement Management techniques were applicable, identify specific individual behavior that should be weakened, shaped, or reinforced, and actually practice their new skills on the job. Members of the training department now periodically visit the station to counsel and guide the trainees. This systematic follow-up is an attempt to further develop the trainees' Reinforcement Management skills.

At the present time, quality-control personnel are taking quasi-baseline measurements for a three-month period to assist in diagnosing target behavior. The primary objective is to isolate problematic trends, such as ticketing and reservations errors and a high ratio of customer complaints per passengers boarded. On the positive side, the ratio of customer commendations per passengers boarded is also being recorded. Local management is monitoring the factors of planning, coordination, and work-force utilization in potential and actual flight delays. Attendance and tardiness records are being analyzed to identify both areas of deficiency and good performance. Once the first three-month baseline is established, the specific measurements will be incorporated into the actual performance goals of the station.

The assistant managers frequently review the lead agents' performance and identify and reinforce good work behavior. The lead agents' success at diminishing counterproductive behavior will be similarly reviewed. In turn, according to the training director, the managers "will frequently conduct performance reviews with their assistant managers to shape and reinforce their attainment of goals such as increased and more evident customer concern, reduced absenteeism, delegation to lead agents, and their reinforcement of lead agents and regular agents."

A number of general intervention strategies and related target behaviors are common to all levels. Among them are the extinction of unproductive complaining and excuse making, the reinforcement of efficient and courteous customer contact, the shaping and reinforcement of good attendance, the reinforcement of problem identification and solution, and the reinforcement of the exercise of good judgment.

The highly unpredictable nature of the passenger airline business, due to daily variances in weather and passenger numbers as well as incidental special handling occasions, makes the identification of specific target behavior on any given day difficult. To ensure the use of Reinforcement Management in day-to-day operations, the company has adopted an approach whereby any behavior judged productive is identified and reinforced on the spot. Conversely, any behavior judged counterproductive is diminished and shaped toward more productive performance. Immediate, contingent evaluation of behavior is stressed.

The training director also stressed that the Reinforcement Management program as implemented in this station is both a supervisory *and* a developmental approach. Strategies and critical steps in achieving performance goals like customer service are being systematically defined. Moreover, everyone now has "something to do" in maintaining and enhancing the quality of *daily* customer service. Both performance and behavioral climate are affected by the Reinforcement Management program.

Preliminary results
of Reinforcement Management

Some doubts were raised at the start of the training period about the advisability of simultaneously teaching Reinforcement Management to managers, assistant managers, and lead agents, even though the managers and the lead agents were in separate groups. It was feared that the two groups would cancel out each other. In fact, the opposite has occurred. Two-way, open superior/subordinate communication has improved at each level. The training director noted that, "Constructive criticism has been found more sincere, less troublesome to give and take, and less clouded by uncomfortable, evasive approaches." Greater confidence and willingness to deal directly with subordinate performance is developing. There seems to be greater mutual understanding of supervisory accountability.

Another interesting fact which has emerged relates to positive versus negative control. Initially, at least, the trainees felt uncomfortable and awkward thanking or sincerely praising an individual for good work rather than punishing an individual for inferior performance. However, the training director said, "Once reinforcement has been learned and attempted it becomes rewarding to one to offer sincere recognition to another, especially when the response is positive and one finds improved effort on the job." More and more, the trainees are focusing their attention on what is *right* with performance and finding ways to reinforce it with praise, recognition, special assignments, and, occasionally, even promotion. The identification and effective use of these reinforcers has been relatively easy for both managers and lead agents.

Initial concern with the manipulative aspect of the technique being taught was overcome by distinguishing between sincere and insincere performance feedback and reinforcement. Insincere reinforcement, the trainers cautioned in the sessions, would soon become as aversive as coercion and other forms of negative control. The training director commented, "Thus, trainees were impressed with the fact that to be an effective leader one must demonstrate a sincere concern for others in relation to their work habits."

Problems the trainees had in attempting to apply illustrative examples cited in training without first analyzing their appropriateness were largely overcome by role playing and practice sessions. As a result, there was less of a tendency to rigidly and mechanically interpret Reinforcement Management. Making each trainee more aware of his impact on others in the work environment also helped. Along these same lines, the objection, "I can't go around doing that all the time," was answered, "Right, just do it when you can." The idea was to get trainees to at least use reinforcement so they would increase their opportunities for experiencing reinforcing results.

A major difficulty in implementing the technique involved a reluctance on the part of the station managers to define specific target behavior requiring attention. Part of the solution came in the form of group discussion on the formulation and attainment of performance goals. However, some still felt that specific target behavior, although observable, was impractical to measure. Reliance on the quasi-baseline measures discussed earlier helped surmount this particular impasse. Operating from these performance statistics, the trainees found it easier to identify desirable behavior that could be reinforced.

This case shows how O. B. Mod. can be taught and applied in the service area. Considering the dramatic growth in the service sector of the U.S. economy since World War II, this case is particularly important. It offers some valuable lessons on how to implement an O. B.

Mod. approach and, particularly, points out the importance of "re-inforcing the reinforcers." In other words, supervisors are much more inclined to consistently use Reinforcement Management if they them-selves are reinforced for doing so. The net result is an organizational climate based on positive reinforcement contingent upon performance. There is no "I win, you lose" strategy in this type of positive reinforce-ment organizational climate. Superiors, subordinates, and, most important, customers benefit from such a reinforcing environment.

THE TOTAL
ORGANIZATIONAL DEVELOPMENT CASE

This case [3] is similar to the last in that it primarily describes the technique rather than systematically evaluates the results. Yet, this case is important because it illustrates how O. B. Mod. concepts and prin-ciples have been applied as an approach to total organization develop-ment (O. D.).

After some localized success with behavior modification principles used as a "troubleshooting" tool, the food-processing company in this case decided to broaden the program and build a complete management system around an O. B. Mod. type approach. The first program was introduced to the company in the form of a first-line supervisory train-ing program. Behavioral learning principles, identification of reinforcers, and management of contingencies were taught to and carried out by supervisors in their respective areas. The training objective was relatively straightforward: teach supervisors some basic behavior modification skills and give them the authority to use them to identify problem behavior and implement appropriate intervention strategies. As part of a shaping strategy, problem behavior was initially identified by the trainers. While this program had relatively good results and adequate supervisory/manage-ment acceptance, it fell short of the overall goal of a complete manage-ment system built around the principles and concepts of O. B. Mod.

At least two problems prevented the initial supervisory training program from evolving into a total O. D. program. First, the satisfactory results tended to be short-lived and too localized in effect. Although some specific behavioral problems were solved, the technique was relegated to a "troubleshooting" tool instead of becoming a total method of managing

3. The authors are indebted to Sam McPherson for providing the fac-tual data for this case. The information is used with permission.

human resources. Second, the reinforcing effect of subordinate self-improvement was overestimated and the necessity of higher management reinforcement was underestimated. Supervisors/trainees who experienced early success with their behavior modification skills eventually showed signs of extinction. Their use of the behavior modification techniques diminished due to a lack of potent reinforcing consequences. Too little attention had been given to shaping and maintaining the supervisors' use of the behavior modification skills.

Another finding showed that the most successful behavior modifiers were also the most effective supervisors prior to the training. In other words, already effective supervisors tended to successfully use the behavior modification techniques but the average and marginal supervisors experienced difficulty in making the transition from modifying assigned behavior problems during the training sessions to exercising self-direction in using the approach back on the job. This latter group of average and low-performing supervisors had problems particularly with discriminating between significant trends in performance data and random, irrelevant data.

In total, although the initial experience with behavior modification as a supervisory problem-solving tool contained encouraging results, the problems mentioned above prevented it from becoming a total O. D. approach. Yet, the training people and top-line management were still convinced that it had the potential for expanded implementation throughout the company.

A new total O. D. approach

Management identified two viable alternative approaches to overcoming some of the problems of the initial program and expanding its implementation. The first alternative involved a more comprehensive training program that would teach the trainees how to discriminate between priority performance data and irrelevant trivia. Concurrently, all managers above the first level, going all the way up to the plant manager, would be trained in how to shape and reinforce appropriate first-line supervisory behavior.

The second alternative involved a program of complete reassessment and reorientation. Rather than focusing on supervisory training, the program would focus on direct identification of key production behavior. Trainer involvement in the initial application of behavior modification had proven insufficient because the trainer's exit left the supervisor in a vacuum of insufficient support. Things fell back into the same old groove as each supervisor found himself sandwiched in between an insufficient source of reinforcement, his boss, and the daily crisis-oriented production floor environment. The second alternative would attempt to organize the entire organizational environment into a contingent system. Operating personnel and three levels of management would be taught to more effectively respond to one another in support of productive behavior at each level.

The company decided to take the second approach. In the words of the training director, "the second alternative was chosen and succeeded. It succeeded to the extent of involving a full-scale organization development project in which floor behaviors were pinpointed and consequated by three layers of line management."

An example in the packaging area

One of the first areas affected by the new total O. D. program was packaging. Packaging is a key results area for any company in the food-processing industry. In this company, it accounts for approximately 10 percent of the value of the finished product. There are strict quality-control criteria for the amount of air, general appearance, and total weight of the bags used in the packaging operation. The effectiveness of the operation greatly depends on the output of the food kitchen, the freshness of the finished product, and the amount of packaging material waste. Thus, the packaging-machine operator is the person in the middle who must "get it all together."

In an effort to pinpoint the operator behavior with the greatest potential pay-off, a detailed performance analysis was conducted. A basic reality associated with the packaging operation is that while the operator skills are difficult and time-consuming to teach, the performance drifts out of line very easily. Because of the importance and somewhat unpredictable nature of the packaging-machine operation, top machine operators are typically described in such vague terms as "a natural" and "born, not made." In fact, personnel requisitions from the packaging area have come through saying something to the effect of "hire me another one just like Tom." Subjective barriers such as these had to be cleared before an objective performance analysis with the purpose of identifying critical performance-related behaviors could proceed.

The performance analysis of the packaging-machine operation revealed monitoring behavior (i.e., gathering information about machine output) as being very critical to packaging performance. Many of the packaging-machine operators demonstrated an adequate knowledge of performance tasks, but when it came to monitoring behavior, the training director stated that "few could monitor the operation in such a manner as to diagnose a machine problem and then effectively select which performance task could improve the output." The performance analysis also revealed that the successful operators spent a greater percentage of their time engaged in monitoring behavior.

After the importance of monitoring behavior was determined, the next step was to break down this behavior into specific, measurable terms in the following manner: (1) periodically gather output data; (2) generate alternative solutions; (3) select the best alternative; (4) implement the solution; and (5) test the solution with a follow-up review of output data. The most effective machine operators reported having a "feel" for the machine while monitoring. Subsequent performance analysis operationally defined "feel" as listening to the machine cycling and periodically inspecting bags of finished product for correct amount of air sealed in the bag, appearance, and weight. Data collected during these informal checks determined what machine adjustments needed to be made. In other words, performance-related task behavior was based upon data collected through monitoring behavior.

The performance analysis uncovered a need for an improved performance feedforward/feedback system. A supportive environment (feedback) was designed for the critical packaging-machine operator's monitoring behavior by starting with the monitoring behavior and working up ("feedforward") through the normal chain of command. The common base for this contingent performance system which spanned four levels in the organization hierarchy was the performance data generated by the packaging-machine operator. In this way an individual machine operator was tied into and became a vital input into the total organization system.

Process Education Program

The new total organization system adopted by this company was labeled the "Process Education Program" or simply PEP. It consisted of two major parts. The first part focused on individual performance (for example, the packaging-machine operator) and was called process education. The second part dealt with effective supervision as a means of performance improvement.

Systematic application of these two parts produced a vehicle for two-way exchange between the individual performer (for example, the packaging-machine operator) and his/her first-line supervisor, and so on up the hierarchy of the company. The first-line supervisor provided process education for his/her superior, the department head, who in turn reinforced performance improvement and provided process education to the plant manager, who in turn reinforced performance improvement, and so on. In this way there was an upward flow of critical performance data and a downward flow of contingent reinforcement for desirable improved performance.

Process education ensured that the individual had a working knowledge of the critical components of his/her task. Emphasis was placed on making sure each individual knew how the critical components were measured as well as how the measures fit into the total picture. Essentially, each individual learned the "what" and "so what" aspects of his/her job. Another important phase of process education involved the generation and communication of critical job data to the immediate supervisor. As explained by the training director, "from that point on, we rely on the second half of PEP to increase the level of involvement and problem solving on the part of the employee. It becomes the job of the supervisor to pinpoint and reward those steps."

For example, once the packaging-machine operators were capable of giving their supervisors the critical performance data, then the operators' performance improvement was stressed. Supervisors were taught how to maintain the flow of critical performance data from the packaging-machine operators. Specifically, they were taught to contingently and positively reinforce the operators' giving of performance data. Emphasis was placed on choosing the proper positive reinforcing consequence and administering it at the appropriate time.

To help structure the performance data which was fed forward to the supervisor, the problem-solving sequence was reduced to a specific chain of measurable behaviors. For example, the packaging operation was broken down into the following questions:

1) Can the packaging-machine operator pinpoint meaningful data for the supervisor?

2) Can the operator identify the cause(s) of problems incurred?

3) Can the operator generate alternatives for attacking the cause of the problem?

4) Can the operator evaluate, weigh, and compare the alternatives?

5) Can the operator choose one alternative and clearly measure its effect on the problem by using his/her data?

6) Can the operator interpret the data such that he/she knows when one solution is not working and another should be tried?

7) Can the operator interpret the data such that he/she knows if the solution has eliminated the cause so the problem will not recur?

This sequence of questions let the operator know exactly what was expected of him/her *and* let the supervisor know what to expect. Perhaps most important, the first-line supervisor's own effectiveness was to be measured by his boss in terms of each of his operators' ability to answer these questions through performance. Each step represented an important link in the operator's behavior chain. The supervisor had to shape the behavior of the operator with positive consequences in order to lead to performance improvement of the operator and, in turn, to performance improvement of the supervisor, the department head, and even the plant manager.

Results of the total O. D. program

Since PEP has just recently been installed at this company, results to date are only short-term and hence tentative. However, some definite trends seem to be developing. Thus far, the procedure has helped pinpoint the lack of job knowledge on the part of operating personnel. Along the same line, supervisory training needs have been identified. PEP seems to possess the potential for acting as a vehicle for employee training, performance measurement, performance evaluation, supervisory development, modeling, and coaching.

Another result is that the upward control experienced by personnel has had a positive impact. For example, the packaging-machine operators are responding well to the "control" they have over their supervisors. Also, the objective performance data provided by the machine operators have freed the supervisors from "watching" behavior and have allowed them to turn their attention to other important matters.

One of the most important outcomes of PEP has been that everyone knows where they stand relative to critical performance areas. In the packaging-machine operation the operator monitors, records, and feeds forward performance data on four critical control points. The first-line supervisor's job is to properly and consistently consequate both this flow of critical performance data and operator problem solving. This supervisory input constitutes feedback on performance for the machine operators. The process continues all the way up to the top.

According to the training director, "the second-level manager's role is to consequate the supervisory behaviors of data analysis and operator training (measured by operator effectiveness). The plant manager's role is to consequate the second-level manager's systematic, data-based machine operator control and the results improvement." So it goes, level to level, the feedforward of critical performance data and the feedback on performance in the form of contingent reinforcing consequences for performance improvement.

The important aspect of this application of O. B. Mod. to human resource management is its "bottom up," total O. D. approach. Rather than concentrating only on a "top down" approach, from first-line supervisors down to operative employees, all levels are tied into a feedforward/feedback system. This case also stresses the importance of systematically identifying critical performance behavior. Critical operating behavior was identified in a formal performance appraisal conducted by management. The responsibility for identifying this important behavior was not left to the supervisor as in the first case discussed. This case sets an important precedent for using O. B. Mod. as a total human resource management/organization development approach.

THE MILITARY CASE

The three cases presented thus far represent various applications of O. B. Mod. to business organizations. However, with the increasingly important administrative challenges facing nonbusiness organizations in our society, we felt that at least one nonbusiness case should also be included. This case [4] involves the application of O. B. Mod. to a military unit. We could have selected a governmental agency, an educational institution, or a hospital because all of these institutions also seem to be in need of new human resource management approaches, but with the movement toward an all-volunteer force and in light of the classic ways that military units have been managed in the past, a military case seemed a particularly interesting choice for discussion of O. B. Mod. applications.

The case concerns a high-ranking Army officer's attempt to use an O. B. Mod. type approach in running his unit. The officer had completed graduate work in psychology and sociology and saw his promotion to Battalion Commander (BC) as an excellent opportunity to put his ideas (called "Performance Management") to a practical test.

The Performance Management approach in this case is similar to the Reinforcement Management approach used in the airline customer service case. Performance Management is based on the concepts and principles of O. B. Mod. but is not as precise as BCM, the method applied in the first case.

4. The facts of this case were drawn from: Fry, John P., "The Army Officer as Performance Manager," HumRRO Professional Paper 13-74, Western Division, Human Resources Research Organization (HumRRO), Fort Bliss Office, Fort Bliss, Texas. Used with permission. The contents of this case do not necessarily represent the official opinion of the Department of the Army.

The setting for the case

An ever-changing environment in a continuous state of adjustment added to the officer's challenge of a new command. The battalion was frequently diverted from its primary mission to a diversity of secondary support missions. This had the effect of reducing the battalion to a number of small support units rather than allowing it to function as a unified whole. As a result, greater command responsibility fell on the subordinate commanders. Unavoidably, the smaller units could only be as effective as their respective commanders. The task of ensuring the unit commanders' effectiveness was the direct responsibility of the BC.

Besides the problem of subunit effectiveness, the new BC was also faced with a high personnel turnover. Turnover ranged from 35 to 40 percent per quarter and battalion manpower varied from 65 to 90 percent of authorized strength. Field training consistent with the battalion's primary mission was carried out whenever possible.

The BC approached his new assignment with two general objectives in mind. First, he had to develop his subordinates' leadership ability and initiative. Second, he had to strengthen subordinate participation in the overall management of the battalion. To accomplish these goals, the BC decided to rely on a combination strategy of Performance Management, participative management in the form of group problem solving and decision making, and performance counseling. The balance of this case focuses primarily on the BC's experience with the Performance Management portion of his strategy.

Application of Performance Management

Due to the unconventional nature of the BC's approach, the implementation of Performance Management initially proved to be difficult. Patience, tolerance, and self-restraint were required on the part of the BC. Often he had to tolerate inefficient or undesirable performance while patiently waiting for reinforceable responses. Though tempted, the officer resisted using traditional punishment for undesirable performance. Initially, he let his subordinate commanders make some "dumb" decisions so that they could develop their problem-solving and decision-making skills and, in general, get a feel for the responsibilities of command. Early performance counseling sessions were designed to provide the BC with feedback on his own behavior. This "reverse counseling" proved to be frustrating to subordinate commanders. The BC did not know whether he was developing the necessary rapport and trust with his subordinates or just permitting pent-up hostility and frustration to surface. Some were heard to refer to the new BC as "weird" or "crazy" and most of his peers avoided him until they saw the results of his approach.

Eventually, as the contingent reinforcement began to take effect, performance started to improve. Fear and distrust of the new approach were replaced by confidence, trust, and sincere effort on the part of subordinates. Contrary to typical military management, the BC consistently and systematically applied contingent reinforcement for the desirable behavior of his subordinates. The BC had observed that the usual approach had been to tell an individual what to do and then threaten negative consequences for noncompliance. Dedicated to the use of positive consequences, the BC deliberately waited for appropriate behavior which he contingently reinforced. Punishment and threats of punishment were deliberately not used. He felt that his subordinates would punish, and thus control, themselves.

Although the BC did not use punishment, he did emphasize the analysis of mistakes and the reformulation of correct solutions. Once the mistakes were corrected, he would deliberately reinforce the corrected, desirable behavior. Some of the wide variety of reinforcers used included praise in the presence of peers and visitors, and letters of commendation. Special effort was taken to ensure that each reward had a personal touch which was deemed to be meaningful to the individual.

Operating in a reinforcing environment where the subordinate was encouraged to assume responsibility, the subunit commanders began experiencing success and accompanying positive reinforcement from the BC. For example, rather than requiring preinspections prior to the annual inspection, the BC simply instructed his subordinate commanders to do as they thought best. Later, when they passed the annual inspection, he verbally reinforced them with references to their ability and initiative. In general, actions were suggested by the BC rather than flatly demanded and subordinate input into suggested actions was maximized.

Results of Performance Management

Over time the unit subordinate commanders got more and more involved with the Performance Management approach. Evidence of self-control began to emerge. The battalion mess-hall incident is a good example.

Although the BC and all the subordinate commanders knew that the battalion mess hall was in serious need of redecorating, the BC refrained from ordering it done. When the BC was absent on temporary duty, one of his subordinates visited another battalion's mess hall and decided his outfit could do better. He proceeded to stimulate a battalion-wide cooperative effort by drawing up plans, determining relevant costs, and persuading his peers to pool their unit funds. When the BC returned from his temporary duty, the project was in the final stages of completion.

The BC deliberately reinforced this effort by giving recognition to those responsible in the presence of visiting officers. In addition to the mess hall getting a long-overdue facelift, the subordinates involved emerged as models for responsible self-direction, effective leadership, and initiative. The probability that this type of self-directed behavior would occur in other circumstances had increased tremendously.

In retrospect, there was no doubt that it took a while for the BC's Performance Management to take effect. Subordinate commanders, conditioned to expect aggressive, domineering, and punitive behavior from superiors, were initially wary of the new BC who offered so few directives and seemed so easy to satisfy. However, as the contingent reinforcement effect took over, the subordinate commanders learned to accept responsibility and exercise leadership and initiative in the absence of direct orders. Operating in an environment of confidence and trust, the subordinate commanders developed an "I don't want to let him down" approach to their jobs. It also became clear very fast that the BC was not "soft" or "wishy-washy." He expected results—only he used different means to attain them.

Although this case involves less precision in content and evaluation than the others in the chapter, it still makes some important points. The application of O. B. Mod. need not be restricted to routine industrial jobs. The case, besides showing O. B. Mod.'s applications in a nonbusiness setting, indicates that the behavior of high-level managerial personnel is subject to environmental control as is the behavior of routine task personnel.

It also demonstrates that in order to be contingent, a manager must exercise a great deal of self-control. For a time, a contingent manager in a noncontingent environment may appear to be an "oddball," as in this case. The absence of demands and punitive control may be confused with overpermissiveness. Subordinate doubt and suspicion may rise during the transition from traditional negative control to positive control. Only a firm conviction in what the manager feels is right and a total commitment to positive control will see him/her through the transition period. However, the results will be worth the effort.

Analyzing Ethical Issues

9

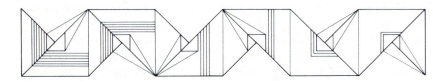

A substantial number of people in our society are genuinely concerned with real or imagined concepts and applications of behavior modification. Time after time we run across people who say, "I'm not sure what behavior modification is all about, but I think it's unethical." This lack of understanding regarding what is involved has been one of the major problems of those critical of behavior modification. At this point in the book, the reader at least should know what O. B. Mod. is all about. This chapter discusses the possible ethical issues involved and analyzes some of the charges and countercharges.

The ethical issues presented in this chapter are drawn from the authors' own experiences in working and talking with people about O. B. Mod. and from the behavioral science, educational, and popular literature on behavior modification in general. We have also attempted to anticipate some of the specific questions the reader may have, especially questions from a management perspective.

THE GENERAL ISSUE OF BEHAVIORAL CONTROL

The whole issue of behavioral control is controversial. One controversy emerges from basic behavioral research with lower animals, specifically the white rat, in highly controlled experiments. Another controversy stems from popular literature. George Orwell's widely read classic *Nineteen Eighty-Four* and the more recent popular novel and critically acclaimed movie *A Clockwork Orange* have contributed to a type of "Big Brother" syndrome associated with behavior modification. Finally, certain basic ethical questions are continually being raised by both laymen and scholars concerning the use of behavioral control techniques.

174

From animal research to human application

Behavior modification is frequently criticized for being too "rat-centered." This criticism is derived from the extensive use of rats as subjects in experimentation. The logic runs as follows: the principles and techniques associated with behaviorism were largely formulated by experimenters using pigeons and rats as subjects; humans are not pigeons or rats; therefore, the principles and techniques of behaviorism will not work with humans.

On the surface, of course, this logic makes a great deal of sense. As Hammer (1971) argued in opposition to the operant conditioning application that Adam and Scott (1971) made to quality control, "Any theory of behavior which effectively equates man with lower animals will . . . be incapable of dealing with the vast majority of human behavior that has no parallels in the subhuman world." Hammer then went on to label the O. B. Mod. type approach as "applied ratamorphism." In a more recent direct criticism of O. B. Mod., Fry (1974), in an article he titled "Operant Conditioning and O. B. Mod.: Of Mice and Men," noted that the behaviorist principle of minimizing the time between behavior and consequence may be important for animals, but irrelevant for humans, since they have developed an ability to remember the past and to expect the future.

Obviously, an O. B. Mod. approach does not assume that humans can or should be equated with rats or pigeons. What the critics fail to realize is that despite the tremendously more complex behavior of humans relative to animals, the controlling mechanisms for both are basically the same. This is much different from saying that rats and humans are the same. While behavior and consequences are obviously different between humans and animals, the fact remains that both animal and human behavior is a function of its consequences. Many people find it uncomfortable to associate animals and humans in any sense, even when it comes to proven laws of behavior. Yet, what would happen to the frequency of a critic's article-writing behavior if it were not reinforced by occasional publication? The law of effect applies to people as much as it does to animals.

The development of modern behaviorism sheds further light on the human–animal controversy. Initially, experimentation in behaviorism greatly depended on animals because they were readily accessible, cheaply maintained, and easily controlled (Skinner, 1969, pp. 100–101). Pigeons were particularly popular because they could emit an easily observable and countable operant response (pecking) at a very high frequency, sometimes exceeding thirty thousand pecks per hour (see: Ferster and Perrott, 1968, p. 280).

All scientific endeavor, including building a science of human behavior, must start off with relatively simple subjects and then move toward the more complex. For example, as Skinner (1969) noted: "Those who study living organisms—say, in genetics, embryology, or medicine—usually start below the human level, and students of behavior have quite naturally followed the same practice" (p. 100). No one seemed to think it was unnatural when the Soviet and American space scientists shot lower animals into orbit around the earth before doing so with humans (concern for cruelty to animals notwithstanding). Good scientific research dictates that early efforts be carried out with relatively simple organisms in highly controlled spaces.

Eventually, the transition was made in behaviorism, both in research and application, from animals to humans. Our history is filled with examples of scientists who turned to new and often radically different solutions to unsolved problems. For example, until Fleming's discovery of penicillin, no one saw the pharmacological value of common mold. Destructive self-mutilation by autistic children, behavioral problems with the mentally retarded, and dysfunctional classroom behavior of special and normal children also required new solutions. Techniques derived from operant conditioning used in the past primarily with animal subjects were successfully applied to these behavioral problems.

Obviously, autistic children, the mentally retarded, and special and normal school children should also not be equated with normal adults working in a modern, complex organization. The point is not that they are the same but that animal, mentally retarded, child, and normal adult behavior is controlled by consequences. The nature of the behavior and the consequences may be drastically different but the mechanism for controlling the behavior remains the same. The applications of O. B. Mod. reported in the last chapter indicate that the transition from lower animals, to immature human behavior, to human resource management can be made.

The Big Brother syndrome

Popular literature sometimes categorizes behavior modification as some sort of tyrannical tool designed for the destruction of democracy and human rights. This view can be labeled the "Big Brother" syndrome. It is largely based on misinformation or a misunderstanding of what is involved in the positive as well as negative control of behavior.

Because of Orwell's (1949) frightening depiction of the future in his book *Nineteen Eighty-Four,* the term behavior modification often conjures up visions of his character Winston Smith being unmercifully truncheoned and electrocuted in the Ministry of Love. Others think of the book and movie version of *A Clockwork Orange* (Burgess, 1963) in which the character Alex, an overly aggressive and sexually promiscuous teenager, is turned into a "nice" boy with drugs and tortuous aversive conditioning.

While popular writing and movies of this type make for exciting entertainment, the behavioral control they describe have nothing in common with an O. B. Mod. approach to human resource management. First of all, the techniques referred to by popular novelists and screenwriters involve aversion therapy. These techniques involve two basic strategies, punishment and classical aversive conditioning (Sherman, 1973).

For example, Orwell's Winston Smith was aversively conditioned with punishment while Burgess' Alex was aversively conditioned through classical conditioning. When Smith answered "No" to the question, "Do you love Big Brother," he was struck on the tip of the elbow and other sensitive spots with a truncheon. Obviously, the "No" responses diminished in frequency. Eventually, Smith admitted that he really did love the symbolic dictator, Big Brother. Loving Big Brother was an avoidance response—verbal allegiance to Big Brother enabled Smith to avoid further cruel physical torture. Obviously, this type of inhuman treatment is inexcusable in a civilized society.

In *A Clockwork Orange*, Alex's fate was somewhat different. After being injected with a nausea-inducing drug, he was strapped into a seat with his eyelids propped open and forced to watch films of bloody beatings, war atrocities, and hard-core pornography. Through simple classical conditioning, Alex learned to associate violence and sex with nausea. After conditioning Alex, his trainers proudly displayed their "new Alex" who became nauseous at mere references to violence or at the sight of a nude female. The ethics of such methods of treating problem behavior is being questioned, as it certainly should be.

Unfortunately for the legitimate approaches to constructive behavior control, however, the Orwells and Burgesses have done more than make their literary point—they have created a generalized fear of anything that remotely suggests behavioral control. This, coupled with the fact that aversive conditioning is sometimes used in behavior therapy, has led to a great deal of confusion surrounding behavior modification in general. It should be remembered that O. B. Mod. is *not* behavior therapy; rather, it is an outgrowth of applied behavior analysis. O. B. Mod. is based mainly on positive rather than negative control and makes no use of aversive conditioning. Hopefully, the preceding chapters have eradicated the Big Brother syndrome surrounding behavior modification.

The ethics of control

Another ethical issue is the whole question of *control* per se. For many the word "control" connotes a threat to freedom. Since freedom is such an important value in our society, the logic goes, any form of control must be bad.

The fact remains that behavioral control, in one form or another, has always been, continues to be, and will certainly remain with us. Popular management terms such as discipline, leadership, direction, persuasion, motivation, and influence are often directly and at least indirectly concerned with behavioral control. Apparently, behavioral control is more acceptable to people when carried out in the name of discipline or leadership. McGinnies and Ferster (1971) succinctly outline the ethical dilemma associated with behavioral control as follows:

> "Social situations have long been manipulated both practically and deliberately. Ever since Machiavelli, and perhaps before, there has been a fear of the control and manipulation of one person's behavior for the benefit of another. With the development of a laboratory science of social psychology, where social phenomena are developed in prototype form and actually shaped and manipulated, a technology is becoming available to influence social situations rationally and self-consciously. This raises questions concerning the ethics of such manipulation" (p. 432).

Skinner (1953) commented that, "We all control, and we are all controlled" (p. 438). But to say that behavioral control is ethical simply because everyone does it all the time is not sufficient. Yet, recognizing that we are all behavior modifiers, constantly attempting to change the behavior of those around us by manipulating antecedents and consequences, we have a point of departure for an ethical analysis.

When we smile, nod approval, frown, make a critical remark, or pretend not to notice someone to whom we choose not to talk, we are experiencing normal, daily social interaction. Each of these social gestures has the effect or is at least intended to have the effect of controlling the behavior of others. Admittedly, such social activity often occurs with little or no formal understanding of the underlying learning theory and principles. However, such activity raises the interesting analytical question of whether the unwitting use of behavior modification is ethical while the purposefuly, systematic use of the same techniques is unethical.

The crux of the ethical issue surrounding behavioral control in O. B. Mod. seems to lie in indentifying the true beneficiary of the control. The above quotation by McGinnies and Ferster mentions the manipulation of one person's behavior for the *benefit of another*. The control of someone else's behavior for purely selfish reasons is, of course, of questionable ethics. In Skinner's classic debate with the noted humanist Carl Rogers, Skinner made the point that, "Man's natural inclination to revolt against selfish control has been exploited to good purpose in what we call the philosophy and literature of democracy" (Rogers and Skinner, 1956). Viewed from the context of achieving mutually beneficial management objectives through an O. B. Mod. approach, the question of ethics should not be a problem for anyone choosing to live in a society where managerial effectiveness is a desirable goal.

Undoubtedly, behavior modification in general and O. B. Mod. in particular can, like any other technology or scientific approach, be misused. There is always the danger that social behavioral control techniques will be misused for the pursuit of selfish ends. Accompanying the benefits of any scientific advance is the professional responsibility for ensuring appropriate application. From an ethical standpoint, any scientifically based technique is neutral until put into use. The point is that behavior modification and O. B. Mod. cannot justly be labeled unethical per se, but their misuse can become unethical.

Individual freedom and dignity

Defining freedom and dignity is like defining hot and cold or high and low. There is always the question, "relative to what?" For example, a prison inmate who has earned trustee privileges enjoys more freedom than the prisoner who has been restricted to a maximum-security cell. Yet, we normally think of a prison inmate as having lost freedom. The terms freedom and dignity are used deliberately in this discussion because much of the controversy surrounding behavior modification is derived from Skinner's book, *Beyond Freedom and Dignity* (Skinner, 1971).

Skinner, while extrapolating his empirically derived behaviorist principles to our culture in the name of increasing human freedom and dignity, has been interpreted by his critics as doing exactly the opposite, i.e., restricting freedom and compromising human dignity. It is not our purpose to critically analyze or defend Skinner's book, but rather to analyze the ethical implications of O. B. Mod., since much of the criticism directed against Skinner is generalized to O. B. Mod.

Erick Fromm (1941, p. 17) opened his classic book *Escape From Freedom* by noting that modern European and American history has centered around man's continual efforts to gain freedom from oppressive spiritual, political, and economic control. Particularly in American society, freedom is a word that stimulates discussion and, when threatened, cues emotional reaction. While many people view any form of behavioral control as a threat to freedom, we would like to suggest that behavior modification which strives to systematically replace negative control with positive control, as does O. B. Mod., may actually enhance human freedom. According to Skinner (Hall, 1972): ". . . The traditional struggle for freedom has been a matter of freeing people from what we call aversive control. . . . Unfortunately, we have come to the conclusion that all control is wrong, that it is something we should escape from." However, behavioral control is present regardless of intent. Conceivably, an O. B. Mod. approach, which strives for positive control in a positively reinforcing environment, could offer a greater measure of freedom and dignity than most contemporary work settings where the work is dull, working conditions are poor, and negative control is always present.

Controlling the controllers

Critics of Skinner's suggestion that we modify our culture with behavior technology are concerned with who will retain the *final* power to decide what behavior is strengthened and what behavior is weakened. In other words, who will control the controllers?

On an organizational level, at least from a management perspective, the problem of controlling the controllers is already settled because an individual organization always operates within a larger sphere of control. For example, top management is responsible to the board of directors in a corporation and is controlled by organizational consequences such as survival, growth, share of the market, and rate of return on investment. In addition, direct and indirect control comes from stockholders, unions, customers, suppliers, government, and general social, economic, and technological conditions. In private businesses, managers unable to meet the required levels of performance criteria, given the environmental constraints, can be replaced. The same is basically true of public, hospital, and educational administrators.

Control carries all the way down the organization. The managerial controllers of organizational behavior are themselves subject to many controlling consequences. In a sense, a hierarchy of consequences leads to a hierarchy of control. The improved performance of an employee on the operative level as a result of systematic shaping with positive reinforcement by a manager contributes to organizational success, which ultimately reinforces top management through favorable organizational consequences.

Recent unique behavior modification applications in education (Gray et al., 1974) suggest a pragmatic solution to controlling the controllers. In one case troublesome students were instructed in the basics of differential positive reinforcement (selecting and positively reinforcing only certain responses). For experimental control purposes, this procedure was carried out without the teacher's knowledge. Needless to say, teachers who were used to handling "incorrigible" students showed great surprise when these students started positively reinforcing them with compliments and other positive reinforcers for helpful and understanding treatment. By "turning the behavioral tables," the troublemakers began to control the controllers and simultaneously change their own behavior. As a result of this unique approach, teacher effectiveness improved and the troublesome students became "good" behavior models rather than "bad" behavior models in the eyes of their teachers.

O. B. Mod. and its accompanying positive reinforcement, shaping, modeling, and BCM techniques are all two-way streets. Just as communication is supposed to flow up and down the organizational ladder, O. B. Mod. can do the same. There is no reason why *countercontrol* cannot be effectively used in today's organizations. For example, subordinates can change the behavior of a particularly cranky boss into friendly, supportive behavior by compliments, rapid and efficient compliance to directions, and other relevant forms of social reinforcement *contingent* upon desirable supervisory behavior. Ideally, all organizational members, superiors and subordinates alike, can learn to use O. B. Mod. to create an environment of mutual positive reinforcement for goal attainment.

THE ROLE OF O. B. MOD.
IN HUMAN RESOURCE MANAGEMENT

Organizations are formed to accomplish objectives that individuals cannot accomplish by themselves. Practical experience over the years and the contingency theory of management (Luthans, 1973b) teach us that there is no one best way to organize human and physical resources for optimum goal attainment. For example, the classic bureaucratic form of organization may be appropriate for a well-established government department working in a stable environment, but inappropriate for a fast-paced, high-technology firm operating in a volatile environment. Because of this situational nature, many types of organizations have emerged. Despite the diversity of organization designs, however, some consistent behavioral problems come up whenever group endeavor is involved. There is always the problem of accomplishing objectives *through* other people.

In answer to this problem, much has been written, said, and carried out in the name of communication, motivation, and leadership. These generally represent internal approaches rather than the results-oriented, external approach taken by O. B. Mod. In O. B. Mod., environmental contingencies are systematically managed to bring about desired organizational behavior changes in the same manner that other organizational factors are typically managed. Management in general is pragmatic; O. B. Mod. is also pragmatic. In terms of a management perspective and goals, O. B. Mod. seems to be a much more appropriate approach than an internally oriented human relations approach.

Undoubtedly, some management theorists and practitioners may feel that O. B. Mod. is inappropriate for modern human resource management. Depending upon their specific interpretation, they may say that O. B. Mod. is not practical or not ethical, or both.

Those who mistakenly see O. B. Mod. as impractical and little more than a "string-pulling" process point out that there are simply too many strings to pull in a complex organizational setting. They view organizations as complex social systems in which the essentially one-to-one behavior modification strategies can only hope to play a minor role. Fry's observation (1974) is typical of this argument. ". . . We can say that individuals will respond in ways that are rewarded, but management is only one of many sources or rewards." Wiard (1972) also cites the practical difficulties and expense of applying behavior technology to large groups of employees in a modern organization.

We answer this argument by returning to the behaviorist's basic premise—behavior is a function of its conseqences. This law holds regardless of the simplicity or complexity of the surrounding environment. The fact that an environment happens to be a complex modern organization does not justify disregarding the rules for predicting and controlling behavior. There is no question that it is easier to manage environmental contingencies and thus control behaviors in relatively uncomplicated and well-controlled environments, but this reality should not automatically preclude an O. B. Mod. approach in more complex settings. This is a challenge rather than an impossibility. Although the theoretical base of O. B. Mod. is well developed, we recognize that much remains to be done in terms of research and practical application. Eventually, we hope that innovative advances for rapidly and efficiently identifying potential reinforcers, such as self-reporting instruments, will increase the practical applicability of O. B. Mod. As Nord states (1969):

> ". . . If, as the operant approach maintains, the conditioning process describes the acquisition and maintenance of behavior, the same principles can be applied to any social organization. The problem of application becomes merely that of engineering. The gains may well be limited only by an administrator's ingenuity and resources."

Not only does O. B. Mod. seem to have a definite role in human resource management, it may very well turn out to be the only practical way of coping with yet unsolved organizational behavior problems and strengthening and maintaining behavior which is consistent with the efficient and prompt attainment of organizational goals. As Edward Feeney (Where Skinner's Theories Work, 1972) pointed out in reporting Emery Air Freight's success with a systematic program of feedback on performance and positive reinforcement: "We do what works . . . what gets a payoff. For us, this behavioral approach got results." The results of the specific applications of O. B. Mod. reported in the last chapter also seem to indicate that the approach works.

O. B. MOD: MANAGEMENT OR MANIPULATION?

There are numerous definitions of management and human resource management. However, the differences in definitions are more semantical than real. Basically, human resource management involves the accomplishment of organizational objectives through people. The word "through" has traditionally been interpreted in terms of communication, motivation, and leadership. This motivational approach is felt not to involve the manipulation of people and therefore, it follows, a traditional motivational approach to human resource management is considered completely ethical.

Behavior modification and O. B. Mod. have been criticized as being manipulative and therefore unethical. We feel that O. B. Mod. is an exacting scientific approach that is no more or less manipulative than any other human resource management approach. As practitioner E. Daniel Grady, a pioneer in applying behaviorism to management, stated: "There is no more manipulation involved in this than there is in the management task of directing people where to go and what to do" (Where Skinner's Theories Work, 1972).

If manipulation does apply to O. B. Mod. any more than to any other approach, it is in the manipulation of the environment rather than the individual. Antecedents and consequences are certainly manipulated in O. B. Mod., but the individual self-adjusts to these environmental contingencies. The idiosyncratic nature of positive and negative reinforcers and punishers also should help dispel the notion that O. B. Mod. is manipulating people. The manager using O. B. Mod. cannot dictate what is reinforcing to an organizational participant.

The stigmatizing of manipulation can be traced as far back as Machiavelli's "end justifies the means" thesis. Skinner (1953) himself is highly critical of a Machiavellian approach. "Machiavelli's pre-scientific insight into human behavior was dedicated to preserving the power of a governmental agency" (p. 437). In other words, a Machiavellian type of manipulative control was selfish control. However, what would be the reaction to Machiavelli's tactics within the context of securing peace, collecting money for charity, or stimulating church attendance? In other words, it seems likely that more altruistic *ends* would take the unethical sting out of Machiavellian *means*.

The discussion of Machiavelli is relevant to the question of manipulation in behavioral control. The issue of manipulation versus no manipulation can be broadened to: manipulation for what purpose? Similarly, we might ask: behavioral control for what purpose? In a human resource management context, if the behavioral problem is great enough or the target behavior desirable enough, why not apply behavioral techniques (e.g., BCM) with demonstrated effectiveness and limited undesirable side effects?

The more traditional human resource management approaches probably escaped the label of manipulation because of their inherent vagueness; the well-known theories of communication, motivation, and leadership are not scientifically precise. In contrast, the precise and systematic nature of an O. B. Mod. approach lends itself to the charge of manipulation. As we see it, the real issue is not manipulation versus management, but rather precision versus imprecision.

A SPECIFIC ISSUE: MEASURING ON-THE-JOB BEHAVIOR

As the reader will recall, the second step of BCM is to measure the performance-related behavior that was identified in the first step. This baseline measure is vital to the subsequent steps of analysis, intervention, and evaluation. Continual measurement is taken even after intervention, in order to determine if the intervention strategy is having its intended effect. This measurement, a vital aspect of any scientific endeavor, plays an important role in O. B. Mod. The question becomes: is it ethical to observe and record organizational behavior without the person's knowledge?

As Chapter 4 pointed out, there should never be a veil of secrecy surrounding O. B. Mod. The manager should be aboveboard and fully describe what he/she is doing. On the other hand, awareness of being measured can in some cases affect the behavioral data being gathered. As a result, the manager attempting to obtain baseline data is often caught in a dilemma. As Brandt (1972) has pointed out:

"Merely close observation of someone, with or without the use of gadgetry, and recording his behavior inconspicuously, when such observation or recording is not expected, can certainly be viewed as an invasion of privacy and perhaps as deceitful also" (p. 40).

Two realities seem relevant to this ethical issue. First, observation and measurement of behavior in a work context is nothing new. In spite of the formal protection of employees' rights afforded by government legislation and collective bargaining agreements, a great deal of employee behavior in today's organizations is under very close scrutiny. This situation is largely the result of industrial engineering procedures that have timed, paced, recorded, charted, and analyzed the minute details of human work behavior in the name of increasing productive efficiency. As a result, over the last fifty years, industrial workers in particular have become remarkably tolerant of (or, perhaps, immune to) managerial scrutiny. For many managers using an O. B. Mod. approach, only the systematic recording of key performance-related behavioral events will be a new factor in the observation of workers. Subjective observation of nonperformance behavior will be replaced by objective observation and measurement of behavior that is critical to performance improvement.

A second reality is the public outcry over invasions of privacy through tape-recording and the indiscriminate use of personal information stored in computer data banks. Government legislation is being proposed to strictly interpret what constitutes an invasion of individual privacy. Some of this legislation will be relevant to employees, some of it will not.

Regardless of the outcome of such legislative efforts, the public debate over an individual's right to privacy will no doubt influence the ethical implications of behavioral measurement. In the final analysis, the question of how observation and measurement in O. B. Mod. can best be accomplished must be answered by each professional manager. Obviously, a manager should not surreptitiously peer from behind filing cabinets or machines, measuring subordinates' behavior. A manager can collect valid behavioral data with an employee's complete awareness, using historical records, various forms of response sampling, key performance results, contingency contracting, and self-observation methods.

In addition, there are some cases where observing and measuring behavior without the employee's knowledge may be justifiable if the purpose is the attainment of both organizational goals and the employee's personal objectives. In other words, as in the other ethical issues discussed, justification rests on the ultimate beneficiary—the individual employee.

Preconditions for Future Development

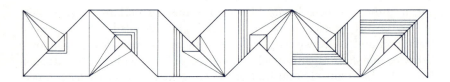

This book is the first to comprehensively integrate operant learning theory and the principles of behavior modification with the management field of organizational behavior. A conceptual framework and method of human resource management which we call O. B. Mod. is the result of this eclectic approach. In this last chapter, we draw some conclusions about what the future holds for O. B. Mod. However, rather than assuming the role of prophesier, we present and analyze some of the preconditions necessary for O. B. Mod. to realize its full potential. While we certainly do not feel that O. B. Mod. is a panacea, we do believe that it provides a viable alternative to traditional approaches and can lead to more effective management of people in today's organizations.

ACADEMIC PRECONDITIONS

Like any new and developing academic discipline, the field of management is very fragmented. Hopefully, this book has provided a sound conceptual framework for an operant-based approach to organizational behavior. No attempt has been made to unify the entire field of management. For its further development, however, O. B. Mod. must be able to close an existing language gap, make further contributions to the thoretical base, and most important, build a body of relevant, research-based empirical knowledge.

186

Closing the language gap

As the short word test in Chapter 1 illustrated, a major problem facing O. B. Mod. is related to language. While behaviorists speak in terms of behavioral events, response frequencies, contingencies and reinforcers, most of today's management theorists and practitioners speak in terms of attitudes, job performance and satisfaction, and motives. The former concentrate on environmental control while the latter continue to search for inner causes.

While we believe that an operant approach leads to better prediction and control of behavior, we realize that both groups are concerned with the same phenomena—human organizational behavior—and we recognize that both approaches have merit. However, the search for improved prediction and control of organizational behavior should not be impeded by language differences. In order for O. B. Mod. to develop properly, the technical language associated with it must be better understood, used, and in some cases even replace some of the vague, but popular, terms used by the other behavioral approaches to management. The human-relations term of "morale," for example, has generally been replaced by the more precise term of "job satisfaction." In the same manner, the distinctions between reward and reinforcer and between negative reinforcement and punishment should be understood and widely used. Even more important, O. B. Mod. terms such as reinforcement and contingency should become as much a part of the working language of management scholars and practitioners as terms like attitudes, motives, and feelings.

Continued development of a theoretical base

Ideally, the progress of a scientifically based endeavor such as human resource management develops in a three-stage sequence: (1) theory, (2) research, and (3) practical application. While each of these three stages exists in any legitimate academic discipline, they may have occurred simultaneously, or in mixed order. On occasion, the sequence may actually be reversed, such as when practical experience inspires academic theorizing and research. For example, the practice of Management by Objectives (MBO) predated precise theory and research. In the case of MBO, theory and research led to the future development and more effective dissemination of an existing technique. On other occasions the impetus for development has come from theory. For example, the theoretical basis of human asset accounting has been around for years without any significant movement toward research and practical application.

The point of these illustrations is that regardless of whether theory precedes or follows some sort of practical application, it gives form, consistency, and direction to an area of study. Although in its present form O. B. Mod. has a sound theoretical base, it can still benefit from the structural influence of further theoretical formulation.

Theoretical formulation of any academic endeavor is but an iterative process of successive contributions and modifications. Additional contributions to the theoretical base of O. B. Mod. will hopefully occur in the future and will, of course, go hand in hand with future research and practical application.

Building a body of empirical knowledge

As the theoretical development of O. B. Mod. proceeds, rigorous laboratory and especially field research must determine which parts of the theory are tenable and which must be reformulated. Some theoretical questions raised in this book require more definite answers derived from sound research. For example: in what specific situations is BCM most appropriate; can self-report instruments really make valid determinations of positive reinforcers? Hopefully, this book will stimulate others to put some of the ideas and tentative answers to the test of rigorous, empirical field research. Only through such a research effort will O. B. Mod. become a truly recognized scientific pursuit.

ORGANIZATIONAL PRECONDITIONS

Along with some academic preconditions which are necessary for the future development of O. B. Mod., there are also some more direct organizational/managerial preconditions. These deal primarily with the more effective application of O. B. Mod. to the practice of human resource management. Two practical problems, already mentioned, are the preoccupation of most managers with an internal explanation of organizational behavior, and the use of negative control on the job.

Managerial attention must be shifted to observable behavior rather than dwelling only on vague internal causes. Negative control must be seen as it really is—an overused, unpredictable, and rather inefficient approach to behavioral control. A concerted effort must be made to create an organizational climate of positive control in which negative consequences are used only as a last resort with extremely undesirable or unsafe behavior. In addition, currently popular and workable behavioral techniques such as job enrichment (JE) and MBO should be integrated with O. B. Mod. to increase the probability of desirable performance-related organizational behavior. A final precondition is the integration of O. B. Mod. with comprehensive organization-wide change strategies which currently fall under the heading of organization development (O.D.)

The transition from internal to external

The distinction between an internal and an external perspective to organizational behavior was the subject of the first chapter. References to hypothetical inner states such as needs, drives, attitudes, and motives are presently the rule rather than the exception in human resource management literature and in practice. Ironically, while managers struggle to control organizational behavior with environmental consequences on a daily basis, management students and management development trainees receive little, if any, exposure to operant learning theory and to proven, empirically based behavior principles dealing with observable behavior and consequences.

Switching from an internal to external perspective is not an attempt to completely disregard the hypothetical *causes* of behavior. Rather, the point is to use workable behavioral *control* techniques for more effective human resource management while the search for causes continues. A comprehensive *combination* of cause and control is a desirable goal for better understanding of human resource management, but for pragmatic prediction and control of organizational behavior, the practitioner should turn more to the concepts and principles embodied in O. B. Mod. However, an external view of behavior is a necessary precondition for the application of O. B. Mod. Unless practitioners, scholars, and students of management recognize the value of dealing with observable organizational behavior, O. B. Mod. will probably not become a viable approach.

A sprinkling of such behaviorist terms as behavioral event, positive reinforcer, contingency, negative reinforcement, and extinction in the practicing manager's vocabulary is not enough. Much more is involved in the transition from internal to external; adoption of an external perspective involves actual behavior observation and measurement, contingency identification and analysis, well-planned intervention strategies, and continual evaluation. In this way the transition from internal to external can contribute to future O. B. Mod. development.

Developing a climate of positive control

This book has repeatedly emphasized that one of the major benefits of an O. B. Mod. approach is the shift from negative to positive control of organizational behavior. Negative control is currently much overused while positive control, which is more compatible with desirable social values and can effectively strengthen and maintain organizational behavior for long-run goal attainment, is little used. Unfortunately, creating a climate of positive control in organizations, although necessary for the future development of O. B. Mod., is not an easy task.

First of all, the term "climate" and the more specific variant, "organizational climate," must be more precisely defined. In everyday use, climate suggests something to do with the weather; it is environmental or ecological. For example, during the cold winter months many people travel south to enjoy the more favorable climate. Climate in this context refers to the daily presence of warm sunshine and cool breezes.

In recent years, the term climate has also been the subject of steadily growing interest to those who study organizations. Psychological climate is generally equated with organizational climate. Grouped under the heading of organizational climate are such characteristics as prevailing sentiments, beliefs, attitudes, or behavior. Consequently, some organizational climates have been characterized as autocratic or supportive.

After pointing out the difficulties associated with defining organizational climate, Tagiuri (1968) suggested the following definition: "Organizational climate is a relatively enduring quality of the internal environment of an organization that (a) is experienced by its members, (b) influences their behavior, and (c) can be described in terms of the values of a particular set of characteristics (or attributes) of the organization" (p. 27). By using this definition as a starting point, we can move toward what is meant by a climate of positive control.

If the prevailing use of positive consequences increases the probability that desirable performance-related behavior will be emitted by a majority of organizational participants, then a climate of positive control exists. Just as sunshine prevails in a favorable geographical climate, contingencies with positively reinforcing consequences prevail in a climate of positive control. Employees working in a positive climate actively perform in order to receive desired positive consequences rather than passively perform to avoid or escape threatened or actual undesirable consequences. This difference is important to the development of O. B. Mod. Defining a climate of positive control is one thing, but actually creating a positive control organization climate is quite another.

Despite the emphasis given to human relations and humanistic approaches, most contemporary organizations are characterized by a negatively controlled organization climate. Negative control may not be an organization's stated policy, but it is a reality in daily organizational behavior: "Come to work on time or get fired"; "Contribute ideas at the department meeting or catch hell from the boss"; "There is going to be some trouble around here if quality doesn't improve this week."

Most managers rely on these types of negative consequences or at least the threat of negative consequences to manage their people. This situation is compounded by the fact that negative consequences become equated with those who control them, thus reducing the ability of that individual to effectively use positive consequences. However, self-evaluation of interpersonal dealings, management development, supervisory training, and the presence of positive control models throughout the organization can overcome the present dependence on negative control.

As the reliance on negative control fades, positive control must be brought in to fill the void. As was brought out in the military case in Chapter 8, the transition from negative to positive takes time and is relatively difficult to accomplish. Patience, perseverance, and a dedication to positive control are required in the transition period. Like any other change strategy, the greater the number of organizational members who are involved with and committed to the shift to positive control, the faster and smoother will be the transition.

Once the organizational climate becomes positively reinforcing, positive consequences will beget more positive consequences. Until this organizational climate is achieved, the transition from negative to positive control will necessarily be a slow, individual-by-individual process. Managers must learn to resist the tempting short-run reinforcement associated with the use of negative control in favor of the more powerful reinforcement associated with the use of positive control. Working with someone to achieve mutually beneficial organizational objectives is much more reinforcing in the long run than resorting to threats and coercion to stimulate a short-lived burst of productive activity.

In terms of both job performance and satisfaction, today's organizations cannot afford to put off the move toward a climate of positive control. In a positive climate attention shifts from what is wrong with performance to what is *right* with performance. Once the desirable behavior of an individual is identified, the manager can begin systematic shaping with positive consequences. Opportunities for negative control are passed up in favor of opportunities to provide feedback on performance, give time off, favorably schedule tasks, praise, recognize, promote, and grant additional responsibility. Such a positive organizational climate is a precondition for the effective future development of O. B. Mod.

Integrating O. B. Mod. with other modern behavioral techniques

For years, motivational techniques proposed in the management literature centered around the lower level needs of Maslow's hierarchy.

According to Luthans (1973a) "Pay, security, hours, fringe benefits, and conditions were the rewards deemed necessary to motivate workers and managers" (p. 511). However, as behavioral science began to play a greater role in the behavioral approach to management, increased emphasis was placed on higher level needs such as affiliation, self-esteem, and self-actualization. Behavioral techniques were developed so that the once-ignored higher level needs could be brought into play to motivate performance and increase job satisfaction. Today, the two most popular among these techniques are job enrichment (JE) and management by objectives (MBO).

Both JE and MBO are more internal in nature than external. However, despite this fact, O. B. Mod. can contribute to their increased effectiveness. In particular, a system of programmed positive consequences seems appropriate to both JE and MBO.

O. B. Mod. and JE • JE is a direct outgrowth of Herzberg's (1959; 1968) motivation/hygiene or two-factor theory of motivation. Herzberg, using a critical-incident research design, found that the hygiene factors stem from the work environment or job *context*. They include supervision, pay, company policy and administration, interpersonal relations, working conditions, and fringe benefits. According to Herzberg's theory, these hygiene factors help prevent job dissatisfaction, but they do not lead to job satisfaction. Factors relating to job *content,* which he labeled motivators, included the opportunity for achievement, recognition, responsibility, and interesting work. It was these motivators which led to job satisfaction.

In JE, the assumption is that greater job satisfaction leads to better performance. Thus, by incorporating the motivators into the job design, the reasoning goes, there will be greater satisfaction and in turn better performance. According to Schappe (1974), motivation through JE ". . . involves modifying job content so that the individual has increased responsibility and autonomy, a wider variety of tasks and more opportunities for achievement and recognition in his work. In effect the work itself becomes a source of motivation for the individual."

As Chapter 1 indicated, there are some severe critics of Herzberg's two-factory theory and of the research design he used in formulating the theory. There is also evidence that JE is not being used as much as is commonly thought and that practitioners are experiencing some difficulties with it (see: Luthans and Reif, 1974; Reif and Luthans, 1972). However, if JE is contingently applied under the appropriate conditions (Luthans and Knod, 1974), it can be an effective behavioral technique for stimulating or motivating human performance. Integrating JE with O. B. Mod. can further improve JE's effectiveness and should be mutually beneficial for both JE and O. B. Mod.

Dull, tedious jobs which fail to promote job satisfaction or which, in O. B. Mod. terms, are marked by low frequency responding may be contingently enriched. For example, a routine task worker who finds Herzberg's motivators reinforcing could have his/her job enriched by integrating the motivators contingent upon improved performance. A formal contingency contract could be used to ensure that the job holder knows exactly what is expected and what the programmed consequences in the form of an enriched job will be. Without this systematic, contingent approach to the implementation of JE, noncontingent enrichment of an individual's job might actually reinforce poor or inefficient performance. Practicing managers should be constantly aware of all of the contingencies they establish both deliberately and accidentally. If an enriched job is a positive consequence for an individual employee, then it should be implemented contingent upon improved performance.

Another way to include O. B. Mod. concepts in JE would be to permit the employee, contingent upon improved performance, to participate in devising ways to enrich his/her job. A third possibility would be to contingently transfer an employee from a critical job that must be done but cannot be effectively enriched to an enriched job. For example, an employee who performs satisfactorily on a undesirable routine job on the first two days of the week or the first week or two of the month could then earn the opportunity to work on a desirable enriched job for the balance of the week or month. This, of course, is the application of the Premack Principle discussed in Chapter 5. Equitability could be achieved by placing everyone in the work group under the same contingency contract. This last approach would seem appropriate for getting a good job done on the unenrichable but very necessary jobs found in nearly every work situation.

Although the respective theoretical bases and terminologies of JE and O. B. Mod. are somewhat different and their proponents take essentially opposite approaches to behavioral control, many possibilities seem to exist for combining the best of both techniques to improve job performance and increase job satisfaction. Nord (1969) noted the similarities between the two approaches as follows: ". . . both job enrichment and job enlargement are apt to lead to what would generally be called greater motivation or what we will call higher rates of desired behavior." The direct result of combining JE and O. B. Mod. is that jobs are enriched as part of a system of programmed positive consequences for improved performance.

O. B. Mod. and MBO • MBO is probably the most widely recognized and used modern management technique. Within the last fifteen years, practically all organizations of any size have implemented MBO to various degrees. The basic MBO format presently comes in a variety of hybrid forms and is sometimes given different labels; however, it generally involves setting objectives and appraising by results. The overriding assumption is that mutual participation between subordinates and superiors in the determination of objectives leads to commitment which in turn leads to improved performance. Appraising by results is an effective control technique because it leads to self-control, which in turn also leads to improved performance.

Depending on the size of an organization, an MBO approach may take four or five years to become an effective management system. At various stages MBO may simply amount to a goal-setting process to improve short and long-range planning or an employee appraisal technique. When fully developed, MBO is supposed to provide a systematic method of giving feedback on specific and overall performance and matching rewards with contributions.

Unfortunately, research on MBO programs in actual use has uncovered evidence that this is not always the case. For example, Raia's (1965; 1966) two-part field study of an MBO program uncovered some interesting facts. Results of the first study made eighteen months after implementation indicated that the MBO philosophy, more than the MBO procedures themselves, had made management more aware of goals, improved interdepartmental communication and understanding, and developed a future orientation in management. However, a follow-up study one year later uncovered some growing disenchantment with MBO. Among the complaints was the feeling that the program had done little to provide adequate incentives for active participation in MBO or for improved performance. In other words, in terms of O. B. Mod., what was missing was a systematic program of positive consequences for making MBO work and for achieving stated objectives. This is an area where MBO and O. B. Mod. can be combined to mutually benefit one another.

Between the process of objective setting (the beginning) and appraisal by results (the end) in MBO, the participant should experience positive consequences for approximating objectives. Figure 10–1 demonstrates how MBO can be integrated with O. B. Mod. The model shows that between each major step in the MBO process, some aspect of O. B. Mod. can be introduced to ensure a closer tie (more precisely a contingent tie) between performance and rewards. Initially, contingency contracting can accompany the setting of objectives. In the language of the expectancy theories of motivation (Vroom, 1964), such contingency contracting can facilitate instrumentality (the performance–reward connection.) Once the objectives have been made operational in the form of specific action plans, shaping and modeling can be brought into MBO to help increase the probability of objective-approximating behavior. Continuous or high-frequency intermittent schedules of reinforcement, and frequent and

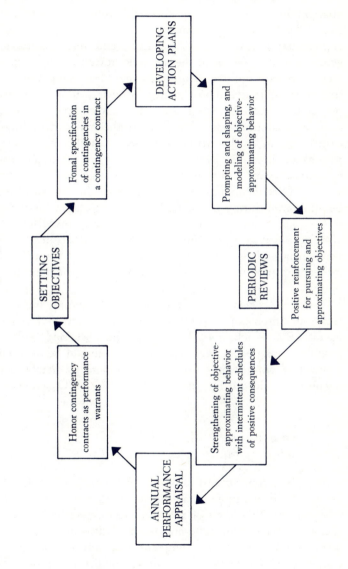

FIGURE 10–1.   Integrating O. B. Mod. with MBO.

perhaps even formally structured feedback on early results should be used at the beginning of the MBO cycle.

Planned periodic review sessions, carried out at least every quarter but more frequently if possible, offer excellent opportunities for formal feedback on performance, contingent positive reinforcement for approximating agreed-upon objectives, and reaffirmation of the contingency contract. Between the periodic review cycles appropriate schedules of potent positive reinforcers should be employed to sustain and strengthen objective-approximating behavior. Finally, as the formal appraisal by results is taking place, the agreed-upon consequences in the contracted contingencies should be forthcoming. Recycling through successive rounds of the MBO cycle begins at this point. On the basis of past experience, new objectives can be more accurately formulated and new contingency contracts can be more realistically determined.

The importance of behavior-controlling consequences should not be minimized during the mutual goal-setting stage, the intervening period, the periodic appraisals, or the annual appraisal in MBO. The attainment of objectives is largely a function of their consequences. Accordingly, key performance-related behavioral events must be identified in the MBO process and positive consequences made contingent upon their accomplishment.

In A→B→C terms, the mutual goal-setting process (A) will increase the probability of the appearance of key performance-related behavior (B), which must be shaped and sustained with a program of positive consequences (C). The net effect should be more effective attainment of organizational objectives and a more predictable and reinforcing organization climate for participants in the MBO system.

Integrating O. B. Mod.
with organization development

In recent years organization development (O. D.) has received a great deal of attention in management literature and in the practice of management. Like most of the other techniques and approaches to management, O. D. means different things to different people. To some, O. D. involves a systematic and comprehensive way of coping with the accelerating rate of change and resulting conflict faced by today's organizations. Others view O. D. as an extension of sensitivity training which attempts to stimulate organizational renewal and/or promote individual knowledge and awareness of self and others. Still others take a broader perspective and equate O. D. with the total field of management. French and Bell's definition of O. D. (1973) represents this broad perspective:

". . . Organization development is a long-range effort to improve an organization's problem-solving and renewal processes, particularly through a more effective and collaborative management of organization culture—with special emphasis on the culture of formal work teams—with the assistance of a change agent, or catalyst, and the use of the theory and technology of applied behavioral science, including action research" (p. 15).

Considering the sweeping scope of a broad approach to O. D., the almost total absence of references to Skinner, behavior modification, or behavioral contingencies in the O. D. literature is at the same time surprising and dismaying. As was brought out in a recent paper by the senior author (Luthans, 1974):

"Even more serious than the absence of a learning theory base in organizational behavior has been the almost total absence of the application of behavior modification to organization development. . . . BCM represents an effective, but up to this point ignored, O. D. technique. . . . Besides BCM, a total O. D. effort can be derived from managing the contingent environment, both antecedents and consequences, of organizational behavior. The antecedent environment can be structured in such a way to increase the probabilities of more productive behaviors at every level of the organization and more positively reinforcing consequences can be made to follow goal congruent behaviors of the total organization."

In sum, we can say that O. B. Mod. techniques such as BCM are actually O. D. techniques and that O. D. and O. B. Mod. are both heading in the same direction, i.e., developing the most effective approach to attain organizational goals. The difference is the emphasis placed on interpersonal processes by the most widely used O. D. techniques (sensitivity training, team building and grid training) as opposed to the emphasis placed on environmental contingencies (both antecedents and consequences) in an O. B. Mod. approach.

O. B. Mod. is not intended to replace O. D. or any of the other approaches to human resource management. However, we do feel that O. B. Mod. can add an important dimension to both the theory and practice of human resource management now and in the future.

References

Adam, E., and W. E. Scott. "The Application of Behavioral Conditioning Procedures to the Problems of Quality Control." *Academy of Management Journal* 14 (June 1971): 175–93.

Addison, R. M., and L. E. Homme. "The Reinforcing Event (RE) Menu." *National Society for Programmed Instruction Journal* 5 (1966): 8–9.

Aldis, O. "Of Pigeons and Men." *Harvard Business Review* 39 (July–August 1961): 59–63.

Argyris, C. *Personality and Organization.* Harper & Row, 1957.

Argyris, C. "Personality and Organization Theory Revisited." *Administrative Science Quarterly* 18 (June 1973): 141–67.

"At Emery Air Freight: Positive Reinforcement Boosts Performance." *Organizational Dynamics* (Winter 1973): 41–50.

Azrin, N., and W. Holz. "Punishment," In *Operant Behavior: Areas of Research and Application*, W. Honig, ed. Appleton-Century-Crofts, 1966.

Bandura, A. *Principles of Behavior Modification.* Holt, Rinehart, and Winston, 1969.

Bandura, A. (ed.). *Psychological Modeling. Conflicting Theories.* Aldine-Atherton, 1971.

Bandura, A., and R. Walters. *Social Learning and Personality Development.* Holt, Rinehart, and Winston, 1963.

Barnard, C. *The Functions of the Executive.* Harvard, 1938.

Beatty, R., and C. E. Schneier. "Training the Hard-Core Unemployed Through Positive Reinforcement." *Human Resource Management* 11 (Winter 1972): 11–17.

Beer, M. *Leadership, Employee Needs, and Motivation.* Ohio State University, College of Commerce and Administration, Bureau of Business Research, Monograph 129 (1966).

Blackham, G. J., and S. Silberman. *Modification of Child Behavior.* Wadsworth, 1971.

Blood, M. R. "Intergroup Comparisons of Intraperson Differences: Rewards From the Job." *Personnel Psychology* 26 (1973): 1–9.

Brandt, R. *Studying Behavior in Natural Settings.* Holt, Rinehart, and Winston, 1972.

Brief, A., and A. Filley. "Contingency Management, Poor People, and the Firm." *MSU Business Topics* 22 (Spring 1974): 45–52.

Burgess, A. *A Clockwork Orange.* W. W. Norton, 1963.

Burgess, R. L., R. N. Clark, and J. D. Hendee. "An Experimental Analysis of Anti-litter Procedures." *Journal of Applied Behavior Analysis* 4 (1971): 71–75.

Burns, T., and G Stalker. *The Management of Innovation.* Tavistock Publications, 1961.

Campbell, B., and F. Masterson. "Psychophysics of Punishment." In *Punishment and Aversive Behavior,* B. Campbell and R. Church, eds. Appleton-Centrury-Crofts, 1969.

Campbell, J. P., M. D. Dunnette, R. D. Arvey, and L. V. Hellervik. "The Development and Evaluation of Behaviorally Based Rating Scales." *Journal of Applied Psychology* 57 (February 1973): 15–22.

Campbell, J. P., M. D. Dunnette, E. E. Lawler, and K. E. Weick. *Managerial Behavior, Performance, and Effectiveness.* McGraw-Hill, 1970.

Cathey, P. J. "Wage Plans: Smorgasbord, Anyone?" *Iron Age* 205 (January 15, 1970): 56–57.

Clark, R. N., R. L. Burgess, and J. C. Hendee. "The Development of Anti-litter Behavior in a Forest Campground." *Journal of Applied Behavior Analysis* 5 (1972): 1–5.

Coch, L., and J. French. "Overcoming Resistance to Change." *Human Relations* 1 (1948): 512–32.

"Conversation With B. F. Skinner." *Organizational Dynamics* (Winter 1973): 31–40.

Cummings, L. L., and D. P. Schwab. *Performance in Organizations: Determinants & Appraisal.* Scott, Foresman, 1973.

Deci, E. L. "Paying People Doesn't Always Work the Way You Expect it to." *Human Resource Management* 12 (Summer 1973): 28–32.

Drucker, P. *The Practice of Management.* Harper & Row, 1954.

Estes, W., and B. F. Skinner. "Some Quantitative Properties of Anxiety." *Journal of Experimental Psychology* 29 (1941): 309–400.

Evans, W. A. "Pay for Performance: Fact or Fable." *Personnel Journal* 49 (September 1970): 726–31.

Everett, P. B., S. C. Hayward, and A. W. Meyers. "The Effects of a Token Reinforcement Procedure on Bus Ridership." *Journal of Applied Behavior Analysis* 7 (1974): 1–9.

Ferster, C. B., and M. C. Perrott. *Behavior Principles.* New Century, 1968.

Ferster, C. B., and B. F. Skinner. *Schedules of Reinforcement.* Appleton-Century-Crofts, 1957.

French, W., and C. Bell. *Organization Development.* Prentice-Hall, 1973.

Fromm, E. *Escape From Freedom.* Holt, Rinehart, and Winston, 1941.

Fry, F. "Operant Conditioning and O. B. Mod.: Of Mice and Men." *Personnel* 51 (July–August 1974): 17–24.

Goodall, K. "Shapers at Work." *Psychology Today* 6 (November 1972): 53–62 and 132–38.

Graen, G. S. "Instrumentality Theory of Work Motivation: Some Experimental Results and Suggested Modifications." *Journal of Applied Psychology Monograph* 53 (1969): 1–25.

Gray, F., P. Graubard, and H. Rosenberg. "Little Brother is Changing You." *Psychology Today* 7 (March 1974): 42–46.

Hall, E. "Will Success Spoil B. F. Skinner?" *Psychology Today* 6 (November 1972): 65–72 and 130.

Hammer, M. "The Application of Behavioral Conditioning Procedures to the Problems of Quality Control: Comment." *Academy of Management Journal* 14 (December 1971): 529–32.

Hamner, W. C. "Reinforcement Theory and Contingency Management in Organizational Settings." In *Organizational Behavior and Management: A Contingency Approach,* H. L. Tosi and W. C. Hamner, eds. St. Clair Press, 1974.

Herman, R., and N. Azrin. "Punishment by Noise in an Alternative Response Situation." *Journal of the Experimental Analysis of Behavior* 7 (1964): 185–88.

Hermann, J. A., A. I. de Montes, B. Dominguez, F. Montes, and B. L. Hopkins. "Effects of Bonuses for Punctuality on the Tardiness of Industrial Workers." *Journal of Applied Behavior Analysis* 6 (1973): 563–70.

Herzberg, F. "One More Time: How Do You Motivate Employees?" *Harvard Business Review* 46 (January–February 1968): 53–62.

Herzberg, F., B. Mausner, and B. Snyderman. *The Motivation to Work* (2nd ed.). Wiley, 1959.

Hilgard, E. R. *Introduction to Psychology* (3rd ed.). Harcourt Brace Jovanovich, 1962.

Hilgard, E. R., and D. G. Marquis. *Conditioning and Learning.* Appleton-Century-Crofts, 1940.

Hill, W. F. *Learning: A Survey of Psychological Interpretations.* Chandler Publishing Company, 1963.

Homme, L., A. Csanyi, M. Gonzales, and J. Rechs. *How to Use Contingency Contracting in the Classroom.* Research Press, 1970.

Humble, J. *Management by Objectives in Action.* McGraw-Hill, 1970.

"Job Satisfaction and Productivity." *Gallup Opinion Index* Report No. 94 (April 1973).

Johnston, J. "Punishment of Human Behavior." *American Psychologist* 27 (1972): 1033–54.

Jones, J. C. *Learning*. Harcourt Brace Jovanovich, 1967.

Keller, F. S. *Learning: Reinforcement Theory*. Random House, 1954.

Krasner, L., and L. P. Ullmann (eds.). *Research in Behavior Modification*. Holt, Rinehart, and Winston, 1965.

Kuhn, D. G., J. W. Slocum, Jr., and R. B. Chase. "Does Job Performance Affect Employee Satisfaction?" *Personnel Journal* (June 1971): 455–59.

Latham, G., and S. Kinne. "Improving Job Performance Through Training in Goal Setting." *Journal of Applied Psychology* 59 (1974): 187–91.

Lawler, E. E. *Pay and Organizational Effectiveness*. McGraw-Hill, 1971.

Lindsley, O. R. "A Reliable Wrist Counter for Recording Behavior Rates." *Journal of Applied Behavior Analysis* 1 (1968): 77–78.

Luthans, F. *Organizational Behavior*. McGraw-Hill, 1973a.

Luthans, F. "The Contingency Theory of Management." *Business Horizons* 16 (June 1973b): 67–72.

Luthans, F. "An Organizational Behavior Modification (O. B. Mod.) Approach to O.D." Paper given at the Thirty-Fourth Annual Meeting of the Academy of Management, Seattle, Washington, August 20, 1974.

Luthans, F., and E. Knod. "Critical Factors in Job Enrichment." *Atlanta Economic Review* 24 (May–June 1974): 6–11.

Luthans, F., and R. Kreitner. "The Role of Punishment in Organizational Behavior Modification (O. B. Mod.)." *Public Personnel Management* 2 (May–June 1973): 156–61.

Luthans, F., and R. Kreitner. "The Management of Behavioral Contingencies." *Personnel* 51 (July–August 1974): 7–16.

Luthans, F., and D. Lyman. "Training Supervisors to Use Organizational Behavior Modification." *Personnel* 50 (September–October 1973): 38–44.

Luthans, F., and R. Ottemann. "Motivation vs. Learning Approaches to Organizational Behavior." *Business Horizons* 16 (December 1973): 55–62.

Luthans, F., and W. Reif. "Job Enrichment: Long on Theory, Short on Practice." *Organizational Dynamics* 2 (Winter 1974): 30–38.

Luthans, F., and D. White. "Behavior Modification: Application to Manpower Management." *Personnel Administration* 34 (July–August 1971): 41–47.

McGinnies, E. *Social Behavior: A Functional Analysis*. Houghton Mifflin, 1970.

McGinnies, E., and C. Ferster. *The Reinforcement of Social Behavior*. Houghton Mifflin, 1971.

McManis, D. L., and W. G. Dick. "Monetary Incentives in Today's Industrial Setting." *Personnel Journal* 52 (May 1973): 387–92.

Margulies, N., and J. Wallace. *Organizational Change: Techniques & Applications.* Scott, Foresman, 1973.

Maslow, A. H. "A Theory of Human Motivation," *Psychological Review* (July 1943): 370–96.

Mathis, B., J. Cotton, and L. Sechrest. *Psychological Foundations of Education.* Academic Press, 1970.

Meacham, M., and A. Wiesen. *Changing Classroom Behavior: A Manual for Precision Teaching.* International Textbook Company, 1969.

Millenson, J. R. *Principles of Behavioral Analysis.* Macmillan, 1967.

Murray, R. "Behavioral Management Objectives." "*Personnel Journal* 52 (April 1973): 304–306.

Nord, W. "Beyond the Teaching Machine: The Neglected Area of Operant Conditioning in the Theory and Practice of Management." *Organizational Behavior and Human Performance* 4 (November 1969): 375–401.

Oates, D. "A Cafeteria Approach to Compensation." *International Management* 28 (July 1973): 14–17.

Odiorne, G. *Training by Objectives: An Economic Approach to Management Training.* Macmillan, 1970.

Orwell, G. *Nineteen Eighty-Four.* Harcourt Brace Jovanovich, 1949.

Pavlov, I. P. *Conditioned Reflexes: An Investigation of the Physiological Activity of the Cerebral Cortex.* Translated and edited by G. V. Anrep. Oxford University Press, 1972.

"Performance Audit, Feedback, and Positive Reinforcement," *Training and Development Journal* 26 (November 1972): 8–13.

Porter, L. W., and E. E. Lawler. *Managerial Attitudes and Performance.* Irwin, 1968.

Premack, D. "Toward Empirical Behavior Laws: I. Positive Reinforcement." *Psychological Review* 66 (1959): 219–33.

Premack, D. "Reinforcement Theory." In *Nebraska Symposium on Motivation,* D. Levine, ed., pp. 123–80. Nebraska, 1965.

Raia, A. "Goal Setting and Self Control." *Journal of Management Studies* 2 (February 1965): 34–53.

Raia, A. "A Second Look at Management Goals and Controls." *California Management Review* 8 (Summer 1966): 49–58.

Razran, G. "Russian Physiologists' Psychology and American Experimental Psychology: A Historical and a Systematic Collation and a Look into the Future." *Psychological Bulletin* 63 (1965): 42–64.

Reif, W., and F. Luthans. "Does Job Enrichment Really Pay Off?" *California Management Review* 15 (Fall 1972): 30–37.

Reitz, H. J. "Managerial Attitudes and Perceived Contingencies Between Performance and Organizational Response." *Academy of Management Proceedings* (1971): 227–38.

Rogers, C., and B. F. Skinner. "Some Issues Concerning the Control of Human Behavior." *Science* 124 (November 1956): 1057–66.

Ruch, F. L. *Psychology and Life* (3rd ed.). Scott, Foresman, 1948.

Schappe, R. "Twenty-Two Arguments Against Job Enrichment." *Personnel Journal* 53 (February 1974): 116–23.

Schneider, J., and E. A. Locke. "A Critique of Herzberg's Incident Classification System and a Suggested Revision." *Organizational Behavior and Human Performance* (July 1971): 441.

Schuster, J. R., B. Clark, and M. Rogers. "Testing Portions of the Porter and Lawler Model Regarding the Motivational Role of Pay." *Journal of Applied Psychology* (June 1971): 187–95.

Schwab, D. P. "Conflicting Impacts of Pay on Employee Motivation and Satisfaction." *Personnel Journal* 53 (March 1974): 196–200.

Sherman, A. R. *Behavior Modification: Theory and Practice.* Brooks/Cole Publishing Company, 1973.

Skinner, B. F. *The Behavior of Organisms.* Appleton-Century-Crofts, 1938.

Skinner, B. F. *Science and Human Behavior.* The Free Press, 1953.

Skinner, B. F. "Operant Behavior." In *Operant Behavior: Areas of Research and Application,* W. Honig, ed. Appleton-Century-Crofts, 1966.

Skinner, B. F. *Contingencies of Reinforcement.* Appleton-Century-Crofts, 1969.

Skinner, B. F. *Beyond Freedom and Dignity.* Bantam Books, 1971.

Sorcher, M., and Goldstein. "A Behavior Modeling Approach in Training." *Personnel Administration* 35 (March–April 1972): 35–41.

Tagiuri, R. "The Concept of Organizational Climate." In *Organizational Climate: Explorations of a Concept,* R. Tagiuri and G. Litwin, eds. Harvard, 1968.

Thorndike, E. L. *Educational Psychology: The Psychology of Learning,* Vol. II. Columbia University, Teachers College, 1913.

Ullmann, L. P., and L. Krasner (eds). *Case Studies in Behavior Modification.* Holt, Rinehart, and Winston, 1965.

Vroom, V. H. *Work and Motivation.* Wiley, 1964.

Watson, J. B. "Psychology as the Behaviorist Views It." *Psychological Review* 20 (1913): 158–77.

Watson, J. B. *Behavior: An Introduction to Comparative Psychology.* Holt, Rinehart, and Winston, 1914.

Watson, J. B. *Behaviorism.* W. W. Norton, 1924.

Watson, J. B., and W. MacDougall. *The Battle of Behaviorism.* W. W. Norton, 1929.

Watson, J. B., and R. Rayner. "Conditioning Emotional Reactions." *Journal of Experimental Psychology* 3 (February 1920): 1–14.

Watson, R. I. "The Role and Use of History in the Psychology Curriculum." *Journal of the History of the Behavioral Sciences* 2 (1966): 66–69.

Wenrich, W. W. *A Primer of Behavior Modification.* Brooks/Cole Publishing Company, 1970.

"Where Skinner's Theories Work." *Business Week* (December 2, 1972): 64–65.

Wiard, H. "Why Manage Behavior? A Case for Positive Reinforcement." *Human Resource Management* 11 (Summer 1972): 15–20.

Wolpe, J. *Psychotherapy by Reciprocal Inhibition.* Stanford University Press, 1958.

Work in America. Report of a Special Task Force to the Secretary of Health, Education, and Welfare. The MIT Press, 1973.

Yukl, G., K. N. Wexley, and V. D. Seymore. "Effectiveness of Pay Incentives under Variable Ratio and Continuous Reinforcement Schedules." *Journal of Applied Psychology* 56 (February 1972): 19–23.

SUGGESTED ADDITIONAL READING

Chew, P. "The Carrot and the Stick." *The National Observer* (May 18, 1974).

Karlins, M., and L. Andrews (eds.). *Man Controlled: Readings in the Psychology of Behavior Control.* The Free Press, 1972.

London, P. "The End of Ideology in Behavior Modification." *American Psychologist* 27 (October 1973): 913–20.

Murphy, J. "Is it Skinner or Nothing?" *Training and Development Journal* 26 (February 1972): 2–8.

Skinner, B. F. *About Behaviorism.* Alfred A. Knopf, 1974.

Skinner's Utopia: "Panacea, or Path to Hell?" *Time* 98 (September 20, 1971): 47–53.

Wheeler, H. (ed.). *Beyond the Punitive Society.* W. H. Freeman and Company, 1973.

Index

Index

Adam, E., 175
Addison, R., 97
Aldis, O., 11, 105
Antecedent events, 42-44, 120, 136, 178, 183, 197; (*see also* Cues)
Applied behavior analysis, 3, 30; relative to O.B. Mod., 30, 177
Argyris, C., 145
Azrin, N., 115, 126

B. Mod. (*see* Behavior modification)
Bandura, A., 59, 89, 113, 121, 137-39
Barnard, C., 90, 132
Baseline, 40, 73-74, 107, 159, 161; practical examples of, 153-57
Beatty, R., 55
Beer, M., 8
Behavior, animal versus human, 175; as a dependent variable (*see* Objective behavior); as a function of its consequences, 3, 25, 32, 41, 108, 175, 176, 182; avoidance, 113-14; causes of, 6, 13; chained, 54; control of, 13, 15, 174, 176; defensive, 122; desirable, 71, 77, 116, 130, 140, 155, 157, 161, 163, 172, 191; environmental model, 6; escape, 113-14; frequency of (*see* Response frequency); internal model, 6; learned, 8, 11, 18, 27, 144 (*see also* Learning); observable, 11, 18, 22, 25, 34, 71, 134, 135, 163, 189 (*see also* Objective behavior); observation and measurement of, 185; operant, 11, 18, 26-28; overt, 3; performance-related, 64, 69-72, 99, 106, 114, 130, 142, 151, 166, 184, 185, 190, 196; problems, 15, 73, 153-57, 176, 177, 181, 184; problem-solving, 135, 152; reflexive, 18; respondent, 11, 18, 26-28; shaping, 55-56; theoretical causes of, 3, 189; therapy, 30, 177; undesirable, 71, 77, 157, 161; unlearned, 8, 11, 18, 35
Behavioral events, 34-37, 64-66, 145, 189; frequency of, 34, 37-41; identifying, 36, 159; time-sampling, 72; (*see also* Behavior; Charting; Response frequency)
Behavioral Contingency Management (BCM), 15, 60-83, 92, 124, 137, 170, 181, 184, 188, 197; evaluating effectiveness of, 158; model of, 70; purpose of, 72; training in, 151-53
Behavioral learning theory, 3; applied to human resource management, 17; related to external approach, 18; Skinner's contributions, 25
Behavioral repertoire, 3
Behavioral scientists, 2, 61, 137; practicing manager as, 60-62
Behaviorism, 3, 175; Skinnerian (*see* Skinner); Watsonian (*see* Watson)

Behavior modification, 3, 12, 13, 15, 67, 160, 174, 186, 197; as a scientific view of human behavior, 34; as a technology of learned behavior, 33; controversy surrounding, 30, 176-77; dependent variable of (*see* Observable behavior); ethical issues of, 174-85; frequency as the basic datum of, 86; independent variables of, 34; intervention strategies, 44-49, 152, 155, 159, 162, 184, 189; principles of, 33-59, 164; procedures and techniques, 44-56
Behavior therapy (*see* Behavior)
Bell, C., 196
Bentham, J., 7
"Big Brother" Syndrome, 176-77
Blackham, G., 97
Blake, R., 61
Blood, M., 94-95
Brandt, R., 71, 184
Brief, A., 135
Burgess, A., 177
Burgess, R., 89
Burns, T., 80

Campbell, B., 115
Cathey, P., 97
Chained behavior, 54, 136
Change, agents, 30, 197; coping with, 196; strategy, 191
Charting, 39, 154; practical example of, 40-41
Chase, R., 10
Clark, B., 10
Clark, R., 89
Classical conditioning, 28, 30, 177

Climate, behavioral, 160; of positive control, 189-91; organizational, 164, 190, 196
Coch, L., 147
Cognitive learning theories, 18
Combination strategies, 46, 123-29, 131, 153
Communication, 90, 168, 181, 183, 184, 194; two-way, 162
Consequences, 108, 159, 168, 176, 178, 183, 194, 197; as named by strategy category, 45; hierarchy of, 180; management of, 28; negative, 146, 172, 191 (*see also* Punishment); relationship to cues and behavior, 14-15; role in modeling, 139; scheduling and timing of, 50; self-management of, 144; (*see also* Learning)
Contingencies, 117, 133, 146; as antecedent–behavior–consequence (A–B–C) relationships, 44; as cue–behavior–consequence relationships, 16; naturally occurring, 93; organizational behavior, 43; systematic management of, 182; unplanned, 58
Contingency, 28, 34, 41, 87, 92, 181, 187, 189; contracting, 148-49, 156, 185, 193, 194; management, 30; questionnaires, 95-98; Skinner's three elements of, 29; three-term, 42; (*see also* Behavioral Contingency Management)
Continuous reinforcement (CRF) (*see* Schedules of reinforcement)

Control (*see* Behavior)

Countercontrol, 16, 181

Cues, 13, 143, 151; behavior of others as, 140; defined, 14; forms of, 14; in Hull's learning theory, 24; (*see also* Antecedent events)

Culture, modification of, 179-80; organizational, 197

Cummings, L., 106

Deci, E., 105

Dick, W., 105

Discrimination, 52-53

Drive-reduction theory, 8, 24

Emery Air Freight, 67-69, 76, 89, 183

Environment, control of learned behavior by, 13; manipulation of, 183

Esposito, R., 159

Estes, W., 115

Ethical implications, 15; of O.B. Mod., 174-85

Evans, W., 105

Everett, P., 89

Expectancy theory, 8-11, 105, 194; Porter and Lawler's model, 10; Vroom's model, 9

External approach, 2, 11, 25, 144, 181, 189; language of, 5

Extinction, 45-46, 48, 81, 124, 152, 161, 165, 189; combined with positive reinforcement, 48; compared with punishment and negative reinforcement, 112-13

Feedback on performance (*see* Performance)

Feeney, E., 67-69, 183

Ferster, C., 50, 52, 175, 178

Filley, A., 135

French, J., 147

French, W., 196

Frequency of response (*see* Response frequency)

Fromm, E., 179

Fry, F., 175, 182

Fry, J., 170

Functional analysis, 29, 35, 113, 127, 128, 152, 159; examples of, 77, 153-57; problems, 79; worksheet, 92

Gellerman, S., 61

Generalization, 52-54

Genetic history, 27

Goal setting, 147-48; in Management by Objectives, 194

Goldstein, A., 142

Goodall, K., 29

Grady, E. D., 183

Graen, G., 11

Gray, F., 180

Guthrie, E., 22

Hall, E., 180

Hammer, M., 175

Hawthorne Studies, 60, 90

Hayward, S., 89

Hedonism, 7, 23

Hendee, J., 89

Herman, R., 126

Hermann, J., 106

Herzberg, F., 7, 102, 192; critical-incident method, 8, 192; motivation/hygiene theory, 7; (*see also* Job enrichment)
Hilgard, E., 22, 37
Hill, W., 24, 131
Histories of reinforcement (*see* Reinforcement)
Holz, W., 115, 126
Homme, L., 97, 148
Hull, C., 8, 24, 26; as a reinforcement learning theorist, 23; (*see also* Drive-reduction theory)
Human relations, 87, 182, 190
Human resource management, 15, 183, 189, 197
Human Resources Research Organization (HumRRO), 170

Imitation (*see* Modeling)
Instinct, 19
Intermittent reinforcement (*see* Schedules of reinforcement)
Internal approach, 2, 144, 181; language of, 5
Intervention strategies (*see* Behavior modification)
Ipsative test, 94-95

Job enrichment (JE), 188; and O.B. Mod., 192-93
Job Orientation Inventory (JOI), 94-95
Job satisfaction, 187, 191, 193
Johnston, J., 115

Keller, F., 18
Kinne, S., 147
Knod, E., 146, 192
Krasner, L., 30
Kreitner, R., 12, 69, 115
Kuhn, D., 10

Latham, G., 147
Lawler, E., 8-10, 91, 105
Law of Effect (*see* Thorndike)
Learning, as an alternative approach, 11; defined, 18; environment, 142; laws of, 3; role of consequences in, 23, 26; technology of learned behavior, 29, 56, 178, 180, 182; theoretical background, 17, 178; (*see also* Behavioral learning theory; Cognitive learning theories; Reinforcement learning theories)
Likert, R., 61
Lindsley, O., 76
Locke, E., 8
Luthans, F., 7, 11, 12, 35, 69, 80-81, 105, 115, 134, 146, 150, 181, 192, 197
Lyman, D., 12, 150

McGinnies, E., 88, 92, 120, 131, 178
McGregor, D., 2, 11
Machiavelli, 178, 183-84
McManis, D., 105
McPherson, S., 164
Management, 183, 186; functions, 146; of consequences, 28, 30; of contingencies, 30;

of the environment, 16; punitive, 122

Management by Objectives (MBO), 64, 134, 147, 148, 187, 188; and O.B. Mod., 193-96; contrasted with shaping, 134

Manipulation, 183-84

Margulies, N., 143

Marquis, D., 37

Maslow, A., 7, 11; hierarchy of needs, 7

Masterson, F., 115

Mathis, B., 133

Meacham, M., 100, 124

Millenson, J., 23, 88

Miller, N., 23-24, 26

Modeling, 137-43, 152, 181; and self-control, 144; imitation, 138; live and symbolic models, 139; strategy for human resource management, 140-43; three basic effects in, 138-40

Money, 91; as a generalized conditioned reinforcer, 88; as a reward, 104-107; schedule of payment, 105-106

Morale, 159; and job satisfaction, 187

Motivation, 178, 181, 183, 184, 192; content theories of, 7; drive theories of, 8; process theories of, 7-8; traditional explanations of, 7

Motivation/hygiene theory (see Herzberg)

Murray, R., 134

Negative reinforcement, 45-47, 81, 123, 189; combined with punishment, 49; contrasted with positive reinforcement, 85, 111; key roles in, 112; versus punishment, 47, 187

Noncontingent, 14; environment, 173

Nord, W., 11, 105, 115, 182, 193

O. B. Mod. (see Organizational Behavior Modification)

Oates, D., 97

Objective behavior, 22, 42, 151; as a dependent variable, 19; (see also Behavior)

Observable behavior, as a dependent variable, 34; (see also Behavior)

Odiorne, G., 132

Operant behavior (see Behavior)

Operant conditioning, 28, 30, 176

Operant psychology, 3

Organizational behavior, 3, 186, 190, 197; as a function of its consequences, 32; as learned behavior, 12; causes of, 6; external approach to, 3, 12, 61; internal approach to, 61, 188; learning approach to, 11; prediction and control of, 6, 11, 16, 189; repertoire, 62-64; understanding, 6, 11

Organizational Behavior Modification (O. B. Mod.), 12, 60, 106, 130, 131, 136, 170, 176, 181-82, 190; actual cases of, 150-73; as a conceptual framework, 186; as an integration of organizational behavior and behavior modification, 12, 186; future of, 186, 197; negative control in, 108-29; positive control in, 84-107; self-control in (see Self-control)

Organizational climate (see Climate)

Organizational consequences, 64-66

Organization Development (OD), 61, 189; integrated with O.B. Mod., 196-97; O.B. Mod. approach to, 164-73

Organizations, 181; and the individual, 145; informal, 79; mechanistic, 80; organic, 80

Orwell, G., 174, 176-77

Ottemann, R., 7, 12, 35, 150

Participation, 147, 171; in Management by Objectives, 194

Pavlov, I., 19-20, 26

Performance, 64-66, 99, 106, 191; analysis, 166; audit, 67-68, 141; data, 168; feedback on, 67-68, 157, 160, 167, 169, 171, 183, 191, 194, 196; goals, 161; improvement, 83, 107, 152, 158, 167, 169, 185; Performance Management, 170; problems, 80

Perrott, M., 52, 175

Piece-rate, 52, 106, 148

Porter, L., 8-10

Positive reinforcement, 45-47, 81, 84, 127, 143, 144, 146, 157, 172, 180; contrasted with negative reinforcement, 85; distinction from positive re-

inforcer, 47, 85-86; timing of as a causal variable, 50

Premack, D., 97, 100-101, 103-104; Premack principle, 103, 193

Punishment, 45-46, 48, 81, 152, 161, 171, 177, 178; combined with negative reinforcement, 49; combined with positive reinforcement, 49; confusion surrounding, 115; functionally defined, 108-110; idiosyncrasy of, 111; noncontingent use of, 58; popularity of, 115-17; undesirable side effects of, 48, 117-22; use and abuse of, 48, 115; use and understanding of, 16; vicarious, 59

Raia, A., 194

Rayner, R., 20

Razran, G., 19

Reflexes, 26-27

Reif, W., 146, 192

Reinforcement, 22, 84, 152, 161, 163, 168, 187; histories of, 92-93, 96, 105, 128, 136; menu, 97; negative (see Negative reinforcement); positive (see Positive reinforcement); Reinforcement Management, 160-64; (see also Reinforcement learning theories)

Reinforcement learning theories, 22-24

Reinforcers, 156, 172, 182, 187; conditioned, 35, 88; functional definition of, 86;

identifying positive reinforcers, 91-92; idiosyncrasy
of, 91, 93, 100, 183; natural
social, 103; positive, 136;
primary, 35, 88; secondary,
35; self-reporting of, 93-99
Reitz, H., 95-96
Respondent behavior (see Behavior)
Response frequency, 37-41, 94,
146; as a dependent vari-
able, 153; future dimension
of, 38; measuring, 39, 73-
77, 152; past dimension of,
38; percentage frequency,
77; time-sampling, 76, 153;
(see also Behavioral events;
Charting)
Rewards, 24, 100, 172, 187, 194;
contrasted with positive reinforcers, 85-86; contrived,
100-102; in learning, 22;
natural, 100-101, 103-104
Rogers, C., 179
Rogers, M., 10
Role perceptions, 10
Role playing, 142

Schappe, R., 192
Schedules of reinforcement, 49-52,
81, 157; continuous and
intermittent, 83, 133, 141,
194
Schneider, J., 8
Schneier, C., 55
Schuster, J., 10
Schwab, D., 105, 106
Scientific perspective, 2, 3
Scott, W. E., 175
Self-control, 66, 76, 80, 172; in
Management by Objec-
tives, 194; in O.B. Mod.,
143-49
Self-observation, 66, 76, 185
Self-reinforcement, 83, 137, 146
Self-selection technique, 97
Seymore, V., 50
Shaping, 55-56, 130-37, 143, 152,
157, 161, 162, 180, 191;
and self-control, 144; by
punishing consequences,
115; meaning of, 131; or-
ganizational socialization
through, 131-32; strategy,
132-37
Sherman, A., 30, 177
Silberman, S., 97
Skinner, B. F., 6, 11, 24-32, 37, 42,
50, 79, 86, 88, 92, 94, 105,
110, 115, 119, 120, 122,
124, 144, 175-76, 178-80,
183, 197; as a reinforce-
ment learning theorist, 23;
controversy surrounding,
25-26, 30; Skinnerian be-
haviorism, 24-29
Slocum, J., 10
Sorcher, M., 142
Stalker, G., 80
Stimulus-Response (S-R), 19-29,
42

Tagiuri, R., 190
Tally sheet, 75
Taylor, F. W., 105
Technology, 73, 81, 106, 181; of
learned behavior (see
Learning)
Thorndike, E., 23, 25-26; Law of
Effect, 23, 28, 42, 86, 89,
117, 175

Time-sampling (see Response fre-
    quency)
Training, 73, 132, 142, 160, 164;
    in Behavioral Contingency
    Management, 151; of hard-
    core unemployed, 55, 135;
    process approach to, 151

Ullman, L., 30
Unconditioned aversive stimulus,
    20-21

Vroom, V., 8-10, 23, 47, 105, 194;
    (see also Expectancy the-
    ory)

Wallace, J., 143
Walters, R., 139
Watson, J. B., 19, 22, 24-26, 42;
    Watsonian behaviorism, 19-
    22, 29-30, 34
Wenrich, W., 34, 110
Wexley, K., 50
White, D., 11, 105, 134
Wiesen, A., 100, 124
Willingness to serve, 90; induce-
    ment of, 90-91
Wolpe, J., 30

Yukl, G., 50